CLEARINGS IN THE FOREST

CLEARINGS IN THE FOREST

On The Study of Leadership

Nathan Harter

PURDUE UNIVERSITY PRESS

WEST LAFAYETTE, INDIANA

First paperback printing, 2008.
ISBN–13: 978-1-55753-475-0

Printed in the United States of America.

Library of Congress Cataloging-in-Publication Data

Harter, Nathan.
 Clearings in the forest : on the study of leadership /
Nathan Harter.
     p. cm.
 Includes bibliographical references and index.
 ISBN 1-55753-381-4 (alk. paper)
 1. Leadership. 2. Leadership—Study and teaching. 3.
Leadership—Moral and ethical aspects. I. Title.
 HM1261.H37 2005
 303.3'4—dc22

                                    2005004923

CONTENTS

FOREWORD

As the field of leadership studies has come of age, it has become a warren of overlapping and often conflicting investigations, analyses, and accounts. These vary in sophistication, from the superficial "airport" books on leadership to serious and rigorous scholarship. Even among the latter, a coherent understanding of leadership is jeopardized by the fact that leadership studies is not a coherent discipline with accepted methodologies, but rather a field of study where scholars from multiple disciplines explore various facets of the phenomena from differing perspectives. The result is a stunning hodgepodge of material under the rubric of leadership. This is not entirely the fault of leadership scholars. The real culprit is the phenomenon of leadership itself. Scholars vigorously debate the very meaning of the term, and it is a commonplace that leadership is a protean construct, ever shifting and re-forming itself in response to shifting times, contexts, participants, and purposes. Is it any wonder that our understanding of leadership has suffered, and the field of leadership studies has become a veritable wilderness?

It is this metaphor of a wilderness that brings us to Nathan Harter's impressive work. Given the current state of leadership studies, the most significant challenge is not the further refinement of any particular line of research, but rather the creation of a synthetic framework that will allow us to see the "forest" of the entire endeavor rather than further investigate the individual "trees" of discrete scholarship. That is, to continue the metaphor, we need a guide to help us navigate the wilderness that is leadership studies. This is what Nathan Harter provides in this book, using, appropriately enough, the metaphor of a guided walk through the forests of leadership.

Let us be clear about the purposes of this excursion. Professor Harter is not providing us with quick and easy answers; indeed, one of his primary tasks is to acquaint us with the complexities of thinking about leadership. The seemingly straightforward query "What is leadership studies?" for example, is rife with hidden ambiguities. Harter helps us to parse out the answer. His objective, however, is far more ambitious than the merely definitional. Professor Harter aims to create an integrated, theoretical treatment of leadership that promises to bring order to our conceptualizations of the construct, and aspires to allow us to conceive of it as a single, coherent object of study. This is no easy task, and Professor Harter's "walk in the woods" is no easy trek. Fortunately, he has had the good graces to invite us along on his journey, and those who stay the course will be amply rewarded.

It remains to say something about the trek you are about to undertake. Professor Harter has his own epistemological framework for understanding leadership. That is to say, he posits a particular way of going about acquiring knowledge concerning leadership. As he says rather early on, "This is a book dedicated to establishing a way of thinking about leadership" (p. xviii). What is this approach? Harter begins by taking the reader down to what he calls the "valley" of leadership by looking to its discrete parts and applications. He then climbs to the higher ground of synthesis, theory, and meaning. Once he has looked to theory and practice, the discrete parts and the whole, Professor Harter proposes several overarching conceptual schemes that promise to bring coherence to this mass of information and perspectives.

To say, however, that Professor Harter's work is an attempt (albeit a brilliant one) to make sense of the tangle of leadership studies is to do it a disservice. For Harter's work is, at base, and at its most powerful, a work of philosophy. More than just organizing leadership studies in conceptually coherent ways, he proposes a philosophy, a "set of principles for mapping our intellectual universe" (p. 78). As Harter phrases it, "We are trying to clarify how to think about leadership, so our work is more philosophy than history or science" (p. 17).

Although he weaves several philosophical strands into the tapestry he weaves, Professor Harter's signal contribution may be his resurrection of a nineteenth-century philosophical tradition and refitting it for use in the study and practice of modern leadership. He sets the stage by identifying two critical problems confronting the student and practitioner of leadership. The first difficulty can be phrased, in Professor Harter's words, as "How do we respond to the question of which theory is the right one?" (p. 20). That is to say, given the morass of leadership theory depicted above, how is the student or practitioner to judge which approach(es) might prove the most illuminating and/or effective? The second issue is inextricably related, and conjures up the frightening complexity of leadership. Again, to use Harter's words, "no two leadership *episodes* are identical," which threatens to throw into a cocked hat all attempts to make generalizations about leadership (p. 24).

Professor Harter responds to these ultimate epistemological challenges by relying upon two philosophical traditions. His first response is to call upon the philosophical approach called "perspectivism," wherein "the whole truth can only be obtained . . . by weaving together everyone's partial viewpoints" (pp. 77). According to such an approach, it might well be that there is no single, correct theoretical explanation for the construct of leadership as a whole. But Harter's book aspires to be more than an erudite compendium of abstract theoretical knowledge. He also intends it for students and practitioners who call out for real guidance in applying such theories to actual leadership challenges. It is here that our good professor has the insight to tap into the nineteenth-century philosophical tradition of pragmatism. In actual, specific leadership situations (as opposed to overarching abstractions), this approach may hold the key to unlock the mysteries of leadership studies. According to Harter, pragmatism "gives us a method for bringing some kind of order to leadership studies" (p. 69). In its essence, "pragmatism advises us to adopt theories that work, that stand up to the tests of . . . consistency and harmony for our purposes" (p. 69). It involves a dialectical reciprocity between reality and theory, yielding a "best fit," and an opportunity for real guidance. His retooling of pragmatism as a means of making leadership studies relevant for our modern world is creative and potentially quite useful. It is as if Professor Harter, upon the completion of our arduous trek through the wilderness of leadership, has given us a parting gift of a compass to guide our future solo forays back into the same tangle.

In sum, this "walk in the woods" with Nathan Harter is both instructive and invigorating. One does not have to agree with all of his analyses to appreciate the scope of his endeavor, and one cannot fail to be enlightened by his argument. By turns profound and provocative, this book will undoubtedly take its place on that rather narrow shelf of the truly informative books on leadership. For those about to join Professor Harter on the trip, *audaces fortuna juvat; mox nox in rem*—fortune favors the bold; let's get on with it!

J. Thomas Wren
Jepson School of Leadership Studies

ACKNOWLEDGMENTS

My thanks to the students who have kept me turning these questions over and over in my mind. I am indebted to the library staff at Indiana University–Purdue University at Columbus (IUPUC) and most especially to Jo Davis for bringing an extensive collection of materials to my desk. A word of thanks to the University of Chicago, the National Endowment for the Humanities, and my colleagues in Professor Don Levine's summer seminar in sociological theory, for an exhilarating experience in 1995 that sent me full of joy into the deep heart of this particular forest.

Thank you, Rachel, for letting me stay with you in Arlington Heights, Illinois, while I completed the first draft in May 2003.

This author repeatedly requires the advice and criticism of others, and I was especially honored by the contributions of a number of colleagues whose generosity and tact made the critical process a pleasure. Specifically, I would like to name Cynthia Tomovic, David Frantz, George Hoffmann, Thomas Wren, James MacGregor Burns, and Michael Harvey. Nonetheless, it is important here at one place to insist that whatever flaws or defects appear in the argument are solely my responsibility.

This book is dedicated to the memory of the Reverend Doctor Nathan F.R. Harter, my father (1920–1997). May my own children understand one day why their Daddy had to spend so much of their time on this project.

To God be all the glory. And to Karin, my heart.

PREFACE

A. WALK IN THE WOODS

"In what follows we shall be *questioning*. . . . Questioning builds a way. We would be advised, therefore, above all to pay heed to the way." Martin Heidegger (1954/1977, p. 3; emphasis supplied) understood that the root of a word such as "questioning" is quest, a purposeful journey through unfamiliar territory. It is a journey of the mind. He wrote: "The way is a way of thinking" (ibid.).

Heidegger chose images of paths through mountain forests, of thickets and clearings, as though his philosophizing were a walk in the woods. It is a compelling metaphor. The material you now hold in your hand uses the same metaphor repeatedly. As you read, you will be invited to follow a number of different paths, making progress in one direction or another toward something you cannot see yet. The words of Heidegger advise caution: do not neglect the journey itself. Pay heed to the way, the way of thinking. One does not rush to a fixed destination when the purpose is to explore.

At the risk of straining the metaphor, let me add that I realize most people want a sure path, a trail through the forest—if not a paving crew clearing the land and leveling its contours to build a highway! Euclid put it sharply, when speaking to his king: "Sir, there is no royal road to learning." Whether the forest can be paved at all is a question I leave to philosophers. (I tend to doubt we can do it.) Even if we could, it would be a mistake, in my opinion, to clear the forest—a kind of disenchantment, yes, the domestication of a wild habitat. Bruce Mazlish talks about the distinctly American "need to redeem the wilderness from the forces of evil" (1990, p. 277). We cherish the myth of the pioneer blazing a trail. It does not have to be the only myth, however. Rather than pass through the forest as though it were an obstacle to our destination, and rather than obliterate it by clear-cutting the trees, the point is to inhabit the forest and move about within it. Rather than redeeming the wilderness, I am suggesting a rival myth: the myth of the deer hunter.

Because this whole book is really only an inquiry or exploration, it invites further discussion and disagreement. Even when the language sounds dogmatic, conclusive, please read behind it a question mark, asking what *you* think. Remember, in what follows we shall be questioning, no matter how definite it sounds, because by means of questioning together we build a way.

Aristotle set up the project neatly. We begin in a state of ignorance, he wrote, and would remain ignorant if it were not for a restlessness, a sense of perplexity and wonder, for then we become aware of our ignorance. Once we do become aware of it, we want to remedy our ignorance, and our journey proceeds from simple, direct questions about ordinary things to the deeper questions about the why and wherefore of existence. Before you know it, we are philosophers! (Voegelin, CW 28, pp. 102–104). In the same manner, therefore, we begin this journey from a state or condition of ignorance, as though lost in the woods. Let us first get our bearings.

B. AN ANALOGY

Taking a walk in the woods will be the dominant analogy for this book, but in order to clarify its purpose let me offer a separate analogy briefly here.

When friends visit the city where I live in Indiana, which goes by the name of Greensburg, I drive them around to see the landmarks and become familiar with my world. We pass the courthouse, the church, the schools, my office—and for each landmark, I tell a story or a joke. The courthouse has a tree growing from its tower, for example, which is our one claim to fame, and natives joke that way up there in the air it gets water from the springs in the old courthouse clock. I work next to the county fairgrounds, so that for about ten days each summer, I can't even park at my own office, but even if I could, I would be unable to get anything done, what with all of the noise from the midway. My neighbor would choose different local landmarks, and even for the landmarks we both would pick, he would tell different stories. That is not the football field where my son scored a touchdown. They are the bleachers where his daughter fell and broke her arm. Even though we move around daily in the same spaces, we occupy different worlds. There is one city, but two versions. They will overlap considerably, but they are not the same.

Now, suppose my visitor plans to move here. He wants advice about living in Greensburg. My tour becomes lengthier, and I add suggestions here and there about the faster routes home and the cheapest groceries. Again, my neighbor would give a different tour, even though we are talking

to the same person about the same exact city. My neighbor knows things I
don't. He values things I don't. And of course once my friend settles here,
he will draw his own conclusions about the place.

There is one paramount reality, but each of us has a slightly different
perspective, a different interpretation.

The forest we are about to enter has been my habitat for sixteen years.
What you are reading is my version of it. Other writers have their own versions. We are describing the same phenomenon—leadership—but each of
us has different stories to tell about different landmarks. Some of mine are
"off the beaten path," as they say. This book presupposes that you are contemplating moving here, that you want to live here, so of course my tour
lengthens and includes things the idle tourist would not need to know. You
are also free to poke around a bit on your own, to draw your own conclusions, which is one reason I include an extensive bibliography.

This is what I've found. This is how I get around. This is my habitation. And I would like to share it with you.

C. WHAT ARE WE STUDYING?

An argument requires structure of some kind. It often helps the reader to see
that structure in skeletal form, as an overview, as it were, and gain some idea
how it all fits together. Writers assist in this by the outline of a table of contents, by a preview of coming attractions in their introduction, by verbal
clues throughout the text in order to explain how one paragraph joins to the
next, like connective tissue; and then, at regular intervals and even at the conclusion of the entire argument, by summaries of what has gone before, to solidify in the reader's mind exactly what the writer had been trying to say.
Publishers then add excerpts and blurbs to compress the argument further.
All of which reminds me of the apocryphal story about Karl Barth, a theolo-
gian and author of the multivolume *Church Dogmatics,* who was asked to
give a public lecture condensing that great work. He tried. At the conclusion
of his talk, during a reception, one woman admitted she had trouble following his argument. Would he kindly give her the upshot? To which he replied
with solemnity, "Jesus loves me. This I know, for the Bible tells me so."

The forest is not linear. It is not squared off or flat. It goes by the
name of "wilderness" for a reason. Even so, it discloses an order to the ob-
servant wayfarer who is in no particular hurry. That is the order this argument tries to approximate. That is the way I intend to proceed. The more
regimented, geometrical, and straight the garden, the less it resembles nature. As we move forward in this book, we shall be descending by stages to
the base *experience* of leadership at the bottom of the valley and then we

shall start ascending from that point toward the uplands of the *meaning* of leadership for individuals, organizations, societies, and history.

This is a book dedicated to establishing a way of thinking about leadership. It devotes several chapters to preliminary matters, before treating directly the phenomenon we all know as leadership. It is more concerned with orientation than progress toward a goal, on the assumption that one should get his bearings before striding into the thicket. The book's purpose has to do with underlying theories and the methods we use to gain our understanding. The deer hunter must be patient. Even when stationary, he studies everything—vigilant to listen and to look. Rather than viewing issues of method as tedium, we might come to experience the stillness of meditation as central to the chase. In the stillness of meditation, we begin the hunt. It is a paradox at the heart of this book. Shall we begin?

Anything we study is tied to everything else in the world. For a moment, in our minds, we have got hold of one strand, one piece that in reality cannot be separated from the rest. Reality is for many people like a huge ball of string, wound tightly together. In the words of Georg Simmel, "A countless number of threads make up the web of reality." The task is to separate what we are studying, taking hold of one strand, only in the sense that we are paying attention to it and not to other things. It is a mental process, and it is artificial, but we do it all the time. We have to. This mental process goes by the name of Analysis.

During an important political speech, just to take one example, the grammarian will notice problems of syntax, the psychologist will notice subtle appeals to subconscious drives, the economist will notice policy assumptions, and the fashion coordinator will notice whether the clothes match. A student has to know what to study: what to notice and what to ignore. As William James is reported to have said, wisdom consists in knowing what to overlook. One of the first tasks in any study would be identifying what to study. Without that, you and I are likely to become confused.

This study is about leadership. Leadership is the "strand" of reality that will occupy us for the rest of these materials. But what is leadership? The term has so many formal definitions—Joseph Rost (1993) has written an entire book about the many definitions for this one word—yet people use it freely all the time in ordinary speech. They seem to know what they are talking about. And to a large extent, they do: the word is useful in ordinary speech. As serious students, however, we cannot be satisfied with street-level meanings, or what are known as first-degree constructs (Calder, 1977, pp. 181f; see generally Schütz, 1953/1962, pp. 3–47). For the sake of precision, we are expected to arrive at a second-degree construct, i.e. a definition that can be tested and measured. The classic method for arriving at a second-degree construct was to identify its class of phenomena and then isolate that which makes it unique within that class—which is what zoologists have done with genus and species. You know: a zebra is a horse with stripes. One step in the process fixes the word within its type (horse), and the second step shows how it is different even within its type (striped). If we were to use this method for leadership, then the first step would be to fix the word within its type, *in genere.* Unfortunately, that could prove trickier than it appears. Even if all we do is arrive at a tentative definition for the time being, that would help. We have to start somewhere.

What then do we mean by leadership? Here are some possibilities:

* Leadership is a sociological form
* Leadership is an interpretation of events
* Leadership is a kind of influence
* Leadership is an organizational tendency toward change
* Leadership is part of the process by which the elite arise to dominance
* Leadership is an art
* Leadership is an exercise of power

A likelier strategy would be to go back and consult those first-degree constructs, to distill into essential elements what people ordinarily mean by the word.[1] What do people seem to intend? We can approach that question in a systematic way. Journalists use a simple device to understand events. Journalists want to know:

* Who
* What
* When
* Where
* How
* Why

That device has merit, as we try to understand leadership. We can ask of those who use the word in ordinary speech:

* When you talk about leadership, who is involved in it?
* What is it they are involved in?
* When does it emerge?
* Where is it going?

- How does it work?
- Why do people become involved?

As a point of departure, then, let us consider leadership to be a sociological form, a relationship, between a prospective leader who has some direction in mind and a prospective follower who comes to accept and move toward that direction as a result of the images they possess (a) of each other as individuals, (b) of each other together in relationship, and (c) of the task they undertake. This compact description obviously requires explanation and elaboration, but at least it gives us a framework for identifying specifically where we might disagree. Within this statement are four core elements of a definition that should meet with widespread popular acceptance (Harter, 1998).

- Leadership must be *interpersonal.* Most if not all people imagine at least two persons in some kind of relationship.
- It must involve *attribution.* The one person in the relationship whom we label as the leader causes or influences the follower to do something he or she would not otherwise have done, regardless of how we define interpersonal causation. We commonly attribute leadership to a leader.
- It must result in *change.* Without change, there is no leadership. There has to be some influence by one person upon the other.
- It must change in a specific *direction.* That direction goes by many names, such as goal, objective, mission, or vision.

During the course of these investigations, one might come to agree with Ludwig Wittgenstein that there does not have to be a single thread running through all uses of the word "leadership"—as though there is an *essence* of leadership. Perhaps the search for a definition of this kind is misplaced. What we might discover are multiple uses of the word that bear a "family resemblance" to each other. We might also discover many other words whose meaning bears a family resemblance to leadership. We will consider in this book, for example, the family resemblance of words such as power and elite. It is distinctly possible that, for people in leadership studies, defining leadership will turn out to be akin to psychologists trying to define the word "soul." The word itself might be indefinable. Such a conclusion however comes at the end of analysis.

Once we conclude the analysis, many chapters from now, there is another part to our study. At some point, the topic has to be understood in context as well. What does that mean? Recall that I wrote that anything one studies is in reality tied to everything else in the world: the task following analysis (which is what we mean by conceptually separating the phenomenon in question from everything else) is known as Synthesis, when the object of study is then conceptually re-connected piece-by-piece to the real world, in order to understand its place in the larger scheme of things.

Naturalists do this frequently. In order to study the zebra—really understand it—you must also study what it eats . . . and what eats the zebra. The zebra has a habitat; it is part of an ecosystem. At some point, you gain a greater understanding of the zebra once you become familiar with African grasses and large African predators on the Serengeti. A zebra in the abstract does not exist. It was just a mental operation to think of it that way, an image. Leadership is also part of a complex world. Leadership never takes place in a vacuum, without real people and their predicaments. Leadership is but a moment in the flux of our social lives, so to be students of leadership we must figure out how it is "embedded" into the rest of that world. But that part comes later.

In the meantime, it is still important at the outset to distinguish to the best of our ability what we are studying from what we are not studying.[2] What is leadership studies all about? How can we categorize it?

1

WHAT IS LEADERSHIP STUDIES?

To some people, "leadership studies" is an emerging discipline, in its infancy and passing through the same stages as any new discipline (e.g., Heilbrunn, 1996). To others, apparently, it is a cult, or at least an academic boondoggle (e.g., DeMott, 1993). For a vast number of people, of course, it is not even a blip on the radar screen. "Leadership studies? Never heard of it." In determining how to study leadership, perhaps it would be best to locate the place of leadership studies in the larger project of amassing human knowledge.

One can assert as a general principle that human knowledge has increased over time in a relatively unstructured manner. Working together, humankind has gradually learned to classify what we know by category. What might have been comprehended at one time by a single discipline, say, by philosophy for instance, has been refracted into a multitude of separate disciplines (see generally Berlin, 1962/2000, pp. 24–35). Last century saw the reification of psychology and sociology. Each of them separated into a distinct discipline. What is to prevent us from expecting further refraction, further fragmentation, further *differentiation*? It certainly has been happening: sociology is a good example. Sociology broke into a variety of pursuits, or sub-disciplines (see Levine, 1995).

Undoubtedly most new disciplines meet with skepticism at first. Some fields prove as barren as phrenology. Others struggle until they stand on their own two feet, relatively mature. To predict which fields might prove barren violates the canon of science. The field in question has to have a chance to prove itself.

The problem is that leadership studies is not a distinct field, like a sub-discipline, so much as it is an application of existing fields to a particular set of predicaments. There is a sociology of leadership. There is a psychology of leadership. There is a philosophy of leadership. And within each of these, as we just stated, there is further differentiation. Again, take sociology: one can study leadership through the lenses of elite theory or group dynamics or the diffusion of innovation. The single beam of light we call leadership refracts into tiny rays, almost one for every scholar out there writing on the topic. To risk yet another metaphor, leadership is a fat subject, a land where everyone may safely graze. (Which bodes ill for it as a distinct academic discipline.) University departments specifically devoted to studying and teaching about leadership have been created in schools of Education, Business, Liberal Arts, and Technology, not counting the programs in military science. Each school has a separate purpose, uses different vocabulary, and rewards distinct methods. The question arises, how to bring order to all of these different investigations (Bass, 1990, p. 888).

The estimable James MacGregor Burns is quoted recently as saying that in his opinion, "[t]he study of leadership has become quite fragmented and some would say even trivialized" (Mangan, 2002). I agree. In response, I believe that leadership studies ought to determine its identity as a field of study.

Ten years ago, Ralph Hummel wrote to his colleagues who studied public administration. He titled it a "call for a philosophy of administration." His words could just as easily apply to what we are doing in this book with regard to leadership. He wrote:

> Recurrently we hear the call for the development of ourselves as a discipline. But we are filled with methodological disputes. How can a field be a discipline when it can't agree on its method? A modern discipline must be able to define the domain which it can dominate. But in modern thought this means possessing a single method; it is method which defines the conceptual relations that are expected to exist between the inquiring subject and objects of inquiry; this determines the content and the boundaries of a theoretical discipline. Displaying that we have a range of methods shows how far we are from having a single method that can delineate and dominate a field while the scholars of the field allow themselves to be disciplined by its techniques. Does this put ourselves at a disadvantage compared to other fields that claim disciplinary status? (1993, pp. 53–54)

Hummel answered his own question: "We actually stand at an advantage in openly asking again and again the questions in which we hear the echo of philosophical concerns . . . : Who or what is it that we study? How can we reliably and relevantly know the object of our study? What are we obligated to do with the results of our study?" (ibid.). It is frankly a good thing to contemplate these questions. In this way, we keep our bearings.

A. "A" IS FOR APPLE

Begin with some object. Imagine studying an apple. The object could have been anything, but suppose it is an apple. How do you study it?

You can describe its qualities and the variation in qualities from type to type, from Pink Lady to Macintosh. There is red, pink, and gold, sour and sweet, and so forth. You can describe the form of the apple, the sensory experience of an apple, the function it serves in the life of the tree, as well as its uses as food, in salads and pies. You can trace the history of a typical apple from blossom to shriveled brown mush on the ground. You can examine the economics of apples: the business and technology of orchards as well as delivery and marketing of apples at the local grocer, where prices fluctuate with the seasons.

If you were so inclined, you could recount the uses of apple as metaphor and symbol, in literature, legend, painting, and ordinary speech. "You are the apple of my eye." The word itself is English. What is the word's derivation? What is the same word in other languages? As property, who owns the apple? What rights do owners enjoy? How is ownership in an apple transferred? Is there a history of the apple tree as a species? Where does it grow geographically? What is the ideal climate?

I stop here to assert that any material object is subject to a similarly overwhelming array of studies. The possibilities are literally endless (Ortega, 1914/1961, p. 168, n. 5, quoting *Adán en el Paraíso,* 1910). Any one item presents itself to the human mind for infinite analysis, from every conceivable angle.[1] Not only can we study the object itself, but we can also study it in relation to other objects: is it larger or smaller, older or newer, warmer or colder? Is it useful to this creature? What about that creature? On and on, giving college professors plenty to publish.

Abstract ideas, such as freedom and duty, are more problematic, since they do not exist in physical nature to be observed and measured. They are "mirages produced on matter" (Ortega, 1914/1961, p. 141). Yet they too generate all kinds of study and debate, in much the same way that an apple would—maybe more, since they do not exist in a state or condition where you can settle things by picking one up. What exactly is freedom, anyway? In the immortal words of pop icon Janis Joplin, "Freedom's just another name for nothing left to lose." The same problems that afflict abstract ideas such as freedom and duty afflict leadership studies. Leadership is not a material thing, like an apple. Nonetheless, it has been studied by a wide range of methods.

None of which is to suggest that leadership can mean anything a person chooses. The word is not so broad and malleable as to include every instance of social or interpersonal change. If it means anything at all, it has to mean something in contradistinction to something else.

The following illustration might help make my point. We laugh at a person from the Borough of Queens who wants to argue that she is from New York City and that someone from the Bronx is not. Yes, Queens and the Bronx are distinct places, yet they are both subsumed by the larger category known as New York City. Both are from the same city. If, by way of contrast, I claim that Greensburg, Indiana, is also part of New York City, you would be entitled to laugh. New York City may be large and include a number of boroughs, but that does not have to mean that it is so large it includes farm communities in the Midwest. In the same manner, the word "leadership" might prove to encompass many different things, yet it is not infinitely elastic. Part of the task for leadership studies would be setting boundaries around the word's usage, no matter how pliable those boundaries turn out to be.

B. POLITICS, SOCIETY, AND THE ORGANIZATION

There is a methodological objection to using works of political science, sociology, and the organizational sciences together in a single study. The political, the social, and the organizational are thought to be separate domains. Universities and academic publishers are careful to preserve these classifications. It is not my purpose to deny that the political, social, and organizational are separate conceptual domains. Nonetheless, we do mix them up promiscuously here in this book, with the result that political scientists find themselves cheek-by-jowl next to business management gurus.

One reason to proceed in this way is that these three domains do interpenetrate; they do affect each other in myriad ways. Marx made this point central to his critique of the state, as early as 1843 (1967, pp. 156 & 175). I prefer another reason to survey them together. In each "domain" there is the same tendency for members to separate into layers or strata, as an inevitable feature of the organizational process. Much will depend of course on whether one is studying a political regime or a voluntary association of, say, hobbyists, and it is worthwhile for scholars generally to keep these domains separate in order to keep separate what makes them distinct, although there is in my opinion much that they share. In other words, what we are dealing with can be said to cut across the domains. In a similarly inclusive vein, James Burnham wrote of the managerial revolution (1960) and Ralph Hummel wrote of bureaucracy (1994), again as features of human organization that cut across these domains.

In the year 2000, at Harvard University's Leadership Roundtable, one of the first speakers "suggested that . . . leadership scholars must develop a common set of leadership concepts that apply across contexts if understanding and practice of this elusive phenomenon is to be advanced" (Pruyne, 2002, p. 23). Bernard Bass agreed. In a 2002 interview, he responded to this very question by saying that despite differences in situation, there are more similarities across domains than differences (Bergstrom, 2003). According to Chemers back in 1984, "if general leadership theory can begin to span the gap between the various levels of analysis (that is, individual, group, organization, society), the resulting theories will provide us with a much stronger base, not only for understanding leadership but also for improving its quality" (Quoted in Wren, 1995, p. 99).

It is therefore with due caution that we proceed—as though the political, social, and organizational are conceptually distinct domains where the same basic phenomenon of leadership will occur. This is the primary reason that leadership studies is interdisciplinary. It also gives us a range of methods to work from, which can be good or bad.[2] The following section of this chapter suggests ordering those different methods for studying leadership under four broad umbrellas.

C. FOUR UMBRELLAS

Leadership studies as a distinct field of scholarly research can be schematized any number of ways. The dominant schema in leadership studies had been chronological. Once upon a time (goes the story) leadership was believed to belong to certain types or classes of people, whether by virtue of heredity, intelligence, vocation, race, or any one of a number of other factors. It was a status or position that leaders deserved or won. Relatively recently, the formal study of leadership took this belief and tried to determine whether there is a specific constellation of traits exhibited by these preeminent persons. The question was: "What is it about them that makes them leaders?" Soon after, scholars turned from traits to investigate leader behaviors and styles of behavior. The question became: "What are they doing that makes them leaders?" Finally, however, the range of approaches to studying leadership expanded in all directions, as scholars spread out to try different approaches, so that today students face a bewildering array of choices.

In other words, leadership studies has moved as Ortega somewhere described it: from static truth, through dynamic truth, to *cinematic* truth. By this I mean we seem to have progressed in a pattern. First, we tried to understand the nature or character of a leader. That is the static truth. Second, we tried to understand what leaders do. That is the dynamic truth.

Now, we are trying to get a more narrative understanding, with multiple *personae* interwoven into a plot or story line that has a beginning, middle, and end. Leadership studies is positioned to become an intelligible, even compelling combination of images, with an emphasis on the way we normally understand the world, as a series of episodes with some kind of emergent meaning. That is cinematic truth. Scholars are poised to produce more work on leadership as drama.

In any event, the chronological schema will not make sense of all of the recent scholarship. Joanne Ciulla recently commented, for instance, in 2003 that the usual linear schema will not work, whether as a series of refinements or replacement theories. We require a different organizing model or schema. This section of my book presents a four-part model for understanding the phenomenon we refer to as leadership. Even though the work of scholars already does tend to fall under these four umbrellas, i.e. these four "ways of understanding leadership," we would all benefit nonetheless from doing so consciously, in a more systematic way. It helps to keep separate types of inquiry separate. And then it also helps periodically to consider how they are interrelated. Collapsing them together prevents both analysis and synthesis, as we have already seen fit to repeat. These four umbrellas are:

- History and past experience
- Science and direct observation
- Logic and theorizing
- The imagination

History and past experience. Leadership studies is presently made up of different approaches. On the bookshelf one might find works of history and, more particularly, of biography that illustrate leadership by particular persons from the past. The reason for including these accounts in a newer discipline would be that exemplars from the past show how it was done, once upon a time. Obviously, if it happened once before, then it is possible. These works show us in narrative form what to do, as well as what not to do. Here then is one approach to leadership studies: i.e. find out what has already happened in the past.

Part of the historical record going back in time includes references to those who are called leaders. We have to understand Caesar in order to understand the conquest of Gaul, and we usually have to appreciate the singular character of General Robert E. Lee in order to grasp what happened during many of the decisive battles of the Civil War. The sociologist Don Levine writes that this process is entirely acceptable. "Practical life depends . . . on the selective reconstruction of past events in relation to their implications for present circumstances" (1971, p. xxiii). Some scholars come within the tradition of Machiavelli by going back to study the past *specifically in order to* draw concrete lessons about leadership, so that in this day and age we get leadership handbooks about Lincoln, Churchill, and Attila the Hun. Leadership has become a distinct topic in historical research.

Robert Kaplan, for example, has gone to great lengths trying to convince us that the world situation today resembles the onset of *imperium* in ancient Rome and China. He wrote that "any new rules for leadership will have to reflect upon [ancient history]. Ancient history . . . is the surest guide to what we are likely to face in the early decades of the twenty-first century" (2002, p. 14). He proceeded to demonstrate this with extensive references to Livy, Thucydides, Tiberius, Sun Tzu, and Machiavelli. And it should be noted Kaplan is a journalist with world-wide experience in the field, engaged in current events. He is not some academic ensconced in his library.

When we refer to "history" we should not overlook less scholarly versions that are if anything more popular and arguably more relevant, which are (a) the memoir and (b) the contemporaneous recounting of the recent past, such as personal correspondence, interviews, and newspaper articles. Publishing houses and periodicals as fresh as the weekly news magazine will attempt to explain our leaders to us and keep us abreast of the latest. They are what has been referred to as the "first rough draft of history." Whatever has survived of this literature from the past is eligible to be used in the present as evidence of some kind, and if the recounting is sufficiently accurate, perhaps these particular works are the best, most reliable information we can have about leadership in the real world.

One way to understand something today is to understand its origins from yesterday. Out of what beliefs, forms, and practices in the past did contemporary leadership emerge? Leadership did not spring, fully formed and complete, from the brow of James MacGregor Burns in 1978. Its history shows how leadership came to be, and that understanding goes a long way toward helping us understand what leadership is and where it might be going. The past tells us something about the evolution of leadership.

Lessons from the past are not enough. Bare tales of what might have happened will not suffice as leadership studies. For one reason, circumstances change, and what works as leadership in one era might not work in the next. Besides, we are dependent for our information on the narrator, who in many instances distorts or embellishes the record. For this reason, one might be tempted to trust more the chronicles of a participant, especially the leader himself, because at least they should know what they were doing at the time, which is why Wren has written that "[t]hose who have been intimately engaged in the actual 'doing' of leadership have a perspective which is unmatched" (1995, p. 451). We ought to be mindful, however, that autobiographies are notoriously suspect as reliable accounts, even if only because of the risk of a self-serving bias. Regardless who writes the narrative, people interpret and recast events in order to draw some meaning from the facts or (worse) settle old scores, with the result that maybe all we can say is that there is no history, but only historians. This includes participants. In other words, everyone "filters." Or, to use another metaphor, each writer uses a theoretical or ideological template, consciously or not, with a variety of unspoken presuppositions. This makes interpretation messy.

Events from the past do serve as objects of study, and they keep the rest of us grounded in reality, which is terribly important, but that is not all we need to consider under this first umbrella of our four-fold schema. From the past we can also use their writings *about leadership*. People have been writing about leadership for centuries. Wren has commented that "philosophers, men of letters, and leaders differed greatly in their perceptions of leadership; nevertheless the rich variety of approaches suggests the insights which may be obtained by the careful reading of the commentators of the past" (1995, p. 47, contra Rost, 1993, pp. 42f; see generally Clemens & Mayer, 1999, introduction). History supplies us not only with events to serve as objects of study, but it also offers writers who in their own historical frame of reference had reason to record their thoughts on leadership. We know for example that Aristotle wrote about rulers and interpersonal influence, as did Machiavelli centuries later. These writings are the unacknowledged origin of leadership studies. Some books remain unsurpassed to this day. Just as psychologists build on Plato's ruminations about the soul and political scientists build on Rousseau's reflections on the General Will, we should be able to build on the lessons of our forebearers. It would be foolish to neglect their contributions.

The next umbrella pertains to science and the rigors of direct observation, as a separate way to study leadership, yet, as Schütz once commented, as soon as a person decides to study anything scientifically, "the scientist enters a preconstituted world of scientific contemplation handed down to him by the historical tradition of his science" (1945/1962, p. 250). Even the scientist must draw lessons from the past. Science itself is a historical process. Even so, leadership studies is not just a sub-field of history.

Science and direct observation.[3] If leadership studies is to gain credibility, it must be grounded in empirical knowledge, for (as we have known since the days of Machiavelli) leadership effectiveness depends on the way people actually behave (1532/1991, chap. XV). The study of any phenomenon has to include the observation of the way things are. Otherwise, we are studying that which does not exist.

In order to test the lessons of experience, scholars have devised a number of methods to observe and measure what happens under specified circumstances. These scholars are the social scientists, who develop a hypothesis and then if possible design a replicable regimen to verify it. Their literature carefully delineates the method and usually offers all sorts of elaborate statistics to establish the relationship of various factors. The social sciences are often distinguished by the "mathematicization" of their subject matter. Indeed, they have added a great deal to our understanding of leadership, and their contributions belong squarely within any discipline of leadership studies worthy of the name "discipline."

Science operates between two intellectual traditions. One of the best characterizations of the history and scope of their tension appears in *The Age of Power*, where Carl Friedrich and Charles Blitzer describe the debates that gradually took shape between such luminaries as Galileo, Kepler, and Bacon, on one side, and Descartes, Hobbes, and Spinoza, on the other side. We label the two sides of this tension: Induction and Deduction (1957, chap. 3).

We may characterize *Induction* as the approach to intellectual questions by which a person tends to gather observations and measurements about the phenomenal world and then after detecting patterns to draw tentative conclusions about the way the world works. Many classroom students appreciate induction's commitment to concrete experience, anchored in the so-called real world, rather than a series of theories spun out of some professor's head.

We may characterize *Deduction* as the approach to intellectual questions by which a person tends to move from self-evident first principles to logical conclusions, in the manner of an algebraic formula. "If X, then Y." In such a manner today, a preacher consults Scripture to establish principles to find how one ought to behave and a courtroom judge applies the Law, that "brooding omnipresence," in particular cases. That is, a person begins from premises to determine what else might be true or right.

Induction builds a bridge from practice to principle, from the particular to the general, whereas deduction builds it the other way around.

Scientists have come to believe the two sides can be reconciled, since they are two ways of building the same bridge. "Maybe we should build it from both ends simultaneously," they say, "and meet somewhere in the middle." That way, deduction gets tied to reality, and induction actually goes somewhere without becoming an aimless series of accumulations of data. Alfred North Whitehead said as much back in 1929–1930: "Theories are built upon facts; and conversely the reports upon facts are shot through and through with theoretical interpretation" (p. 11).

The hidebound tension between Induction and Deduction persists in leadership studies, as one set of writers still leans toward induction and the other still leans toward deduction.

Experience often serves the inductive process, as leaders accumulate lessons from the past to use in the present; we all formulate schemata from what we experience about the way the world works, and then, as we live our lives, we test the schemata. We observe and experiment with our lives. Leadership studies takes a systematic approach, turning anecdotal evidence and accumulated wisdom into findings of fact. This at least is its aspiration. Hughes, Ginnett, and Curphy are right to admit that leadership studies is an immature science (1996, p. 7). Nonetheless, it proceeds apace. Going down my personal bookshelf, I can find a few typical examples. Bennis and Nanus (1985) selected ninety successful people to interview. Kouzes and Posner (1987) describe their research as including surveys and interviews of hundreds of managers. (Appendix B) Kotter (1988) combined interviews, questionnaires (with nearly a thousand responses), and personal observations (preface). This does not include the various forms of memoir that represent the inductive conclusions of practitioners, including Max DePree, James Autry, Charles Handy, and (foremost among them) the late John Gardner.

The same bookshelf includes studies of a different sort. They tend to be more deductive. Rost devised a model for leadership first and then asked academics and practitioners to adopt it (1993, pp. 126–128). Block does much the same thing (1993, preface). Wheatley & Kellner-Rogers (1996), for all their avowals of looking to science for guidance on questions of leadership, mostly import findings from the natural sciences and use them as metaphors for us to consider in our own private ruminations. They do not pretend to have gone out and derived their findings from induction. They want us simply to reconsider our premises. Senge (1990) does something similar to Wheatley, offering systems thinking as a way of understanding leadership, a template. From this vantage point, then, we should be able to understand leadership better. Drath (2001) offers a more recent example of the deductive process that is also more candid (pp. 28–29).

Few credible studies today are pure types of either induction or deduction. The scientific method as it is currently practiced incorporates them both. Some would argue that science—if it truly qualifies as science—always did incorporate both. This was Whitehead's assertion. Goethe had made similar remarks.

"The highest wisdom would be to understand that every fact is already theory." Elsewhere, he explained, "Merely looking at a thing can tell us nothing. Each look leads to an inspection, each inspection to a reflection, each reflection to a synthesis; and hence we can say that in every attentive glance at the world we are already theorizing." (Cassirer, 1945, p. 82, citing *Maximen und reflexionen* and *Naturwiss. Sch.*)

Scholarship operates *between* the general and the specific, the theoretical and the practical. Perhaps studies in leadership could be arranged along a continuum, between inductive and deductive, as they differ by degrees in one direction or the other, but that would be a tiresome exercise and frankly of little use. Authors often neglect the extent to which they are moving in both directions, by alternation: they use both induction and deduction, whether they say so or not. Even so, we are advised to make this pattern explicit and bring it to consciousness.

Charles Sanders Peirce, a scientist we shall meet in the next chapter, preferred the term *abduction* for a process by which a scientist gathers data, makes assumptions explicit, proposes hypotheses, then tests these hypotheses against experience, as well as the experiences of others (Nahser, 1997, p. 72). In a manner of speaking, Peirce gave a name to the process that scientists had finally accepted as a way to transcend opposition between induction and deduction. For this reason, it would be advisable for leadership studies to undertake abduction consciously, beginning with Peirce's explanation of it (e.g., 1940/1955, chap. 11; 1997, lecture 6). Juan Fontrodona has already begun this project in his 2002 book *Pragmatism and Management Inquiry*.

Scientists have much now to contribute. Nonetheless, I would argue that, just like the historians, they too operate according to certain theoretical or even ideological precepts. (In his classic book *The Structure of Scientific Revolutions*, Thomas Kuhn [1970] used the term "paradigm.") The question is whether these precepts are explicit and adequate.

Let me back up first to emphasize the importance of rigorous observation. By this means, we avoid many of the weaknesses found in the historical record. It hardly needs repeating that the rise of the scientific method has led to an explosion of information and useful technologies. There is a reason that the hard sciences are held in such esteem. Their successes are astounding, and they inspire great confidence (e.g., Voegelin, CW 24, pp. 205–215). For the sake of thoroughness, however, we have to remind ourselves of the limits of science. It is a piece, but only a piece, of the puzzle. To say this is as much as to cast aspersions on the scientists, which is not my intention. In a scientistic culture such as ours, the status of the scientist rarely comes under attack.[4] What sort of "attack" do I intend? None, really. What follows is not meant to be an exhaustive list. I am simply trying to illustrate my larger point, which is that science has to be but a partner in the study of leadership.

(a) It is a hollow complaint, for example, to argue that social scientists are content with likelihood, that is, with probabilities. We could have expected that, inasmuch as Aristotle warned us of it long ago. John Stuart Mill put it this way: "an approximate generalisation is, in social inquiries, for most practical purposes equivalent to an exact one" (1988, p. 34). Sigmund Freud made a similar remark: "It is actually a sign of a scientific mode of thought to find satisfaction in these approximations to certainty and to be able to pursue constructive work further in spite of the absence of final confirmation" (quoted in Mazlish, 1990, p. 22).

Science proceeds in the short term at the expense of concrete and individual nuances, those "stubborn facts" that Pascal once said have the power to destroy any general proposition (Friedrich & Blitzer, 1957, p. 57). This is true since the goal of a particular experiment is to verify or arrive at an abstract law or correlation. It is probably safe to say that no scientist is interested in a one-time event that will never recur. The whole point is to discern patterns and gain some predictability about the future (cf. Popper, 1965, pp. 339–343). Why? According to Francis Bacon, "the chief glory of science lay in the fact that it increases the power of man" (Friedrich & Blitzer, 1957, p. 54, citing *Novum organum* [1620]). By necessity, therefore, science has to isolate certain recurring factors for study and get past the notion that every situation is unique. The process has to begin with the assumption that abstract conclusions are possible.[5] Mind you, this is not really a complaint about science. It is a key component of science, and one of its strengths. Without it, science has no utility. Nonetheless, it is a limitation that subsequent students must remember, for as one study selects certain factors to observe and measure, it just as assuredly overlooks the rest (Handy, 1994, p. 221; Wheatley & Kellner-Rogers, 1996, p. 26). One has to hope that over time the sheer volume of research will gradually encompass all of the truly relevant factors. But then this leads to my next assertion . . . .

(b) The sheer volume of information has to be organized and interpreted in order to comprise a single science. It is not enough to have at our disposal a vast list of unrelated findings; we need some coherence among them. This was purportedly one of Francis Bacon's errors: his exclusive trust in "the mere amassing of factual data" (Friedrich & Blitzer, 1957, p. 55). It must be the next step, after analyzing the discrete parts of a phenomenon, to synthesize them, to explain how the parts are related to each other. In so doing, one follows in the path of Galileo and Harvey (and later, Newton), whose work "was neither mere induction nor mere deduction, but a sound combination and blend of both" (Friedrich & Blitzer, 1957, p. 56). We shall try to do the same thing in this book.

Karl Popper once insisted that "all observation involves interpretation in the light of our theoretical knowledge, . . . [Otherwise] pure observational knowledge, unadulterated by theory, would, if at all possible, be utterly barren and futile" (1965, p. 23; Mazlish, 1990, p. 30).

One way to imagine this is to picture a line originating in the present and extending backwards in time. This line serves as the base of experience, the set of all findings. A discipline (as leadership studies aspires to be) requires such an empirical base. There has to be a record of observation, measurement, and experimentation. And as we stated before, there stretches into the past a whole set of essays, histories, treatises, and assorted chronicles that include material on leadership. Onto that "base," in order to make sense of it all, there rises a vertical superstructure of theory. Theory is in a manner of speaking (and only in part) the integration into one useful whole of many acts of induction.

If for instance a study finds that juries tend to select the oldest male as their foremen, we can try to comprehend the meaning of this fact, and our efforts will tend to fit a certain theory about human behavior. It tends to happen that juries select the oldest male. That is the backward line established by observation. What vertical superstructure shall we overlay? Is this fact about the oldest male an example of gender-based patriarchy at work in our subconscious actions? Or is it evolutionary biology driving the assertive and dominant male to lead the temporary "pack" for the sake of carrying forth his DNA? Perhaps it derives from religious scruples about the headship of the father and husband as symbolic representatives of the divine. One explanation might stem from insights that male property-owners (as opposed to renters and men who live with relatives) have been socially conditioned in their role to sharpen those analytical and verbal skills that jurors value at such moments. I could go on. The point is that science takes part in theory-building, or it remains stuck in simple fact-gathering and goes nowhere. Thus, it matters a great deal what theory is at work, and in many instances within leadership studies that theory is not explicit.

(c) Consider as well how scientists begin their work. They begin with a definition of leadership, as though we can agree what the word even means, which of course we cannot do in what Rost calls this "culture of definitional permissiveness and relativity [in which] one scholar's definition is as good as another's" (1993, p. 6). So the scientists have to identify what they are studying, to delimit the field of their research, and then trust that the rest of us agree that it is in fact leadership. Easier said than done, as we are swiftly finding out.

And, as we shall have occasion to explain later, the language of leadership comes from ordinary or street-level usage, which is notoriously sloppy. When a scientist tells you what she means by the term, you quickly discover not everyone concurs. A science of leadership will have to get past that problem somehow.

(d) Another criticism, which I am uncomfortable making, is the postmodern claim that knowledge is a social construct, i.e. a conclusion that derives its authority from the consensus it enjoys among those whom we regard as experts. Kuhn refers to this consensus as the hallmark of "normal" science (1970, chaps. 2, 3). According to postmodernists, we are supposed to beware all kinds of mischief in the choices that scientists make. The argument is that the choice of topic (like other decisions) is influenced by the power the researcher (or her source of funding) hopes to gain from the results; we should be as skeptical in studies of leadership as we are when a tobacco company pays for a study on the effects of cigarette smoking, because it is (according to postmodernism) the same thing. Objectivity and strict neutrality is a crock. Look for the hidden agenda. (See generally e.g., Lyotard, 1984/96.)

Such cynicism can be attributed to the increasingly esoteric nature of scientific discourse. According to Jacques Barzun:

> As things stand, despite the conscientious work of many trained minds, the reports of "science" on a wide range of subjects are contradictory, equally publicized, and the laity cannot decide what to believe . . . an intelligent opinion about them cannot be formed. And when there is evidence that business and politics affect more than one "scientific" pronouncement, gone is the confidence in science felt and voiced in the 19C. (2000, p. 751)

Decades ago, James Burnham dismissed this objection on behalf of all scientists, when he wrote the following:

> [T]hough our practical goals may dictate the direction that scientific activity takes, though they show us what we are trying to accomplish by the scientific investigation, what problem we are trying to solve; nevertheless, the logic of the scientific inquiry itself is not controlled by the practical aims but by science's own aims, by the effort to describe facts and to correlate them. (1987, p. 35; see also Schütz, 1945/62, pp. 245f)

(e) The main problem that I have with studying leadership scientifically is that leadership depends on the understanding the parties have of themselves, since leadership is not a tangible event in nature, like two chemicals poured into a beaker (Hughes, 1958, chap. 8, interpreting Weber). What happens happens in the minds of the participants, which is a place notoriously beyond the reach of any scientist to observe directly. Leadership takes place inside a "black box"—the individual human mind—where external observers cannot see. Thus, the scientist must resort to questionnaires and interviews and dubious instruments that are mediated by the parties, who might be confused, inarticulate, devious, self-serving, suggestible, or entirely oblivious to what has been happening (Bass, 1990, pp. 888–890; Rost, 1993, pp. 33–35; Hughes, Ginnett, & Curphy, 1996, chap. 4; Fontrodona, 2002, p. 51; see generally Hayek, 1955).

For these and other reasons, leadership studies will depend in part, but only in part, on science.[6]

Logic and theorizing. Since science itself relies on logic and epistemology, it would have been tempting to include these under the second umbrella of the four-fold schema, but they are distinctly the province of philosophy. Science and philosophy are related, of course; Stanley Jaki has written "that science is not only a rich field for philosophical reflections but . . . it also presents considerable philosophical problems" (1990, p. 184). The study of leadership has a place for philosophy. Perhaps for many scholars *it goes without saying* that the study of leadership depends on sound logic and certain fundamental precepts of epistemology. Nonetheless, this is a separate component. It is not grounded in direct observation (e.g., Peirce, 1997, p. 151). It does go to the reliability and meaning of what is observed, and I am eager to illustrate what I am saying, as it applies to the study of leadership.

Suppose that a mob gathers in agitation at the steps of a building. A solitary man emerges from the building and speaks to the crowd. At the conclusion of his oration, the mob turns as one body and, now with that solitary man at its front, marches off in another direction, still agitated. In our little scenario, we have behavior that suggests interpersonal influence, if not outright leadership on the part of that solitary figure. Observation is one thing; logic allows us to draw inferences. If we knew what the man actually said to the mob, we would have more evidence to work with, and it might strengthen the plausibility of our inference, but the accuracy of our observation is something different from the validity of our reasoning. The overall reliability of our conclusions depends on the quality of both. We do not know what the participants were thinking. We can never know with 100% confidence, *even if they tell us.* Thus, it matters a great deal just how close to 100% we are permitted to get, under the circumstances. In effect, we must engage in hermeneutics. That is, we must interpret events.[7] And interpretation requires good logic.

It might help to show the importance of good logic by presenting an example of poor logic. One evening, a teacher explained the following assignment to his class. He told them to sit back and listen to what a sample of acknowledged leaders in a particular field have to say for public consumption, and by this means one can learn what kind of leadership works best in that field of endeavor. Accordingly, the class listened to snippets of speeches by the Pope, Billy Graham, and Mother Teresa, in order to come up with a profile of "religious" leadership. The next week was to have been devoted to military leadership, and so forth. Here then is a sampling of my immediate objections:

(a) The list of religious leaders does not include non-Christians. For that matter, the list does not include religious leaders from other eras. Do we know that speakers A, B, and C are representative of the set?

(b) The pronouncements they made were not particularly about leadership. In fact, just as the list of religious leaders was selective, so also was the choice of public pronouncement to use as representative of their leadership. So, again, with regard to these pronouncements, do we know that speeches A, B, and C are representative of their views about leadership? Are their views on leadership even relevant to their actual leadership?

(c) Pronouncements made for public consumption are notoriously suspect, and serve only as examples of how a number of acknowledged leaders saw fit to communicate for a specific purpose. The instructor is using A (what they said) as an example of B (how they tend to lead). Where is the logical nexus between A and B? This was never explained.

(d) The classification "religious leader" is too broad and not analytically useful. A Billy Graham will lead sinners to Christ by means of preaching, and that is his claim to fame, whereas a Pope manages an elaborate bureaucracy and tries to sustain an international institution. To say that (i) a fundamentalist crusade in a single auditorium for the sole purpose of getting as many as possible to "make a decision for Christ" is of the same type as (ii) the reading of an encyclical on, say, economic justice to millions of ethnic Catholics, including scholars, rivals, ecumenical partners, and borderline schismatics, negates the usefulness of the entire assignment. The instructor wants to put leaders A, B, and C into a set they cannot really share.

(e) Furthermore, where is the proof that these religious leaders were as a result of these particular pronouncements particularly successful? Is there some kind of tally? Perhaps the success rate was miserable. Can we know that pronouncements A, B, and C are examples from the set that interests us?

(f) Does one brief pronouncement, such as the students watched on video-tape, usually take place in a vacuum, without build-up, without context? It would be crucial, I think, to incorporate that contextual information as well. The pronouncement A is just a part of the process B, and A probably makes no sense taken out of this context.

I could go on. The classroom exercise fails repeatedly on grounds of logic. One does not have to be an exacting pedant to recognize the trouble. (One does have to wonder how often its like is repeated throughout the discipline.) Poor logic ruins the best data. Good logic makes even the slightest data useful. If leadership studies is ever to establish its credibility in academe, it had better be logical.

This very book belongs to this particular umbrella as an approach to studying leadership. It falls within none of the others. We are here trying to clarify how to think about leadership, so our work is more philosophy than history or science.[8]

The imagination. This chapter has advanced in the following way: In our understanding of leadership, we draw on certain experiences from the past, but back of that set of experiences is a scientific method that we follow in order to gain reliability, although back of scientific method are certain rules of epistemology and logic we must observe. Science and history rely on theory. To take it one step further, it is entirely plausible that back of logic, epistemology, and theory is psychology, and more particularly the psychology of the imagination.[9] Psychologist James Hillman has stated emphatically that "psychology inherently assumes superiority over other disciplines" (1975, p. 131). We intend to make the case in a subsequent chapter that leadership studies involves an understanding of the imagination. Indeed, the book rests on this very foundation. As Fontrodona put it, in his explication of Peirce, "We may stand before phenomena, but in the absence of imagination, we cannot connect them in any rational way" (2002, p. 145, citing *Collected Papers* 4:611).

One might conceive of the imagination as directly opposed to the previous three umbrellas. History, science, and philosophy exist as disciplines partly to prevent the imagination from distorting our understanding of reality. For many persons, reality and the imaginal realm (as it is sometimes known) are separate, if not antithetical. We study something in order to replace our imaginings with knowledge, since the imagination seems too closely akin to superstition. It can seem that by adding the imagination here we shall have been slipping the fox back into the henhouse. In my own defense, I explicitly favor keeping this umbrella separated from the other three conceptually, since it is distinct. It gets its own umbrella, but it does get an umbrella, for reasons that should become evident.

D. CHAPTER SUMMARY

So there you have it: four umbrellas for leadership studies. (1.) History, based on the record of human experience. (2.) Science, based on regulated observation and measurement. (3.) Logic, epistemology, and theory based on rules of inference. (4.) Psychology, based on the imagination. Historians look back, to see where we have been going; scientists look around, to see where we are; philosophers look above, at the peaks and the stars, to fix our location; and psychologists look down, at the path we tread. The sooner this nascent discipline incorporates all four of these together into one common project, keeping them properly distinct, the quicker it will emerge as a distinct and reliable field of study, because its credibility depends on a deliberate blending. These four ought to be (and actually are) interdependent.[10] From this four-part schema, we can proceed.

And make no mistake, this is a book about theories, of which there are plenty.

2

PRAGMATISM IN LEADERSHIP STUDIES

> *"Theories become instruments—not answers*
> *to enigmas, in which we can rest."*
>
> **—William James, 1907**

A. "WHICH ONE IS TRUE?"

Student resistance to academic theories of any type is widespread and well known. Resistance seems to increase for the social sciences when students are expected to learn multiple theories about the same phenomenon. In the physical sciences, one theory tends to replace or transcend another. In the social sciences, however, they tend to accumulate, until at last the poor student wonders what to think when even the experts cannot agree. There are so many theories. It is a fair question, therefore, tinged with exasperation: "But which theory is true?"

I teach about leadership. Theories about leadership abound. In order to teach about leadership thoroughly, most textbooks present students with the whole range of theories and let it go at that. They try not to take sides. Students then complain.

When they are asked to answer for themselves why there are so many rival theories at one time, students give three kinds of answers. "Why do you suppose there are so many competing theories about leadership?"

(1) Some students believe these theories are numerous attempts to explain a single thing, namely leadership, so that eventually we might one day gather them together, interweave them in such a way that the evidence holds, and voilà: leadership theory. Existing theories are thought to be insufficient versions of one big thing, like the blind men describing the elephant. Some theories are probably better than others, although none is complete yet. "So which one is true?" Why, all of them, taken together. (2) Other students believe that a single true theory is impossible. Why? Maybe because the topic is too big for one theory. Maybe because leadership isn't one thing, but many. "So which one is true?" None of them can be, separately or combined. (3) Not a few students believe theories are like faces: everyone has one, and despite similarities, no two are alike. Needless to say, their trust in the value of theories generally is pretty low, on the order of "that's what you think."

In any case, learning all of these theories one right after the other is bad news. Bad news for students turns out to be good news for researchers, writers, consultants, gurus, and publishing houses, for as one of my colleagues exclaimed, "The whole field lies before us. We can go in nearly any direction and say something new."[1] Which means that the books and audiotapes and conferences will proliferate, making matters obviously worse for the student . . . especially for students clinging to the hope that at some point they will find a right answer. So long as there are royalties to be earned and tenure to be won, the proliferation will continue.

In light of this situation, what can teachers offer frustrated students? How do we respond to the question about which theory is the right one? Such is the classroom predicament that spawned this entire book.

One possibility lies in a distinctly American approach to questions of this kind, and that is pragmatism, an approach Louis Menand sees as increasingly relevant in the post–Cold War, postmodern world. He admits in the best seller *The Metaphysical Club* that pragmatism can seem strange to us now (2001, p. 442), but I think part of his purpose in writing the book was to explain (or explain away) the strangeness of pragmatism, so that we can pick it up again and apply it, without the unnecessary baggage (about slavery, for example, evolution, and the role of statistics in science). Richard Rorty has also felt the need to defend it recently, since "pragmatism is usually regarded as an outdated philosophical movement—one that flourished in the early years of [the last] century in a rather provincial atmosphere" (1982/1987, p. 31).[2] Nonetheless, to this day Rorty looks for ways to use it as well. Richard Bernstein even wrote an article in 1992 on "The Resurgence of Pragmatism." With the same spirit, this chapter is being written in order to open a line of inquiry: to what extent might pragmatism help students understand the phenomenon we know as leadership?[3]

B. DESCRIBING THE APPROACH

First, what is pragmatism? Menand shows that its founders did not always agree, and one of them rejected the name. Arch-Pragmatist William James once admitted that "brief nicknames are nowhere more misleading than in philosophy" (1897/1995, p. 97). Bernstein has written that pragmatism has been characterized by "heterogeneity, diversity, and sharp internal conflict" (1992, p. 824). Be that as it may, we can describe the central features of pragmatism in this way, according to five features.

- ❖ Radical empiricism
- ❖ A pluralistic universe
- ❖ Antecedents and consequences
- ❖ The method
- ❖ Oscillations

1. Radical Empiricism. William James gets the first word. "The essence of life is its continuously changing character; but our concepts are all discontinuous and fixed" (1909/1996, p. 253). This would be true about leadership, both as an experience and as a concept.[4] It is just as well that we seek "conceptual order" about the world, so long as we appreciate that the world keeps changing around us, oblivious to what we say about it (p. 217). Otherwise, if we are tempted to treat our concepts as reality (and worse, an unchanging reality), then gradually the correspondence between the two will crack, break apart, and eventually make no sense whatsoever (pp. 218f). James insisted: "Reality, life experience, concreteness, immediacy, use what word you will, exceeds our logic, overflows and surrounds it" (p. 212). "The whole process of life is due to life's violation of our logical axioms" (p. 257). With a wry grin, he also wrote that our intelligence "must at any cost keep on speaking terms with the universe that engendered it" (p. 207).

In other words, James spoke up in favor of a radical empiricism. The touchstone for anything even resembling truth would have to be human experience. According to pragmatism, what we should want to know about leadership is what happens in fact. What is it that happens which we call leadership? Once we come up with a concept of leadership, we must continually go back and test it against changes in the world. What was experienced as leadership in 1907 might not be what we experience today. Our concepts have to be grounded, in other words, in a state of flux, and therefore they must be subject to change (James, 1970, p. xxxi).[5]

Charles Sanders Peirce, another founder of the pragmatist movement, held that "the scientific spirit requires a man to be at all times ready to dump his whole cartload of beliefs, the moment experience is against them" (1940/1955, pp. 46f; James, 1880, p. 457). Peirce referred to this as the idea of fallibilism (1940/1955, p. 356). We could be wrong. We must be open to the possibility we are wrong. Students often expect theories to be made of sterner stuff, but James was clear that pragmatism means we must be willing "to live without assurances or guarantees" (1970, p. 229). It is all provisional and tentative. Hannah Arendt apparently referred to this as thinking "without banisters" (Bernstein, 1992, p. 838). That is a nice image.[6]

James was especially concerned that theories have a tendency to take on a life of their own and become more real to people than the reality that spawned them. We latch on tightly to our favorite theories, yet they come to interfere with their original purpose. We can trace this tendency to (what James labeled) "vicious abstractionism"—in which the conception of something in reality *replaces* reality (1970, p. 249). We become so convinced of our abstractions—our models, concepts, schemas, and theories—that we quit paying attention to reality. In time, we lose touch with reality and find ourselves lost and inept (1909/1996, pp. 218f). We shall have plucked a piece of reality from the flux of experience and neglect how that piece had been related to the flux to begin with. No theory should become a vicious abstraction.[7]

Leadership itself—not the study of leadership, but leadership as an experience—has a similar tendency to calcify or congeal, solidifying into a more permanent relationship than the parties had originally intended. (See, e.g., Jean Miller [1976, 1986], in Wren, 1995, pp. 223f.) Leadership reinforces itself, perpetuates itself, long after the motives for it have gone. Leaders often settle themselves into becoming rulers, overlords, and bosses—in other words, into an *elite*. On this, James observed that "most human institutions . . . end by becoming obstacles to the very purposes which their founders had in view" (1909/1996, p. 96). Pragmatism offers a way of understanding this tendency and empowers the participants to guard against it.

As for radical empiricism, Peirce was adamant. There is a paramount reality out there, independent and inevitable, and this reality eventually determines thought (Fontrodona, 2002, p. 81). Over time, by proper methods, within a community of right-minded seekers, we can come to know it. Our many perspectives and hypotheses converge into a complex image that matches or corresponds with lived experience (ibid., p. 122). According to Juan Fontrodona, "the fact that thought is determined by reality is what enables reality to be distinguished from fiction and allows us to come to agreements on what we perceive as real" (2002, p. 76, citing Castañeres, 1994). In other words, our method would have to be anchored in experience in order to arrive at the truth (Fontrodona, 2002, p. 108). Elsewhere, Fontrodona wrote that "experience and nature are the masters and ultimate correctors of theory" (ibid., p. 95).

Alfred Schütz was a social scientist who struggled to clarify what is meant by experience and reality, since it is possible to experience things that are not externally real, such as dreams and hallucinations. Because that is true, Schütz argued that there are multiple realities. Experience tells us as much. Nonetheless, he agreed with Peirce that there is a paramount reality, "one objective world, the universe within which we all live as psycho-physical beings, within which we work and think, the intersubjective life-world which is pregiven to all of us as the paramount reality from which all the other forms of reality are derived" (1945/1962, pp. 251f). In the words of James, it is "the world otherwise known" (ibid., p. 237, quoting *Principles of Psychology* II:289).

Already, radical empiricism permits us to detect the outline of an approach to the problem of multiple theories. One reason for their emergence could be that as the world has changed, so too have the theories meant to describe it and rightfully so. Theories are like snapshots of a golf swing, no one of which is capable of showing the entire motion. Each theory would be a freeze frame in the ongoing attempt to understand leadership. To ask which theory is true is to ask for too much, like asking which freeze frame in the golf swing is the only true representation of an entire swing. Peirce insisted, "We cannot know that there *is* any truth concerning any given question. . . . [Nonetheless,] questions do generally get settled in time, when they come to be scientifically investigated" (1940/1955, p. 288). Peirce especially was attached "to concreteness and observability" (White, 1972, p. 154). If that were the extent of pragmatism's answer, then all we have to do is match experiences of leadership with concepts, leaving open the possibility of new ones all the time. And that is part—but only a part—of the pragmatist's answer.

2. A Pluralistic Universe. The world of experience is comprised of many things and phenomena. We all know the world to be filled with different items affecting us in different ways—vehicles, pleasures, toys, odors, symptoms, animals. Rorty refers to this as "an undifferentiated manifold" (1982/1987, p. 38). James had been typically more colorful when he talked

about an infant's impression of the world "as one great blooming, buzzing confusion" (1890/1950, p. 488).[8] Despite our disconnected experiences of it, many writers have argued that the whole collection is really just one big thing we call a universe (or Being, or Creation). In response to those who insist that all of it is really one big thing, William James asked why it was so important to deny the obvious, which is that we never experience that one big thing. All we experience is the multiplicity, the variety. Maybe—just maybe—we live in a multiverse, rather than a universe, or in other words, a hopelessly divided and pluralistic existence. That way of thinking is closer to the world we experience. That way of thinking also opens up new possibilities for studying leadership.

Writing in 1907, James expressed himself this way: "That there may be one sovereign purpose, system, kind, and story, is a legitimate hypothesis. All I say here is that it is rash to affirm this dogmatically without better evidence than we possess at present" (p. 145; cf. Fontrodona, 2002, pp. 46, 65). Until then, we experience a "common-sense world, in which we find things partly joined and partly disjoined" (ibid., p. 161).[9]

Why is this notion of a pluralistic universe important to students of leadership? This very book opened with the image that all of reality is like one big ball of string. Consistent with this, we have been attempting to detect patterns in social behavior that we can classify as leadership, as though it were one thing throughout the universe, and then we have been trying to formulate better methods for leading, so that we might be in a position to offer sound advice on the subject. (Leadership studies has always been both descriptive and prescriptive.) The pluralistic universe sends us back to our experiences, as we have been saying, where many different kinds of leaders have done many different things to lead others. One has to wonder whether there is one object or phenomenon out there to call by this one name. How exactly are Hitler and Gandhi alike? Or Billy Graham and Lee Iacocca?

In fact, we might be justified in saying that, even when the parties are the same—the same leader and the same follower—no two leadership *episodes* are identical, in which case the sole purpose of leadership studies gets thrown into doubt, for if no two episodes are identical, and if we live in a pluralistic universe, then the connections we have been inferring from one episode to another could be conceptual illusions. The search for an "essence" of leadership, leadership-in-itself, that quality of leadership-ness and so forth, is misplaced. There is no such thing as leadership. Or, to be more precise, we have insufficient evidence to conclude that leadership is one thing. There are incidents we interpret as leadership as a way of grouping similar events. (For a fictional version of this approach by a noted semiologist, see Eco, 1990; for a recent version of this approach to leadership, see Drath, 2001.)

The pluralistic universe enables us to explain why there are so many theories about leadership: leadership is not a thing or phenomenon. Leadership is an interpretation of events, and we interpret events in different ways, depending on the patterns we detect. James MacGregor Burns did it his way. Fred Fiedler did it another way.[10] Peirce once wrote that "everything in the psychical sciences is inferential. . . . Very difficult problems of inference are continually emerging in the psychical sciences" (1940/1955, p. 69). There is nothing in external reality to use as a universal and infallible measuring stick, as a way of demonstrating which inference is right. Life gives us a variety of experiences. Leadership too would appear to be an undifferentiated manifold.

None of what I have just been saying about a pluralistic universe should lead the reader to conclude that pragmatists have no sense of reality, that they deny reality. On the contrary, reality is the testing ground for all theories. A theory must refer to the paramount reality and yield satisfactory results in reality (James, 1970, p. 191). Pragmatism means to be anchored in reality. Thus, the truth of any theory must be relevant to a real world situation and promise to serve some "subsequent utility" in that real world (1970, p. 216). Other realities, such as delusion, cannot serve as the paramount reality, "the one spatio-temporal fact-world" external to myself, resisting my will, and shared with other people (Husserl, *Ideas toward a Pure Phenomenology,* in Barrett & Aiken, 1962, p. 175).

None of what I have just been saying about a pluralistic universe should lead the reader to conclude that pragmatists treat all theories the same, as forever and inherently equal. It is not true that for a pragmatist, one theory is as good as another.[11] The method of pragmatism exists in order to separate the wheat from the chaff. Pluralism does not have to mean equality or relativism. It would be logical then to ask how pragmatists deal with the plurality of theories and get to a useful conclusion, knowing there are plenty of plausible theories at any given moment.

3. Antecedents and Consequences. Despite the undifferentiated manifold surrounding him, a pragmatist is interested in detecting patterns or trends within the flux of experience. What seems to happen again and again? One-time events, never to be repeated, are incapable of being understood and certainly are incapable of verification. One does not need a reason to explain what happens only once. What we want to find are generalities or regularities (Peirce, 1940/1955, pp. 265, 318).

Put this another way. Pragmatism is not so concerned about things (such as an apple) or phenomena (such as the wind) in a pluralistic universe. That alone would be unhelpful. Pragmatism is concerned more with certain *relationships* among things and phenomena, specifically between antecedents and consequences (James, 1970, p. xxxvi; Copleston, 1966, p. 68). If in our experience X precedes Y with some regularity, then we might ask what exactly is the nature of their relationship. Is there one, in fact, or was the regularity a coincidence? If there does turn out to be a relationship between X and Y, how does it seem to work? Is there another factor, such as Z, influencing the relationship? With what confidence can we say, as a matter of scientific law, that X precedes Y?

The flash of lightning tends to precede thunder. Are they related to each other? How? Did the flash of light (X) in any sense cause the thunder (Y), or were both light and sound caused by some third thing (Z)?[12]

Of primary interest to students of leadership is the relationship between an idea or belief about leadership, expressed in the form of theory, on the one hand, and actual conduct in the real world, on the other (James, 1970, p. 163). As Peirce was to put it: "In order to ascertain the meaning of an intellectual conception one should consider what practical consequences might conceivably result by necessity from the truth of that conception" (Copleston, 1966, p. 67, quoting from the *Collected Works*, vol. V, ¶ 9). In the event it turns out that some idea or belief really makes no difference in the way a person lives his life, then we have no reason to say it is true (or false). We should discard it as a useless distraction from the real work at hand, which is testing ideas and beliefs that *will* make a difference (James, 1970, p. 52). A pragmatist wants to know the consequences of a theory before taking sides for it or against it.

4. The Method. Pragmatists keep themselves open for new evidence from the empirical world, as we have seen. They also keep themselves open for new hypotheses, since all hypotheses emerge out of the flux (James, 1907, p. 79). The key to pragmatism is what pragmatists do with these hypotheses. It is after all a method, a method William James explained by which we should be able to determine what practical difference the hypothesis would make (pp. 45f, 51).[13] "In what respects would the world be different if this alternative or that were true? If I can find nothing that would become different, then the alternative has no sense" (p. 48). We look at consequences, in other words, as we saw in the previous section (p. 55). The value of these consequences gives us what James calls the "cash value" of that hypothesis (1970, p. xxix). Rorty has written that a particular belief has to be judged as

"a more useful belief to have than its contradictory, or than some belief expressed in different terms altogether" (1982/1987, p. 38).

Pragmatists did not entirely agree how this method plays itself out. Peirce, for example, did not believe that a hypothesis had to be practically verifiable, despite his "attachment to concreteness and observability," so long as we are "able to conceive its practical consequences" (Copleston, 1966, p. 70; Fontrodona, 2002, p. 117). Elsewhere, he explained "that the whole 'meaning' of a concept expresses itself either in the shape of conduct to be recommended or of experience to be expected" (1940/1955, p. 272). This effort of the imagination is what Peirce meant by "experimentation" (p. 271).

Peirce summarized the pragmatist approach to our problem of leadership by saying, "The most perfect account of a concept that words can convey will consist in a description of the habit which that concept is calculated to produce" (1940/1955, p. 286). What is likely to happen? We want to be able to draw the following conclusion: "If a normal person were to perform an operation of kind O . . . , he would observe results of kind R" (White, 1972, p. 155, quoting from the *Collected Papers*).

James took a slightly different approach. It was not that he disagreed with what Peirce was saying. He simply wanted to know in addition how a theory would fit other beliefs or concepts we already use satisfactorily. Each new possibility has to be checked against beliefs we possess, like introducing a bride to her in-laws. "Will they approve? Are they going to force me to choose between them?" For James, part of the measure of a theory is the extent to which it is congruous with what he called "residual beliefs" (1970, p. 60). In other words, James was adding a second part to the criterion of usefulness. Or, more accurately, he was reinforcing the criterion of usefulness by asking whether the theory fits residual beliefs or requires that we abandon them, which in turn threatens overall usefulness. He wrote that theories would be "'true' in proportion as they facilitate our mental or physical activities and bring us outer power and inner peace" (1970, p 65). James the psychologist was concerned that a theory "yield the most satisfactory total state of mind" (1970, p. 88; see also p. 192). Peirce, on the other hand, was not so interested in using as a standard one's "mental activities" or "inner peace" or "state of mind." These are too private and idiosyncratic. (But see Fontrodona, 2002, p. 95, citing *Collected Papers* 7:606.)[14] James knew nonetheless that the pragmatist finds himself in a pickle—both logically and psycho-logically—if he believes that two incompatible theories are equally useful and therefore equally true. (See White, 1972, pp. 157f.)

Ultimately, pragmatists agree to define "belief" as "that upon which a man is prepared to act" (Peirce, 1940/1955, p. 270, citing Baine). One has to imagine how it would influence behaviors that form into habits in the real world. James encapsulates it neatly: "Concepts signify consequences" (1970, p. 275).

5. Oscillations. The method of pragmatism establishes a particular rhythm to the way we investigate the world. The rhythm of pragmatism is outlined by Peirce in a famous essay titled "The Fixation of Belief" (1940/1955, chap. 2). A person operates according to a relatively fixed set of theories about the world. (We all have a pretty good idea what we mean by leadership, for instance.) That set of theories is exhibited in modes of acting or habits (Levine, 1995, p. 255). A state of mind of knowing what to do and why, is pleasing. It feels good. At worst, we have no reason to notice it at all, as we go happily about our business. However, as life goes on, the flux of reality confronts a person with new experiences that do not fit the prevailing set of theories. In other words, a person experiences some disruption that raises the specter of doubt. Doubt is an unpleasant state of tension. Nobody enjoys uncertainty. So a person in doubt will try to restore a sense of order or stability. Pragmatism sees in this struggle the "creative potentialities of periods of doubt alternating with periods of fixed belief and habitual action" (Levine, 1995, p. 266). It is only in this way, as a person learns to reconcile the two, that we experience growth (ibid., p. 267).

If all theories are fallible, subject to review upon experience, then how would a pragmatist proceed? The objective is to anticipate doubts and think through the implications of a theory before adopting it. To do that, a person will constantly scan the horizon for alternative theories and new experiences. In the meantime, he will hesitate to insist too strenuously that his present set of theories is true for all situations. The pragmatist is especially wary of imposing his beliefs on others, for as Louis Menand explained it, pragmatism was initially a response to the horror of the American Civil War. Pragmatists had learned from it that "certitude leads to violence" (2001, p. 61). Better, they thought, to pull back and reflect on the consequences of a theory. Better to exercise humility and openness. People who do *not* pull back, reflect, or exercise humility are more likely to shoot each other.[15]

Rollo May captures the spirit nicely:

People who claim to be *absolutely* convinced that their stand is the only right one are dangerous. Such conviction is the essence not only of dogmatism, but of its much more destructive cousin, fanaticism. It blocks off

the user from learning new truth, and it is a dead giveaway of unconscious doubt. (quoted in Hitt, 1992, p. 3)

Gaetano Salvemini was more succinct: "Whoever is convinced of possess-
ing the infallible secret for making men happy is always ready to slaughter
them" (quoted in Bobbio, 1995, p. 90).

In addition to scanning and anticipating, the pragmatist will also engage in conceptual housekeeping, putting the various theories and beliefs
he does possess into some coherent order, perhaps in a hierarchy, so that
they form a relatively stable system of useful beliefs (James, 1909/1996, p.
235). The individual theories become integrated to form a whole worldview that affects choices. In short, a theory must be coherent in relation to
both the experiences of reality and to the rest of one's beliefs. Life gives an
individual repeated opportunities to re-think those theories, which means
that he or she will continuously oscillate between belief and doubt, but always in the direction of more accurate (that is, more useful) beliefs. Each
turn away from doubt should be a turn toward an improved set of beliefs,
in a never-ending progression of enlargement and refinement. This at least
is the goal of pragmatism.

Speaking of doubt and belief, it is not too much of a distortion to say
that we live by faith. Pragmatists want us to adopt our faith as a result of a
"deliberate process" (Fontrodona, 2002, p. 122). That process is a process of
oscillation.

C. CHAPTER SUMMARY

Students want to know which theory about leadership is true, since the experts disagree. According to pragmatism, however, that turns out to be the
wrong question. What does pragmatism advise? First, pragmatism is an approach fixed firmly on what people actually experience and not on concepts, models, and technical terminology. In other words, theory serves us
to understand experience; it is meant to be instrumental. Wherever necessary, theory yields to experience, and not the other way around.

As it happens, we experience leadership in many different ways: different types of leaders use different styles in different contexts. So for any
theory of leadership to remain viable, it will have to be sufficiently rich to
embrace them without jumbling them all together. Probably the best place
to start is the relationship of antecedent to consequence: what happens in
conjunction with what other events that people call leadership? And most
important is the question asking which theory about leadership (as an antecedent) results in the most effective outcomes (consequences)? The truest
theory is the one that works best. Better still is the theory that provides for

its own improvement down-the-road, something like the amendment clause in a constitution or legal contract, in case it becomes advantageous later to change yet again. Leaving room for subsequent revision is part of what it means to be a fallibilist.

Whatever you or I conclude about the truth of leadership theory, we are advised by pragmatism to put these beliefs to work while at the same time remaining open to new information, alternative schemata, and any evidence of the impact we seem to be having on the world and on the people around us. The goal is not to discover the one immutable truth about leadership. For all practical purposes, there is no such thing. (We limit ourselves, and even become dangerous, the moment we believe that there is.) According to pragmatism, the goal is to make continual progress toward a more complete and realistic understanding that makes a difference.

The following chapter attempts to take a closer look at leadership specifically, to engage in some of that conceptual housekeeping we were just talking about. When a person talks about leadership, what does she mean?

3

LEADERSHIP AS EXPERIENCE-THEORY-SYMBOL

Let me be blunt: facts have no meaning. Facts are the fruit of reality, dangling, thick in a jungle of facts, awaiting interpretation. Nothing that is, and nothing that happens, has any meaning whatsoever—not inhering, that is, not as an attribute or quality. Standing alone, a fact is raw data, information, artificially singled out from that vast storehouse of facts we call reality. It just is.

Humans experience reality. (This too is a fact.) What is more, we seek to understand and explain reality. In so doing, we engage in rudimentary philosophy. We shall be proceeding in this book on the assumption that it would be better to do philosophy more effectively. But to do it more effectively, we need the right tools. This and the following chapter present several tools that help us to understand and explain leadership. These tools originate in philosophy as part of its technical apparatus. It is my opinion that an investment of time and effort learning how to use these tools will make the rest of this book, as well as other studies, that much easier. In other words, the practical effect of philosophy is to improve our understanding, which in turn improves our choices in life. Since the intended audience for this book would be scholars, educators, and theorists, the "cash-value" of the following chapters will be determined by their contributions to your work. For the time being, I urge patience.

Just as the study of a zebra relies on biochemistry, with all of the abstract principles of chemistry, seemingly detached from the animal itself, so also the study of leadership gets around to issues of method. A zoologist might prefer to study the snorting beast in the wild, but part of the discipline requires sufficient scientific background first. In the same way, we have to devote time and effort to the following issues before examining a living, breathing leader—in the flesh, as it were.

A. MORE PRECISELY, THEN, WHAT IS LEADERSHIP?

Leadership studies (as a collective noun) exists to prepare students to lead and lead well. It is intended to be practical. Implicit in this purpose is the belief that without study, a person might lead badly. Leadership, like medicine or law, can be done badly, so leadership studies exists in order to help students prevent that outcome. Presumably, we all want leaders to lead well. In order for its lessons to be valuable, leadership studies wants to teach students what will work in the real world—to educate them, in other words, not only to recognize and value good leadership, but also to go out and do it themselves. This presupposes of course that leadership can be learned. Otherwise, why bother teaching it? Leadership studies exists because instruction is presumed to help. It also presupposes that judgments about leadership, such as whether a leader has been effective or ethical, are possible. Thus, by the end of his or her studies a student comes to understand what it means to lead and lead well. A student also learns proven techniques to do it. I think I am right in saying that this is the objective in leadership studies (see Pfeffer, 1977, p. 108).

Behind all of this, however, leadership studies presupposes that we can know what leadership is. Knowing what leadership is would seem to be a prerequisite for judging whether it is even good or poor leadership. "Good for what?" If I were to promise to teach you leadership, and instead I taught you how to remove rotting teeth, you would recognize instantly that something is wrong. Dentistry is not leadership. You would declare it to be nonsense were I to insist that dentistry is what I mean by leadership, because "they say leadership is like pulling teeth around here." That's plain silly.

Accordingly, one would think that teachers of leadership already know what it is. In fact, to the extent they also conduct research on leadership, writing monographs and giving lectures at academic conferences, they must have *some* idea what they are studying. Otherwise, of what use is all that research, especially for prospective leaders? Most people understand that biologists do not study rocks. They study living organisms and not rocks. That is what makes it biology. What, then, is leadership studies? What exactly does it study? We return to that deceivingly simple question.

The sad truth is that experts in leadership studies cannot agree. Joseph Rost has complained about this. "There is no possibility of framing a new paradigm of leadership for the twenty-first century if scholars and practitioners cannot articulate what it is they are studying and practicing" (1993, p. 6). The disarray has worsened to the point that some teachers and writers no longer care what leadership is precisely, and even say so, yet they go along teaching and writing about it. They apply for grants and earn tenure. Rost recently argued that leadership studies "has a culture of definitional permissiveness and relativity. . . . The culture allows anyone to give a definition of leadership, and ipso facto it is as accurate and acceptable as anyone else's definition" (1993, p. 6; cf. Bass, 1990, chap. 1, especially p. 11). Participants at Harvard's Leadership Roundtable considered ignoring the issue of a definition altogether (Pruyne, 2002, pp. 23, 26). The report of their first session had this to say: "At this time there is no agreement among leadership scholars and educators . . . as to how to approach the semantic confusion surrounding leadership terminology" (ibid., p. 27; see also p. 6).

What then is the confusion over leadership? Why do they not know what it is? These would seem to be basic questions, feeding into the more practical question of whether it makes sense to value something and teach it when you simply do not know what it is. We usually expect paid professional teachers to know what they are talking about. Here, it seems, they do not. Why is that? Richard Barker recently aired his suspicions about the motives of people engaged in this enterprise. He wrote, "Could it be that leadership scholars are not really scholars, but marketing representatives, developing programs for consumption by persons with business and political ambitions? Or, are leadership scholars simply less sophisticated than their counterparts in the physical sciences?" (2001, p. 470) He supposes that, at most, leadership studies constitutes "conventional knowledge" on a par with knowing how to cash a check (ibid., p. 475). Benjamin DeMott suspected much the same thing back in 1993 when he skewered what he called the "leadership cult . . . a no-less-perfect specimen of late-twentieth-century academic avarice and a precise depth gauge of some recent professorial descents into pap, cant, and jargon" (p. 61). To their way of thinking, leadership studies resembles an open air bazaar, teeming with hubbub, fraud, and confusion. Their advice to an unsuspecting student: *caveat emptor.* "Buyer beware!" The suspiciousness about leadership as a meaningful object of study is sad because so many talented people have been laboring in the vineyard in unstructured, if not incoherent ways, talking past each other and preparing students poorly for an important social role—which defeats the purpose of leadership studies to begin with.

Certain questions arise. Is the confusion in leadership studies intractable? Is there no hope for order? If there is none, then why persist? Better to fold up our tents and go home. That will not happen, of course, since there is too much money, too many careers, too much momentum for us all now to quit. DeMott was not far wrong: "As leadership scholars snuggle to the new public teat, a new industry and special interest are born" (1993, p. 66). It appears the growth will continue.[1]

In this book—yet another book—we will stubbornly consider those theoretical questions.

The next section of this chapter approaches an understanding of the word "leadership" as a symbol, a theory, and an experience. Along the way, it contrasts first-degree constructs used in ordinary speech with second-degree constructs used for purposes of science. (We alluded to this distinction earlier.) The second section of the chapter warns against taking a postmodern turn toward denying reality altogether and detaching the study of leadership from the experiences that engender it. The following chapter introduces the importance of the role of images and the imaginal realm to the leadership process, as well as to the study of leadership. Then, by way of illustrating how to begin using these conceptual tools, it introduces two distinctions from the work of Eric Voegelin.[2]

B. WHAT'S IN A WORD?

What we seek in this chapter is the meaning of a specific word, so the place to begin is how we know the meaning of words generally. What is a word? Stated simply, a word such as "leadership" is a symbol or sign for something humans experience. The phrase "human experience" is very important, primarily because human experience is a comfortingly empirical place to start. Even so, leadership is not an object in the world, like a rock or a tree. One does not simply perceive leadership by using the five senses. An observer might perceive behavior *consistent with* leadership, yet it requires an extra step to draw that conclusion, as we mentioned earlier. The observer has to interpret his or her perceptions in light of a theory symbolized by the word "leadership." The word is a symbol for a theory.

"The word is a symbol for a theory?" With this proposition, we tumble down the rabbit hole of technical philosophical terms . . . without landing (one hopes) in what DeMott dismissed as "pap, cant, and jargon." The following paragraphs are not for the faint of heart. Despite my best efforts, they are tedious and intricate and some would say scholastical. All of which may be so without taking away from the fact they are also *necessary*, if not long overdue within the so-called "meta-narrative" of science (Lyotard, 1984/96). The following passages lead directly to the dark heart of the forest. So, what does it mean to say that the word "leadership" is a symbol for a theory?

The word "leadership" presupposes something about the way the world works. We have to remember it is possible to theorize otherwise. One of the simplest ways to demonstrate the claim that the word symbolizes a theory is to consider a theory that does *not* permit one to speak intelligibly of leadership. The novelist Leo Tolstoy, to pick one prominent writer, rejected the role of leadership in the affairs of life. Human events such as war are just too complicated, confusing, and powerful, he wrote, for any one person to make much of a difference. It could well be *comforting* to believe differently. We would like to believe we can control fate. Nevertheless, that does not change history's inexorable march. Leadership is not something that (according to Tolstoy's theory) it makes any sense to study, let alone to attempt as a career. (See Pfeffer, 1977, p. 109, for a recent version of this critique.) If that is what Tolstoy believed, one can see that the very existence of leadership studies stands in opposition to Tolstoy's "theory" about the inefficacy of individual human beings. Another theory of some kind must be at work.

To use the word "leadership" is already to imply a theory about the world.[3]

The specific contours of Tolstoy's theory are more elaborate than anything suggested here. We shall have reason at the end of the book to consider the disagreement in greater detail. The sole objective of this paragraph was to illustrate that back of leadership studies is a theory that has been symbolized as "leadership." Part of that theory has to be that individuals *do* make a difference. Without that, the whole project of leadership studies becomes meaningless (Bass, 1990, p. 8; Harter, 2003, Summer).[4]

There is a theory, in other words, lurking somewhere in the use of that term, but what does it mean to say of a word that it serves as a *symbol* of a theory? What is a symbol?[5] Symbols can represent experiences based on encounters with the environment, such as stepping on a sharp rock, and symbols can also represent theories as formulations about the nature of the environment, such as the law of gravity. Whitehead breaks these down into presentational immediacy (experience), causal efficacy (theory), and symbolic reference (1927/1955, p. 18). One could think of these simplistically as direct and indirect experiences of the world. Symbols represent both. They grow out of experience (Voegelin, OH-5, p. 38). (Symbols have other functions as well.) By the same token, theories are constructed of symbols. And experiences are mediated through a person's symbolization. In this way, experience and theory grow out of symbols. Each of these three "grows out of" the other two. Thus, we need three technical terms: Experience—Theory—Symbol. All three together are compact, like a tight knot, and difficult to separate. In actual fact, they cannot be separated. They have to be understood only by means of each other, as terms "concurrent and mutually determining one another." Their differentiation into three separate things is a mental process of separating that which cannot be separated in fact. What we are doing here in this chapter is symbolizing a theory of language to get at the meaning of a word that has something to do with human experience.

The point to remember is that none of these three serves as the foundation for the other two. None is preeminent or absolute. Even experience, the touchstone for pragmatism's radical empiricism, fails to meet the test (Voegelin, CW 12, p. 123). There is instead something more basic, beneath all three, which we shall reach as we descend further to the valley floor. We are just not there yet. (See generally Ealy, 2002.)

We have explained briefly what we mean by a symbol. What exactly is a theory? We had reason to use the term earlier, in our consideration of science as one of the four umbrellas for understanding leadership. Theories are not things in the material world. They are mental artifacts, abstractions, attempts to fix in the mind some particular feature of the world we experience. (See Ortega, 1940/1946, p. 35.) A theory is not plucked completely from experience, however, like the experience of pain, since theory includes inference and speculation and other mental feats. A theory tries to explain experience and fit it into the other experiences and theories we have had. In other words, the theory on which judgments of leadership rest represents an explanation about events that humans experience. Leadership is meant to explain something people go through.

There is a simpler way to say this: theory uses symbols to make sense of experience. But one has to be careful. Theories can be unintelligible to those who cannot make a similar connection between the symbols that are being used and their own personal experience.[6] According to Eric Voegelin, "Theory as an explication of certain experiences is intelligible only to those in whom the explication will stir up parallel experiences as the empirical basis for testing the truth of theory" (1952, p. 64). We could not talk intelligibly about leadership if our theories about it are wildly different. This does happen sometimes, as for example when someone refers to Adolph Hitler as a leader. Too many people simply reject the possibility of an evil leader and dismiss it out of hand, on the grounds that leadership is inherently moral. Hitler was not moral. Therefore, to call him a leader is to speak nonsense. The conversation grinds to a halt, if we are not careful. For the sake of intelligibility, therefore, we end up having to align our experiences, our symbols, and our theories with the experiences, symbols, and theories of others. We do this because variations in our experiences, symbols, or theories can leave us baffled. And is that not the situation in leadership studies today? People are baffled. Bafflement is uncomfortable. Thus, for the sake of intelligibility, we must examine our different alignments and consider making adjustments in light of what others tell us.[7] (It might even become necessary to abandon the word "leadership" altogether.)

If it is any comfort, people adjust their alignments all the time anyway. Language is full of common symbols representing experiences and theories. Without it, community becomes difficult, if not impossible. People "align" themselves at the market, in the workplace, and on the street. They adopt certain conventions of speech or "usages" for the sake of their daily interaction (Ortega, 1957, chap. 10). Specifically, people use the word "leadership" successfully on the street. It is not an esoteric symbol. Does that mean people in the street have already done the hard work for us? Perhaps ordinary usage warrants a look. That is the reason for cataloguing ordinary usage of the term. When he attempted to define a term, Aristotle began by looking at the way ordinary folks used it, partly because usage represents a long and elaborate process of testing and consensus that he was reluctant to ignore (Voegelin, 1952, p. 28, citing *Politics*). One does not discard ordinary usage hastily. Ortega once commented, almost in passing, that "the real meaning of a word appears when the word is uttered and functions in the human activity called speech. Hence we must know who says it to whom, when, and where" (1940/1946, p. 12). One reason we cannot afford to ignore ordinary usage is that we would risk intelligibility, as we said in the previous paragraph, because lay people will mean one thing while scholars mean another (Bass, 1990, p. 37, citing Glaser & Strauss, 1967). Paying closer attention to ordinary usage is one way to avoid "pap, cant, and jargon." Meindl et al. remind us that "leadership" comes directly from the street anyway. It is their word. It was never invented by scientists to be a term of art (1985, p. 339, citing Calder, 1977; see also Voegelin, 1952, p. 27).

There is a difference nonetheless between street level usage and science, as we stated earlier. Street level usage, which is made up of what are known as first-degree constructs, can be sloppy for purposes of science (Calder, 1977, pp. 181f; cf. White, 1972, pp. 152f, citing Peirce, *Collected Papers*). Here are a few of the problems with ordinary usage. On the one hand, the same experience can be known by two different symbols, such as teeter-totter and seesaw. Science cannot tolerate that. On the other hand, the same symbol can represent two entirely different experiences, such as the word "ball" meaning both "spherical object" and "formal, festive dance." Science has trouble with that as well. Science abhors ambiguity (Pfeffer, 1977, pp. 105–106; Heifetz, 1994, p. 14, citing Calder). Besides, usage changes over time. At one time, the word "gay" denoted a happy manner, but then it came to refer to homosexuals. Complicating things further, science aspires to universality, whereas we still use entirely different languages in the street. People do not use the precise word "leadership" in Mandarin Chinese or Aramaic. These languages might have had equivalent words, at best. I don't know. Rost tells us the word "leader" did not even exist until the year 1300 (1993, p. 37, quoting Bass, 1981). Does that mean the experience on which leadership is based did not happen until the English word came into existence and only among those who spoke English? Rost thought so (1993, pp. 42f). I happen to disagree. There had to have been equivalent experiences and equivalent theories of interpersonal causation.

In addition to these problems, usage tends to reflect a lot about a person's private and possibly idiosyncratic perspective. No two people have had the same experiences, and no two people structure their various theories about their experiences in quite the same way. On the street, we do not all think alike. You and I might have flunked the same spelling test in elementary school on the same day, but you tend to believe that this failure reflects on your worth, so you go home horrified or depressed, whereas I believe that so long as I try my best, that's what counts, since I am really not particularly gifted when it comes to spelling anyway. No big deal. In one sense, we had the same experience. In another sense, we had completely different experiences.[8] Another problem with ordinary usage—lampooned by Socrates in ancient Athens—is that people confidently use many words they cannot define, so that if it is a definition we seek, they might not be of much help (Barker, 2001, p. 475; White, 1972, pp. 152f, citing Peirce, *Collected Papers*). If anything, they look to us to define their words for them. (With all due respect to Socrates, the key is not how they define a term, but how they use it in daily speech.) Finally, people are regrettably free to use language for dishonest purposes, abusing others by abusing the language, through distortion and deceit. That also happens all too often on the street, so for yet another reason ordinary usage cannot be trusted for purposes of science.[9]

Science aspires to move from first-degree constructs (and all of their sloppiness) to second-degree constructs, which are intended to avoid these and other problems at the street level. That is the primary reason science tends toward mathematicization (if I may borrow an ugly word). Mathematics and its proofs are wonderfully neat and universal. There is a reason so many sciences drift in its direction. Am I saying that leadership studies must be reduced to mathematical formulae? I would not be the first person to say so, but I am a long way from drawing that extreme conclusion. Instead, I am trying to show how leadership studies must proceed about the term "leadership," taking it from ordinary usage and testing it for its scientific utility . . . without entirely detaching it from its origins on the street (Meindl et al., 1985, pp. 339f; Voegelin, 1952, p. 28).[10]

Let me say this another way. Leadership studies takes in language and ideas from the street, casts it all in scientific forms, studies it carefully, and then, to complete the task, helps people in the street understand what the science reveals. It is part of a positive feedback loop to enhance knowledge and understanding. Regrettably, that does not always happen. I remember attending a conference on leadership where, at a breakout session, leadership educators explained that their job was to attract both external funding and prospective students to leadership programs on campus based on the street level usage of the term, because that usage is more appealing to the man in the street, but when back on campus, they change the meaning of the word, in ways that most people would not recognize, teach the new (and even contrary) meaning to the students, and at graduation send them back out into the world. Starting the program, kids often want to lead, and benefactors often want to fund the training of leaders, but these educators confided that they tell a student, once he or she comes under their power, that leadership is by definition inclusive, participatory, collaborative, empowering, and altogether inconsistent with conventional usage. The distortions can be surreal. Kids are graduated either uncertain what they just learned or incompetent to lead, in the conventional sense. And the benefactors who send good money to colleges and universities get something in return that is at odds with their expectations. This appears to be a problem. One participant in the breakout session I just mentioned conceded that teaching is a subversive activity. In other walks of life, we call it fraud.

Right or wrong, at least they were clear in their own minds what they are doing. I suspect that most leadership educators are not. They are flailing somewhere between first- and second-degree constructs, making a mess of things. Hence, the confusion.

The symbols of science are not identical to the symbols on the street. Science finds it necessary to drop some and create others, yet "there exist . . . two sets of symbols with a large area of overlapping phonemes" (Voegelin, 1952, p. 29). In some instances, the efforts of ordinary persons to make sense of the world serve the purposes of science admirably, and a number of symbols work just as well as first- or second-degree constructs. Then, there are symbols that end up serving incompatible purposes. "This complicated situation inevitably is a source of confusion. . . ." (ibid.).

Ernst Cassirer, who wrote exhaustively about the use of symbols, recognized the difficulty. On the one hand, he wrote, we use theories and symbols in a bloodless process of intellect, drawing us further and further into that proverbial ivory tower and away from the experiences on which it is all based, even though we promise to help people function in the world we ourselves seem to have left behind (1921/1953, p. 113). It is a conundrum, or at least an occupational hazard.

It is a conundrum we are obliged to contemplate, over and over. Our work has to be grounded in reality. And the solution does not lie in using the word "leadership" any way it pleases us, like Humpty Dumpty in Lewis Carroll's *Through the Looking Glass* (1862–1863/1991, chap. 6), who uses words to mean whatever he likes, so that a "rooster" is what the rest of us know as chocolate, or a "haystack" is a river.

> "When I use a word," Humpty Dumpty said in rather a scornful tone, "it means just what I choose it to mean—neither more nor less."
>
> "The question is," said Alice, "whether you can make words mean so many different things."
>
> "The question is," said Humpty Dumpty, "which is to be master— that's all."

The path away from confusion is not the path toward such patent, solipsistic nonsense. Science should not quit being science. Sadly, not everyone can agree, even on this.

C. THAT'S WHAT YOU SAY . . .

The postmodern move is to assert that truth is socially constructed. If we change usage, then the truth also changes. All we need in order to change usage is power. Power is the basis for all truth, and has been, in the Western world since the beginning (e.g., Foucault, 1977/1984, pp. 67–75). Males had the power to determine truth and used it to keep women oppressed (e.g., Mendus, 1995). White people had the power to determine truth and used it to keep blacks oppressed (e.g., Malcolm X, 1965, chap. 10). Scientists and industrialists have had the power to determine truth and use it to keep the rest of society oppressed (e.g., Marcuse, 1992). The disempowered have clung to the postmodern critique because it does two things for them. First, it allows them to explain their difficulties in life as something on the order of a dirty trick. They are victims. This bolsters their self-esteem (Babbitt, 1924/1979, p. 104). Second, postmodernism instructs them how to respond to life's difficulties: not by engaging in the oppressor's language games rigged from the outset to reinforce status, but rather by accumulating power to dictate the terms of engagement. In his article "Towards a Semiological Guerrilla Warfare" (1967/1983), Umberto Eco declared simply, "Today a country belongs to the person who controls communications" (p. 135). The battle rages over who gets control. Social control determines what is true. Out of this logic, of course, comes political correctness, a pejorative label for what the disempowered say is the process of their liberation.

Everywhere one looks, postmodernism and science clash, though especially so at colleges and universities. It all resembles the "two worlds" thesis of C. P. Snow, as English lit professors snipe at departments of mechanical engineering, which in response get their revenge by no longer requiring their graduates to take English courses: they create their own courses in technical writing and by that method starve the academic departments that aggrieve them. As enrollment goes down in the English classes, the influence of English lit professors dwindles on campus, to the point that budgets shrink and faculty are let go. This kind of conflict then serves as proof to the postmodernists that indeed it was all about power, so they cast about for some power of their own, making alliances with women's studies and black studies or infiltrating other programs that would appear to the outside world as relatively benign. (Programs such as leadership studies?)

Eric Voegelin once referred to the "intellectual grotesque" when "the reality of reality . . . is simply denied" (1966/1978, p. 161). Postmodernism at the margins denies reality. People who deny reality have to replace it with something, says Voegelin, so they replace it in their imagination with a second reality—a condition Voegelin labeled as pneumopathological, which means a disease of the spirit. Why is it a disease? It means that a person is ignoring reality, turning away from it, choosing at some level of consciousness to reject it. That might be a comforting strategy in a crisis or as a diversion, and one could argue that on occasion a person has to deny reality for a moment as a practical matter for the sake of inner peace, like an escape or a cooling off period, but as a condition for living, it will not work. Ortega once defined reality as "that which must be reckoned with, whether we like it or not" (1940/1946, p. 20).[11] Freud used a similar principle for mental health. One cannot disprove or even debate the merits of a second reality. Fiction is fictitious. In the Land of Oz, Scarecrow can most certainly speak without lungs or vocal cords, and children of a certain age understand that it is just a fantasy. Adults, on the other hand, who abide in their second reality, who believe that scarecrows can talk, will refuse to respond by means of argumentation anyway. They do not see why they should have to. "This is my reality. I'm entitled to it. You can have whatever reality you need. It all rests on power anyway and not on things like evidence or logic." Goodbye, Enlightenment. . . .

None of which is to suggest that we entirely discard the postmodern critique, as though that were even possible. A number of serious scholars have been trying to work within it (e.g., Meindl et al., 1985, with regard to leadership and Lyotard generally, 1984/96). It certainly exceeds the scope of this book to work through all of its ramifications. One of the reasons for this digression on the hazards of postmodernism is to contrast it with the approach to leadership studies I have been urging, while at the same time folding it into that approach at the proper place. I agree with Bernstein, who wrote "that a properly developed pragmatic orientation can lead us beyond many of the sterile impasses of so-called 'modern-postmodern' debates" (1992, p. 818). Regrettably, much of what this book offers will resemble straight-up postmodernism, which is not my intention. So I ask you, the reader, to set aside what you might know about postmodernism, temporarily.

The symbols and theories we use in the sciences might differ from first-degree constructs, and they probably should to an extent, as we have already noted. One difficulty is that this difference might lay scientists open to the charge of creating their own second reality. After all, their language looks different from ordinary language. When the physicist refers to quarks that nobody can see, the layman might become suspicious. Is the relationship of Reality to Second Reality the same as the relationship of first-degree construct to second-order construct? Science does indeed have to guard against the temptation that its work might spin off into science fiction.[12] But the task of science is not in and of itself pneumopathological. Moving from first-degree constructs to second-order constructs is not the same thing as creating a second reality. Second realities fail to correspond with the paramount reality we all experience. Sometimes that is even intentional. They are fanciful and false. Second-order constructs, on the other hand, correspond closely to the reality we all experience. They had better. Otherwise, it is not science. This is what Voegelin meant when he wrote, echoing Heraclitus, that "only if the [scientist] speaks the common *logos* of reality can he evoke a truly public order" (OH-5, p. 26). Scientists can disagree, of course, about the best way to do this, but that is a separate thing from resisting the project altogether (ibid., p. 35).

We have lingered long enough within the tension of experience-theory-symbol. Their complex relationship determines how we communicate about leadership, because they determine how we think about leadership. They lie deeper, in a sense, than the lessons and literature most of us in leadership studies use on a daily basis, yet there is a level deeper even than this, a level no one can thoroughly describe or explain because it lies "beyond articulate experience" (Voegelin, CW 12, p. 124). That level is the absolute bottom (ibid., p. 129). For our purposes, we shall refer to our participation in it loosely as the imagination.

Just because some persons might resort to the imagination in order to replace reality is no reason to impugn the imagination altogether, as the next chapter explains: the imagination helps to construct our understanding of reality. Indeed, it is necessary. Voegelin's objection to Second Realities does not extend to the imagination *per se*. This is important to remember. It has to do, rather, with the purpose and manner in which the imagination is used. The Spanish philosopher José Ortega y Gasset wrote about this in his inimitable style: "The fact is that weak races may turn this strong drug of the imagination into a vice, an easy escape from the heavy weight of existence" (1914/1961, p. 132). We should want to avoid that here.

D. CHAPTER SUMMARY

In summary, people use the word "leadership" as a symbol for experiences they have in their social life. The symbol makes sense only within a certain crude theory they have about the way social life works. It becomes the task of leadership studies to examine the relationship among the symbol, experience, and theory people refer to collectively as "leadership"—although to do that in a sufficiently rigorous and useful manner, leadership studies has to detach the words people commonly use to describe leadership and subject them to certain tests in order to avoid many of the problems inherent in ordinary language.

In the next chapter, we take a closer look at leadership as image. It is the longest chapter in the book, dealing with epistemological difficulties rarely of interest in leadership studies, but do not despair, because immediately afterwards we take a brief rest to stop and get our bearings. Then, we finally get to turn our attention to leadership itself.

4

LEADERSHIP AS IMAGE

"Do not use the word hypothesis, *even less* theory, *but mode of imagining."*
— *Georg Lichtenberg (n.d.)*

A. IMAGE IS EVERYTHING

As scientists revise and devise their symbols and theories in light of experience, they have to use their imaginations (Voegelin, OH-5, p. 38). The trouble, as we seem to keep saying in different ways, is that imagination untethered to the project of understanding human experience is the very source of second realities and of trouble.

Meindl et al. explain that scientists have been moving "away from the personality of the leader as a significant, substantive, and causal force on the thoughts and actions of followers." What, then, are they moving toward? They are starting to place "more weight on the images of leaders that followers construct for one another" "It is the personalities of leaders as imagined or constructed by followers that become the object of study" (1985, pp. 330f; Pfeffer, 1977, p. 110; see generally Bass, 1990, pp. 7f). As we have known for some time, leaders *use* symbols and images. They dress for success, choosing power words, power seats at the table, and otherwise managing impressions to achieve their purpose, yet they are themselves symbols because they are images. (See, e.g., Gardner, 1990, pp. 18–20.) Leadership truly is in the eyes of the beholder.

One reason for highlighting the imagination as a separate faculty is that leadership is to a large extent an affair of the imagination. I have come to agree with others that leadership is essentially imaginal (e.g., Mazlish, 1984b & 1981). (And I do not use the word "essence" casually.) Accordingly, on the leadership bookshelf, next to empirical research and historical anecdotes, we will find works of the imagination, all the way from playful texts by Max Dupree and Margaret Wheatley to outright fiction, such as *Zapp!* and *Habits of the Heart.*[1] One of the most effective uses of story-telling to teach about leadership is Wilfred Drath's 2001 book *The Deep Blue Sea.* While we are at it, we might as well incorporate classical and popular literature, inasmuch as we can and do learn about leadership in epic poetry, novels, scripture, comic books, and cinema. The Hartwick Humanities in Management Institute has developed an entire curriculum around leadership in feature length films. Pfeffer refers to a *mythology* of leadership (1977, p. 111). In effect, one can say that leadership studies has for its object the mythology of leadership.

There can be problems basing a scientific study on the imagination. The imagination is believed to possess several disadvantages. For one thing, according to Gilbert Durand,

> The image has a specific logic of its own, which requires complete surrender of the principle of identity as well as its famous corollaries: non-contradiction and exclusion of the middle. Having abolished the chronology of time and the three-dimensionality of space, the image is not bound by linear thinking and bivalent logical sequences. (Sells, 2000, p. 59; Eliade, 1991, pp. 9, 37)

The world of the imagination more resembles dreams, delusions, and cartoons than the rigid, mechanistic structure once detected by means of science. Perception we understood to be a filtering process, so we took that into account. Patricia Berry argues that imagination is unlike perception because it is an altogether different operation (Sells, 2000, p. 94). We have only to compare a photograph of the Spanish landscape with the surreal mindscape portrayed by the painter Salvador Dali. One of them we call "real." The other is, what, no more than art? How can a science proceed to make sense of what seem to be crazy fantasies? Are we saying here that leadership *is* part of a second reality, indistinguishable from fantasy? Are we not all postmodernists now?

The simple act of communicating about the imaginal realm distorts it (Sells, 2000, p. 101). "[I]mages . . . express more than the subject who has experienced them could convey in words" (Eliade, 1991, p. 17). Berry has written, for example, about dreams (though one could ask why it would not apply to other parts of the imaginal realm as well), where she explains that they "are like knots of condensed implications . . ." (Sells, 2000, p. 104). A terrific simile, that. Images are knots of condensed implication. Images are, in the words of Eric Voegelin, compact, whereas science operates by a process of differentiation, as we will have occasion to explain shortly. Hillman concedes that this approach through the imagination will not lead to validity or certitude (1975, p. 142), and in fact we should not take any of it literally (ibid., p. 150), but is that not what leadership studies would be seeking? Again, is this not the postmodern move? It is not.

The imagination refuses to fit our conventional models for doing science. This much is true. For this to serve as an objection, however, is to impose a sense of science that violates one of its own, most basic precepts, which is that science ought to be the investigation of what is. And imagination plainly happens (Babbitt, 1924/1979, p. 171). It not only happens; it pertains to leadership in crucial ways. It will be the burden of this subsection to indicate the plausibility of approaching the study of leadership by means of the imaginal, and to offer a few guidelines.

Benjamin Sells, introducing a set of articles on archetypal psychology, has asserted that "every act, every thought, every gesture, every dream, every impulse of whatever kind, if experienced at all is mediated and presented through the soul's images and imagining capabilities. . . . [T]he image is not only what is experienced but how it is experienced" (2000, p. 5; Voegelin, OH-5, p. 37). In one of those articles, Henry Corbin called the image "primordial . . . unconditional and irreducible" (Sells, 2000, p. 85). Berry added, "On the image level evaluations cannot apply, for the image simply is" (ibid., p.108; Peirce, 1997, pp. 146–147, 200, 203).

The most popular living spokesman for studying the imaginal realm is James Hillman. And his most comprehensive defense appears in a book titled *Re-Visioning Psychology* (1975). (It would be too ambitious to summarize it here.) Of particular interest is the premise that images are the basic structure of the psyche. We embody them. It is because images are the basic structure that we have such difficulty recognizing their importance. "[I]t is virtually impossible to see the instrument by which we are seeing" (1976, p. 103). Yet we must become aware of the imaginal realm, in some way.

Another articulate spokesman for the epistemological importance of images for the social sciences, namely Kenneth Boulding, holds that "behavior depends on the image" (1956, p. 6). He includes images of fact, such as the image of an apple on a tree, as well as images of value about what is good, safe, and beautiful (ibid., p. 11). He is careful to avoid saying these images are altogether private or idiosyncratic. We all certainly operate on the assumption that our images of the world are shared by others, that is, that they are public and objective (ibid., p. 14). We frequently talk about our images and compare them with each other (ibid., p. 15). We tend to believe that from our vantage point anyone would see the same thing in the same way. (See also Schütz, 1955/1962, pp. 315–316.)

When it comes to studying leadership, we can be more explicit. The relevant images are images of interacting persons—(a) images that the follower has of himself and of the leader, (b) images that the leader has of herself and of the follower, and (c) images that the observer has of both the leader and the follower. Out of these images, or identities, the participants together construct a relationship. Fontrodona, explicating the work of Peirce, once put it this way:

> When two people meet, their primary encounter is as living bodies, through which they express meanings, purposes, and intentions. Each one is, for the other, a series of signs, words, or gestures, acts or omissions that must be interpreted. (2002, p. 82)

In ordinary speech, when people use the language of leadership, they usually refer to specific persons and to specific events. One could accumulate instances of leadership in this way and catalogue them, abstracting from usage in order to arrive at meaningful classifications. "X was a leader. Y was a leader. Z was a leader." Such a project would be useful. Where in all of this is the imagination?

What usually happens in ordinary experience when people have impressions of each other? They try to make sense of those impressions according to preexisting schemas. When I am introduced for the first time to another person, I tend to slot the other person into preformed categories: she is an elderly, white woman who seems kind, weary, weak, and impoverished. She is probably a grandmother. Over time, I learn to cluster certain traits or characteristics together into distinctive types—the bully, the Bible-thumper, the nerd, and the supermodel. It might be advisable ordinarily to operate according to the law of individual differences, which holds that every person is unique (Newstrom & Davis, 1993, p. 12), yet in the mind we tend to use these types as a kind of shorthand, so we can say of a person quickly that he or she is a "typical" something-or-other. A type helps to economize the mind's energies. It simplifies the task of dealing with new people. Where does a type come from? A type is a composite image made up of images; we construct types out of our imagination and memories—memories of previous acquaintances and memories of previous encounters with the same person, if any. We organize our impressions into an ordered unity and give it a name.

"In order to know a man," wrote Georg Simmel, "we see him not in terms of his pure individuality, but carried, lifted up or lowered, by the general type under which we classify him" (1971, p. 10).

A number of writers have already begun the work of identifying and categorizing these images. Johannes Steyrer, for example, relying heavily on Oswald Neuberger, identifies four distinct leader-images: the Father, the Hero, the Savior, and the King (1998). Gladwell describes Mavens, Connectors, and Salesmen (2000). F. H. Heinemann had his leaders, scouts, lieutenants, pseudo-leaders, and wardens (1979). In 1991, Manz & Sims offered these four types: strong man, transactor, visionary hero, and super-leader (in Wren, 1995, p. 215, table 1). Peirce himself came up with artist, practical man, and scientist (Fontrodona, 2002, p. 97). There are other taxonomies, going all the way back to Plato (e.g., Wills, 1994; Hughes, Ginnett, & Curphy, 1996, p. 189, citing Kroeger & Thuesen, 1988; see generally Bass, 1990, chap. 2).

Max Weber classified three types of legitimate domination, which are in a sense three groupings of images. They are suitably famous to illustrate how this works.

- Legal domination
- Traditional domination
- Charismatic domination

First is *"legal" domination*, grounded in accepted procedures such as elected politicians or CEOs hired to shake things up. The followers might not have actually chosen the leader, but they accept the process by which the leader rose to dominance, so they acquiesce. The ordinary citizen cannot ignore legal commands by saying "I didn't vote for you." Accepting the process means that you accept the outcome. This includes leadership based on the promise of reward, when I agree to follow you because you will do something for me in exchange.

Traditional domination rests on the past—on habit, custom, precedent, a continuation of what was already accepted. Many leaders rise to dominance because they fit the traditional model. They are the eldest son in some organizations, or the next in line. Of course, once a leader rises to leadership, his or her dominance is likelier to persist than not—all things being equal—out of sheer inertia (if one may think in those terms). The person you accepted as leader once before must be acceptable again (or still), barring some kind of disruption in the meantime.[2]

Charismatic domination has drawn considerable attention from leadership studies, and a number of writers seem to have decided that this alone qualifies as leadership. (See, generally, Hughes, Ginnett, & Curphy, 1996, chap. 11.) In a few words, what is it? It derives from Christian usage about the divine gifts a leader possesses. God spoke to the leader, or God endowed the leader with extraordinary talents and abilities, or the vision that the leader represents impresses the rest of us as inspired by God. For Weber, there is still today an element of the divine, but a more neutral characterization might be that the leader earns followers because the followers yield to something distinctive about the leader. He (or she) seems smarter or more physically imposing or some such. The follower's attention is drawn to the leader, like the figure to the ground.[3]

Leaders from each type might find themselves in conflict with other leaders. Two leaders can vie for legal domination in an election, for example, but also a traditional leader might find himself in competition with a charismatic rebel. Within types and across types, prospective leaders vie for dominance. Weber was not saying that in these rivalries and struggles only one person *deserves* to lead. Instead, the follower's basis for following can be said to fall within one (or more) of these three categories. The *follower* determines which person deserves to lead. It is also important to recognize that the same leader might lead one person out of legal legitimacy and another person out of charismatic legitimacy. These are not mutually exclusive in reality. They are different conceptually. And for the sake of thoroughness, we should acknowledge that a leader such as Fidel Castro might begin his career with charismatic domination and then remain in power by means of traditional domination.

It would appear that an important task for leadership studies is to describe the family resemblance among all of the different images we have for leadership. At the end of the day, there would be no definition of leadership so much as "overlapping and criss-crossing" relationships. In any event, to catalogue and describe all of these images thoroughly requires entering the depths of the imagination. There seems to be no other way around it.

To be blunt, leadership studies involves an understanding of the imagination. It has to. Pfeffer put it this way: "[L]eadership is of interest primarily as a phenomenological construct. Leaders serve as symbols for representing personal causation of social events" (1977, p. 104). Later, he wrote that leadership "is attributed by observers" (ibid., p. 109). It is their interpretation of people and events that "create" leadership to begin with. To the extent participants and observers engage their imaginations, then, consciously or not, scientists hoping to understand the process must appreciate the role of the imagination.

Mircea Eliade wrote in terms of symbols and their basis in imagery.

> Symbolic thinking . . . is consubstantial with human experience[;] it comes
> before language and discursive reason. The symbol reveals certain aspects
> of reality—the deepest aspects—which defy any other means of knowl-
> edge. Images, symbols and myths are not irresponsible creations of the psy-
> che; they respond to a need and fulfill a function, that of bringing to light
> the most hidden modalities of being. Consequently, the study of them en-
> ables us to reach a better understanding of man—of man "as he is," before
> he has come to terms with the conditions of History. (1991, p. 12)

The postmodern critique, despite its apparent hostility, can accept a
science of the imaginal, so long as science respects it and adapts its methods to the nature of the object of study. Science that dismisses the imaginal
as childish or backward assumes the form of intellectual imperialism, ad-
judging parts of reality as inferior or inadequate because they do not conform to accepted models (Lyotard, 1984/96, pp. 80–81). It is unnecessary
for a postmodernist to reject science and scientific method (ibid., p. 87). It
is equally unnecessary for science to reject the imaginal. What is required
under the postmodern critique is, according to Lyotard, two-fold. First,
students must recognize and to some extent tolerate the "sloppiness" of ordinary language and leave themselves open to shifts and refinements due to
the "heteromorphous nature of language games." Second, students must
make explicit, and attempt to share, what they are doing and how they are
doing it—to search for a "local" and tentative consensus, even if it might be
possible to go off in a thousand different directions, because without that
local and tentative consensus, there is no understanding and no hope.
Consensus binds together. The tentativeness permits us to bracket certain
doubts and alternatives for a limited duration and for limited purposes,
without pretending they don't exist. Consensus is what this book attempted at the very beginning when it identified four core components of
a tentative definition of leadership: relationship, attribution, change, and
direction.

What Lyotard has requested in the name of postmodernism greatly
resembles pragmatism: an openness to change, a search for functional consensus, and fallibilism.

B. VOEGELIN'S TOOLKIT

It would be useful, in my opinion, to import two lessons from the work of Eric
Voegelin, who is one of the least heralded of the great philosophers of the previous century.[4] These lessons deal with fundamental distinctions that would

assist anyone trying to grapple with the fruits of the imagination. The first lesson distinguishes "primal" images from "thought" images. The second lesson, which takes longer to explain, describes the distinction between compact and differentiated symbols.

1. PRIMAL IMAGES < > THOUGHT IMAGES. Eric Voegelin's early work on the role of images in human experience included a helpful distinction between "primal" images and "thought" images. The purpose of this first subsection is to explain and then illustrate this distinction.

The approach I refer to as the "early" Voegelin appears in *The History of the Race Idea* (CW 3), where he distinguishes between two German terms, *Urbilder* and *Denkbilder*. These terms had specific meanings for Voegelin, so we should explain those meanings. We are assisted in this by the editor's introduction to the English translation (V-3, pp. xiii–xiv).[5]

a. Vondung translates *Urbild* as "primal image" (p. xiii). "Primal images" have to do with the images we use to see the world. These images are not to be judged true or false, since they are simply the way a person sees the world. To this extent, "they are all true"—even when they are contradictory (p. 16). As Voegelin asserted, "There is no argument against a primal image" (ibid.; see Whitehead, 1927/1955, pp. 6f). They can change over time. The primal image of what is human (to use Voegelin's example) has evolved in the West. And why not? Primal images are impressions we have. I happen to prefer translating *Urbild* as an impression, a word that comes from translations into English of the work of José Ortega y Gasset.

> Ortega gives the name "patent world" to that part of reality which is revealed without any effort except that of opening our eyes, that is, to the world "of mere impressions." (Marías, 1961, p. 175, n. 10, quoting Ortega, 1914/1961, p. 66)

Ortega went on to explain that this patent world is a world "of sensuousness, of appearances, of surfaces, of the fleeting impressions which things leave on our stimulated nerves" (1914/1961, p. 83). "Impressions form a superficial tapestry from which ideal paths seem to lead us toward a deeper reality" (ibid., p. 74). That "deeper reality" has to be depicted by means of *Urbilder*.

b. In order to complete the distinction, we must now explain the meaning of that other term, *Denkbilder*. According to Vondung, a *Denkbild* would be an "image of thought" (xiii). These images, unlike the primal images grounded in experience, are concepts, theories, judgments, and so forth, the philosophical apparatus for thinking *about* our experiences. These are mental tools and mental constructs to help a person make sense of experience.[6] (Under pragmatism, we saw this in the interplay between [i] the flux of life that presents itself to us as impressions and [ii] our beliefs.) Unlike primal images, these thought images *can be challenged* by means of argument. Some are better than others.

A critic can attack images of thought in two ways. (This is an important section of the forest trail, as we will refer back to it repeatedly throughout the rest of our journey. Pay heed.)

First is "intrasystematic consistency," which requires a coherent, valid set of propositions, so that for instance a person doesn't simply contradict himself heedlessly. "All men are mortal, and all men are immortal." That sort of paradox is not usually helpful. At least it raises red flags. Speaking up for intrasystematic consistency is the kind of argument that William James encouraged for the sake of conceptual housekeeping, as we noted in the chapter on pragmatism. Conceptual housekeeping has been a problem particularly for leadership studies (Bass, 1990, p. 913). The second kind of argument has to do with the degree of correspondence or "harmony" of thought images with the prevailing primal images.[7] A perfectly valid system can fail because it relies on impressions the rest of us do not share. For example, a philosophy based on a primal image to the effect that all humans are rational maximizers will never gain traction with folks who see humans exclusively as tangles of nonrational drives. Even if they use the same words, they are not talking about the same things.[8]

At any given moment, a stable society will probably tend to share certain primal images, in the manner we mentioned earlier, though among the educated classes thought images constantly struggle with each other. Politicians, college professors, and journalists traffic in competing symbolizations. This means that the relationship among all of these images constantly changes. As Vondung put it, "Primal images and philosophical images of thought correspond with and influence each other; they can be in harmony with each other but may also diverge widely" (p. xiv). In the flux of images, thought images that become "detached" from their primal origins lose power. As Voegelin observed, "thought images alone . . . are bloodless shadows that have no effect on us and have nothing to say to us" (p. 17). There is a chronic need therefore to determine whether there are thought images "better suited to the new way of seeing" (p. 15).

If the primal images and primal ways of seeing change, the philosophical thought images must change with them, and if the rational requirement for consistency within the thought images cannot be met, doubt spreads out from this failure and makes careful examination of a philosophy's primal images necessary. (p. 12)[9]

In summary, therefore, let Vondung have the last word.

The analysis of the actual subject matter is divided into two parts [i.e. thought images or "theories" and primal images or "ideas"] in accordance with Voegelin's conviction that theories of a scientific status must not be mixed up with [primal images]. Theories, which try to describe and explain reality, must be tested under the terms of theory, i.e., with respect to the validity of their premises, the logic of their reasoning, the rationality of their argumentation. [Primal images], however, present a different task and have to be treated in a different way. Since [primal images] form a part of political, or social, reality itself, they have no place within theoretical reasoning. The task is rather to find out how they originate, how they function, and how, for instance, they contribute to the formation of groups and societies. (V-2, p. xiv)

Vondung cautions that the "early" Voegelin left us a less adequate set of thought images than the later Voegelin, so that a thorough examination of his mature writings would extend this line of development, but Vondung also assures the reader of the early Voegelin that what appears here is not radically inconsistent with his later works. Rather, it is (to use his words) less precise and less differentiated (p. xiv, referring also to Heilke, *Voegelin on the Idea of Race*, pp. 7–35).[10]

2. COMPACT < > DIFFERENTIATION. Voegelin also found it helpful in his later work to distinguish between "compact" and "differentiated," as well as the process by which the compact *becomes* differentiated. It is the purpose of this subsection now to explain these terms.

Eugene Webb offers the simplest place to start. "Compact. Voegelin's term for experience having distinguishable features yet to be noticed as distinct." "Differentiated. Voegelin's term for consciousness in which the distinguishable features of a previously 'compact' field of experience are noticed as distinct" (1981, p. 279). In other words a differentiation brings to consciousness differences within an experience or symbol that were previously unnoticed, such as the compact image of a circle being differentiated by various arcs or pie shapes or concentric circles.

Voegelin found the distinction especially useful in his study of history. In the first volume of *Order and History,* he set forth three principles that had "emerged in the course of this study" for the purpose of clarifying a problem he referred to as "the problem of civilizational form." The last of these principles is that "[t]he structure of the range [of human experience] varies from compactness to differentiation" (OH-I, p. 60). Put another way, the terms "compact" and "differentiated" describe stages or increments along a continuum, in much the same way that we use the terms "youth" and "adult."

What he intended to show was one way to measure changes in civilizational history. Over time, communities adopt symbols to interpret their experiences; then they adapt them, when symbols that are more adequate become available. "Compact blocks of the knowable will be differentiated into their component parts and the knowable itself will gradually come to be distinguished from the essentially unknowable. Thus, the history of symbolization is a progression from compact to differentiated experiences and symbols" (OH-I, p. 5). That is the direction to imagine the process taking place, from compact to differentiated.

A word of caution. By using the word "progression" in the foregoing quotation, Voegelin was definitely *not* trying to say that "compact" is "more primitive than 'differentiated' [since] symbols of each sort can be evaluated as to their adequacy in representing truth" (McClain). One is not superior to the other, in that sense. The compact symbol might actually be richer, more complete. Voegelin makes the interesting assertion that "our differentiated vocabulary is not adequate to [some] compactness" (OH-I, p. 41). That is, the differentiated symbols might deprive us of appreciating the richness of the compact symbols out of which they arise. We could very easily differentiate ourselves away from a more adequate understanding of experience and get lost in subtleties that ignore the press of reality. Whatever we shall have gained by means of differentiation can be offset by losses.[11]

A differentiation of Tchaikovsky's sixth symphony into three movements and a finale scarcely begins to explain why we know it today as the *Pathétique.* After all, Beethoven's third symphony has three movements and a finale, but we know it as the *Eroica.* The compact experience of the music retains the reason for these names—reasons that we are at risk of losing when we start differentiating the compact experience, breaking it up into pieces. What Voegelin was saying is similar to claims in the literature on leadership about synergy, for example, and systems thinking. It is his cautionary note to remember that analysis (the separating) requires synthesis (the reattaching) in order to get at the most thorough understanding.

To give another instance of what can be lost, Voegelin noted that the links holding things together in compact symbols tend to be overlooked once those "things" can be thought of as separate. In this way, "the world ceases even to be experienced as a 'world' in the full sense, implying unity and order, but dissolves into a set of discrete particulars" (Webb, 1981, p. 137).

Even though he defended the image of a pluralistic universe, William James (a philosopher and psychologist whom Voegelin respected) also warned against the temptation to overlook the connective tissue of reality for the sake of discrete ideas.

> Thus it comes that when once you have conceived things as "independent," you must proceed to deny the possibility of any connexion whatever among them, because the notion of connexion is not contained in the definition of independence. For a like reason you must deny any possible forms or modes of unity among things which you have begun by defining as a "many." (1909/1996, p. 219)

Again, the process of differentiation tends to isolate "independent" parts of the compact whole, not only from each other but also from the whole of which they are a part, and this would be a mistake.

Nonetheless, differentiation is a gain of some sort. It exists in response to the realization that a compact symbol standing alone is inadequate, precisely because it failed to separate component parts. So, to reject the insights of differentiation altogether is to move backward. The task is to keep the compact experience as the *context* for further and further differentiation (Webb, 1981, p. 138, citing OH-IV, vol. 4, p. 175).

One of the difficulties is that, as a community differentiates its symbols, the various new symbols pile up without coherence. The community finds itself burdened with a variety of differentiations, which means a variety of new symbols. Voegelin wrote, "The symbols are many, while being is one. The very multiplicity of symbols can, therefore, be experienced as an inadequacy, and attempts may be undertaken to bring a manifold of symbols into a rational, hierarchical order" (OH-I, p. 8). Voegelin calls this the problem of the "seemliness of symbols," when a community risks confusion over all of the un-integrated symbols. They have proliferation without coordination. In this confusion, the community needs, not just further differentiation, which always has some potential value, but a coherence among the resulting symbols. Bernard Bass makes a comparable assertion in his guardedness about typologies and taxonomies about leadership (1990, pp. 21, 36). What Voegelin seemed to be cautioning was that it is just as possible to suffer from *too many* differentiated symbols as it is to suffer from too few. Whitehead offered a vivid image for what we are talking about.

> No account of the uses of symbolism is complete without this recognition that the symbolic elements in life have a tendency to run wild, like the vegetation in a tropical forest. The life of humanity can easily be overwhelmed by its symbolic accessories. A continuous process of pruning . . . is a necessary function in every society. (1927/1955, p. 61)

The objective is not to limit the proliferation of new symbols, which is a kind of willful ignorance, but rather to integrate them in some meaningful way. William James referred to the power we possess "of translating the crude flux of our merely feeling experience into a conceptual order" (1909/1996, p. 217). And so, to cope with the *plenum*, we seek patterns, inasmuch as "without patterns, memory is swamped" (Barzun, 2000, p. 768).

The sequence in history, then, is from compact to differentiated and from unstructured differentiation to structured differentiation.

A distinction between "compact" and "differentiated" serves more than the study of civilizational history. It is a distinction of some use in the study of many things, including leadership. How might it be used?

a. First things first. Differentiation is a process. The creation story of Genesis wonderfully illustrates the material process of differentiation, in which an inchoate, compact stuff (Chaos) is divided into simple dichotomies, such as light from darkness, heaven from earth, dry land from sea, living things from inanimate material, animals from simpler organisms, and humans from animals. According to its own terms, the creation story attempts to tell the process by which these dichotomies came into being. Curiously, it also parallels the process by which any one person comes to consciousness during infancy. Even though none of us remembers what happened immediately after birth, we understand the process generally of learning, first, simple distinctions, such as light and dark, hungry and full, me and you. What Voegelin intended to study was the process by which a person comes to a more adequate symbolization of a reality that is altogether and inescapably compact, and that study is precisely what we need in leadership studies.

b. One of the best ways to get at the process of differentiation is to study the usual organization of stimuli. We begin with the five senses—seeing, hearing, tasting, touching, and smelling. This alone is a differentiation, because the brain encounters the world as a compact unity, "as one great blooming, buzzing confusion"—even though we experience it through five completely different modes. Next, the five senses can be subdivided. The visual world, just to take one example, can be differentiated by light and dark, and by color. In fact children learn colors by a process of differentiation, beginning with three primary colors before learning the color wheel and then the visible spectrum, which itself begins simply as ROY G BIV (red, orange, yellow, green, blue, indigo, violet) and progresses into a complete spectrum of indistinguishable degrees between infrared and ultraviolet.

Remember, part of the task, according to Voegelin, is making sense of the differentiations. With regard to color, not only does the visible spectrum help to categorize differences we experience in the world, but the other differentiation of light and dark enables us to take that spectrum and further differentiate hue and tint. The same shade of green can be lighter or darker, making for distinct colors. Painters and fashion coordinators are expected to master the nuances.

The same basic process applies to the other senses, as the listener detects differences in tone and pitch, and the taster learns to distinguish sweet, sour, salty, and bitter. What I am trying to do is argue that the process of differentiation happens all the time. In infancy the child has no basis for telling one adult from another, but then gradually he learns males from females, family from strangers, until as an adult he encounters one unique human being after another, despite the tendency even then to associate each new acquaintance with someone from his past. "This new employee is a lot like my cousin Dave." "That woman at the next table has the same laugh as a girl I knew in school." After countless attempts to symbolize and classify these differentiations, we arrive at a very extensive organization of the world we experience by means of perception.

c. The conventional university as an institution of higher education serves as another example of the same extensive organization of the world we experience. After differentiating into humanities, arts, and sciences, we can further differentiate the sciences into the physical (or "hard") sciences and the human (or "soft") sciences. Among the human sciences, we find psychology, for example, anthropology, and sociology, to name just a few. Within sociology, we find subdivisions. Don Levine identifies national traditions of sociological theory, which of course is only one way to slice the discipline (1995). Some sociologists will emphasize a distinction between quantitative research and qualitative research. Some will insist on the Weberian "fact/value" distinction. Similar breakdowns can be made in chemistry and geology, et al., to the point that each doctoral candidate—no matter what the discipline—must demonstrate the ability to specialize and become a classification of one person, *sui generis,* alone in the history of the world as the expert on her topic.

d. I have found it helpful in my teaching career to illustrate differentiation by reminding students of the famous utterance whenever the comic book hero Superman appeared. "Look, up in the sky. Is it a bird? Is it a plane? No, it's Superman!" At the risk of dissecting a clip of popular culture to death, let us notice the differentiation. First, the listener is directed to look, to use his or her eyes, rather than other sense organs. But look where? In the sky. (The words bring clarification with alacrity.) But only now does the differentiation begin in earnest. What is it we are looking at? The first option, a bird, is what every child knows to expect flying through the sky. (It's certainly no fish or pig, let alone a rock or a daisy.) The mind turns first to the most familiar alternative, but upon further inspection, that classification isn't quite right, so a further differentiation comes to mind, between "animal" and "human" flying things. "Bird" is a symbol that doesn't work. Except that the most likely *human* flying thing, an airplane, isn't quite right either. The impression is not familiar, except as something human, and yet this thing is beyond what we have come to know about human flying things; it is above the human, a new classification that we can only categorize as "super" human. It takes its name from the extent to which it differs from what we already know. A new symbol for a differentiated experience is born.

e. One could take this process of differentiation and look to see whether it adequately describes the evolution of leadership itself. Freud told the story of an Ur-leader, the primal father, who embodied leadership at its most compact, only to be supplanted by an increasingly complex arrangement of rival warlords and so on (1921/1959, chap. 10). Simmel also hinted at the process, without developing the idea further (1971, p. 21). It was his contention that, over time, relationships have become more complex, numerous, and heterogeneous. We have gone from very few kinds of leadership to many, from very few societal contexts to many. What we have now are versions of the original, variations on a theme. The differentiation of leadership would be part of a more elaborate and deep-seated tendency. Voegelin devotes much of *Order and History* (volume 1) to describing the differentiation of ancient Israel's leadership from single patriarch/warlord through judges and their chieftains distributed throughout the twelve clans to the complicated struggle for command among kings, priests, and prophets. From the one undisputed king, Saul—identified by the last of the judges, Samuel—rivals for the office emerged almost immediately, primarily young David, and, soon after Solomon, the kingdom itself split into two. In addition to the importance of military generals, a priestly class gradually assumed control of rituals and writings, surrounding the king with bureaucracy and clericalism, exercising influence over the community and especially over its continuity, while less structured bands of prophets—some being nearer to the center of immanent power as official prophets and some on the periphery, in the wilderness, in contraposition to the king's court, even at times in direct conflict with the king's court . . . until the solitary holy man in the desert, exemplified by John the Baptist, but wildly diverse among themselves as to type and talent, stood in radical opposition to all formal authority, completely outside the power structure. The story tells how authority shifted ultimately to these idiosyncratic characters, before the Romans came and destroyed the temple.

This process of differentiation must be treated with the same care as Voegelin treated it in his study of history. That means, first of all, we ought to remain perpetually open to further and further differentiation, to avoid willful ignorance, but we should not discard the more compact symbols as having been superceded in the process. These compact symbols bear a richness that differentiated symbols cannot match. The compact is the context for the differentiated and cannot be ignored. Also, as stated earlier, we can generate *too many* differentiations and *too many* new symbols, without any real coherence. Thus, we must engage in the further discipline of bringing unity and order to all of the differentiations we amass. Otherwise, they become a jumble and lose their usefulness—and in due course bring confusion and frustration, leading to permanent attitudes of apathy, cynicism, or despair. That would be the condition this book hopes to prevent or repair.

3. USING THE TOOLS. How can we apply these "tools" to leadership studies? To start, we have to remember that we are interested in the images we have of specific other persons, against the more general image of what it means to be human. The more general image of what it means to be human can change. A change in the primal image of humanity must be embodied or "realized in a historical person" (3). That is, somebody exhibits or demonstrates or exemplifies some trait or attribute or way of living. There has to be an exemplar, a model, a living-breathing source. Voegelin illustrated what he meant by naming Plato, Caesar, and Jesus of Nazareth (17). Their lives changed the way we see what it means to be human. These are particularly vivid and enduring characters, but (as he went on to explain) the same basic process of change occurs in ordinary life. An individual's private understanding of what it means to be human changes as he or she encounters exemplars, no matter how local, such as parents, teachers, athletic coaches, or rock musicians. How we "see" hu-

manity *generally* derives from what we have encountered in humans *specifically*.

At this point it would be helpful to read Voegelin in his own words.

> We are faced with the historical fact that people have to varying degrees the character of primal images; rare men . . . have it to the utmost degree, and their images shine through the millennia; other people surround them in narrower and wider circles and receive the law of their lives from the primal image at the center; they may be more than mere followers and imitators and modify the primal image out of the wellsprings of their own aliveness and may themselves become a center, a model for others—in an infinite interlocking of circles and ranks, down to the closest connections of the present day and the example every living person is to all around him. Throughout history human society has been structured according to the rising and falling of these images and according to the degrees of authenticity and inauthenticity with which people followed them (ibid., p. 17).

What Voegelin has described is a vast network or web of interpersonal influence, with some persons having a greater impact on society than others. Even down to the most intimate relationship, people influence each other's way of seeing what it means to be human. And, as he pointed out, as members order themselves (and in that way as society structures itself), they do so according to their primal images. A society structured on the model of St. Francis of Assisi will differ from a society structured on the model of Napoleon. Thus, change originates in the life of an exemplary human being, whose impact on others can be found at the level of imagination.[12]

Elsewhere Voegelin made this comment: "The class of ideas about persons contains all formations of ideas that nourish the experience of political reality from the figure of a great ruling person (ideas of caesars, dictators, kings, priest-kings, leaders, and the like)" (CW 2, p. 4). Athanasios Moulakis (2000) has described the exemplar as "The exceptional, creative, mystical individual, who draws the substance of order out of the depth of his psyche, moved by and against the corruption and obtuseness of his age and who creates a social field that we recognize as political order by his compellingly persuasive effect on others."

The exemplary human being who embodies a primal image is only part of the equation. There have been countless cranks, heroes, and avatars who had little or no influence whatsoever. They never served as "primal images"—not necessarily because they were somehow inadequate in and of themselves, but rather because the other persons around them did not or would not recognize them as exemplary. Instead, these might-have-beens were overlooked, misunderstood, or rejected. In other words, according to Voegelin, the time must be ripe (CW 3, p. 3; see generally James, 1880, pp. 447f). Other persons in the role of observer or follower must be willing or able to see it in them.

In light of the foregoing, leadership studies can be understood as trafficking in thought images about certain impressions we refer to loosely as leadership. Since thought images are subject to argument, then leadership studies would be engaged in argument of two kinds, as we noted earlier, i.e. intrasystematic consistency and harmonization with primal images. Let me now give a couple of examples about how these arguments begin.

Part of the project of leadership studies would be testing claims about leadership for coherence and validity, as for example determining whether the captain of the National Guard can be said to "lead" his troops when his objective is to preserve the status quo and *prevent* change to the regime. Not a few theorists claim that leadership has to entail change. They argue that without change there can have been no leadership, by definition, just as a haircut in which no hair is cut does not deserve the name "haircut." There must have been some discernible change. No change, no leadership (e.g., Shriberg et al., 1997, p. 216; Bardwick, 1996, p. 131; cf. Rost, 1993, pp. 77, 115 ["Change is the most distinguishing element of leadership"]). So, how can a leader bring about change when his task is to *prevent* change? The process of sorting through the apparent inconsistency is one kind of argument: is it possible both claims can be true? How so? Resolving that kind of problem—simple though it is—is one of the tasks of leadership studies.

The other kind of argument, as you will recall, pertains to the degree of correspondence or harmony between thought images and the underlying impressions of leadership. This is the argument from radical empiricism. For example, Joseph Rost asserts that leadership cannot take place in a simple dyad. The leader can be a leader only of a group (1993, pp. 109f). He makes this assertion flatly, with little justification or explanation. He believes we already possess adequate terms for dyadic relationships. Leadership is, in his words, "larger, more complex, and less intimate than a dyadic relationship typically is" (ibid., p. 11). Rost claims to be doing everyone a favor when he narrows the field of inquiry by removing dyads. One must observe, however, that in ordinary usage most people use the term "leader" in simple dyads all the time, which Rost acknowledges. This use of the term is entirely consistent with their "primal images." What is more troubling for Rost's assertion is that many, if not most colleagues in the field schematize leadership in the simple dyad of leader-follower (e.g., Chemers, 1984/1995, p. 91, citing George Graen and associates regarding Vertical Dyad Linkage and the LMX theory; Bass, 1990, pp. 335–336, 890–892). In other words, the dyad as a thought image suits their purposes, which means that Rost is being unnecessarily, if not mistakenly, restrictive. He argues for a thought image that seems to be at odds with some existing primal images, and for that reason alone we should doubt the utility of his thought image.[13]

In my opinion, one way to think of the work of Ralph Stogdill on "Personal Factors Associated with Leadership" (1948/1995) is that he had been trying to get at what the primal images of leadership might be. In his words, he tried "to determine the traits and characteristics of leaders" (ibid., p. 127). He admitted "[t]here is no assurance . . . that the investigator who analyzes the biographies of great men is studying the same kind of leadership behavior that is revealed through observation of children's leadership activities in group situations" (ibid., p. 128)—the very sort of caution called for by Voegelin. Then, Stogdill warned against a trait theory of leadership that fails to take into account the situation, echoing the words from Voegelin about whether the times are "ripe." None of which is to suggest that Stogdill was even aware of Eric Voegelin. That is not the point. He was engaging in the project Voegelin recommended for the social sciences, of determining the degree of correspondence or harmony between thought images and the underlying impressions of leadership. Searching for the traits or characteristics of leaders would be part of this process.

Another way to illustrate the role of these two kinds of argument is to look at the claim that in order to qualify as leadership, the leader must be moral, ethical, or principled in some sense. This is not an unpopular claim (e.g., Burns, 1978, chap. 2; Panichas, 1996, p. 311; Grob, 1984, p. 269).

An argument of intrasystematic consistency might begin by seeking clarification: to what does the adjective (moral, ethical, or principled) apply? Is it meant to apply to the leader *per se* (Franklin Delano Roosevelt as human), the reputation of the leader (FDR as president), the objective a leader claims to seek (peace and prosperity), the objective a leader actually seeks (self-aggrandizement), the methods used by the leader (lies and manipulation)? (This is part of the confusion surrounding the relevance of the moral lapses of President Bill Clinton.)[14] Another angle might be questioning what standard of morality to apply, e.g., biblical, Aristotelian, deontological, utilitarian, and so forth. Yet another angle might be the epistemological and investigative question, how we can even know whether a leader is moral, ethical, or principled. As it happens, there is plenty to talk about.

Yet it is also appropriate to inquire whether the primal images of leadership seem to require that the leader be moral, because this is not self-evident. Some writers will challenge the claim outright, perhaps by referring to Attila the Hun, the Borgias, and Hitler as leaders. The point is not whether these persons were in fact moral. Instead, the issue is whether we are willing to entertain the possibility that a leader can be immoral. In other words, can a single person consistently hold that both of the following propositions are true?

    a. X is a leader.

    b. X is not moral.

Jacob Heilbrunn complained that "the science of leadership has devoted too little attention to what might be called the darker side of the question. Ruthlessness, mendacity, dishonesty, and cunning—all are qualities that the leadership theorists flinch from" (1996, p. 10). In effect, what he was calling for was a greater correspondence or harmony of our thought images about leadership with the primal images that most certainly exist out there in the real world.

Voegelin's schemata are not just handy as a model for leadership studies to mimic; he was writing directly about leadership. I believe this because leadership is fundamentally about the imaginal. Each act or moment of leadership is a response to and a refinement—a fleshing out of—the follower's primal images. This is why so much of leadership education consists of impression management, such as dressing for success and making a positive first impression. The entire literature on impression management reinforces the argument that leadership is grounded in image (see Bass, 1990, pp. 210–212).

In his book *The Deep Blue Sea* (2001), Wilfred Drath does an exemplary job of doing what Voegelin recommended.[15] Drath tries to describe the evolution or progression of our understanding of leadership through stages toward a new "knowledge principle" that he admits threatens our existing understanding. The experience of leadership changes and so does the way people "see" their relationship. Drath reminds the reader that each new "knowledge principle" somehow incorporates the old, yet the participants have felt the need to transcend or refine the old. The existing primal images have shifted, so our thought images must adjust as well. This leads to a period of uncertainty and doubt. Some people want to go back to the old ways, but the organization cannot afford to.

By telling a story as the book develops its argument, Drath gives realistic images of a corporation and its characters to accompany the conceptual work. This was clever. It is also consistent with Voegelin's approach about looking closely at primal images. Each character represents or personifies a stage in the process. Using the imagination in this way in order to come to understand leadership ties Voegelin together with an earlier section in this book. Drath even concedes he is not trying to *prove* anything. One doesn't prove primal images, if you recall. He does offer, however, an image of thought (*Denkbild*) we might want to employ in order to understand the process of changing primal images. Further, Drath notices that differentiation about leadership had become nearly unmanageable without some new organizing principle to fit it all together. His new principle happens to allow room for further differentiation and even one day a new organizing principle, so that unlike dogmatists who want a closed process, Drath keeps his perpetually open. One can disagree over his conclusions, but the effort deserves respect, for it follows in the tradition set by James to reconcile new hypotheses with residual beliefs while remaining a fallibilist.

Voegelin's terminology about truth and reality might seem grandiose for leadership studies, but the predicament he describes is precisely our own. What is that predicament? Many thinkers resist the existing symbols for leadership, as well as leadership itself as a symbol, because they sense that human experience is not being adequately represented by them (Voegelin, OH-5, p. 39). The symbols just don't work. In order to get behind the symbols, therefore, they must resort to the imagination. What they in their turn create or discover to be the new symbolization will succeed only if other people respond to it and if the organization of their lives is changed in some way for the better. Otherwise, what was the point? Inevitably, the new symbolization provokes four typical responses. (a) Adherents of the old symbolization will defend their symbolization and resist change. (b) Other discoverers will urge their new symbols and present them as superior alternatives, so that multiple possibilities jostle for acceptance, the more so as existing symbols crumble. (c) The resulting confusion, such as exists today in leadership studies, will provoke a measure of skepticism: people now have reason to distrust the old symbols, but they are unsure which of the new ones to adopt, so it occurs to many people that maybe it would be best to give up the project altogether as hopeless. (d) Finally, of course, the new symbolization will meet with considerable indifference and incomprehension (Voegelin, OH-5, p. 25). It would be naïve to expect anything less. Thus, in order to overcome these four typical responses—from defenders, rivals, skeptics, and dullards—the thinker who proposes a new symbolization "has to tell quite a story indeed" (p. 25). The thinker must expose the existing disorder and describe the resistance he or she has felt, leading to the search for new symbols, grounded in actual human experience, until fresh or refined symbols make themselves known. What is left to do is explain the consequences, in ordinary life and in the real world, of making the switch from disorder under the old symbols to the new symbolization (Voegelin, OH-5, p. 25). This is what Wilfred Drath has tried to do, so we have in leadership studies an example of what needs to be done.

C. CHAPTER SUMMARY

What students find is that leadership happens in the imagination or the imaginal realm, so that what they are studying ultimately are images that inform people about themselves, each other, and the way things happen among them. For the study of these images, we have introduced two basic distinctions from the work of Eric Voegelin: the distinctions between (a) primal images (or impressions) and thought images, as well as between (b) compactness and differentiation.

At this moment, we find interwoven into a single strand the experience, theory, symbol, and images of leadership—compact and undifferentiated in reality and therefore frequently confused and often confusing to students of leadership. Nonetheless, despite their intimate relationship in reality, experience-symbol-theory-image must be separated conceptually in order for us to make scientific sense of the phenomenon. Then, the task will be to explain their relationship, as it occurs in reality, for the sake of the original, practical purpose of leadership studies.

With all of that in mind, we also have to acknowledge several limitations. For example, the symbol "leadership" refers to a variety of experiences and theories and not just one. Also, other symbols—such as manager, ruler, coach, and hero—overlap. The symbol "leadership" is even subject to change and disputation. It is not a fixed thing. As leadership studies progresses, it poses new questions and presents new lines of inquiry. Add to these challenges the puzzling logic of the imagination, and one discovers that there is much work to do. How is that to be done? Eric Voegelin gave us a couple of tools, and subsequent chapters take a more conventional approach.

In our woodland hike, we have been moving down, following slopes and watercourses to the lowest level. At the bottom of valleys are the creeks and streams that cut them, so that even at the base of the forest, at the lowest point, there is a distorting film of moving water between us and the absolute depth. Our imagination is that moving stream, and despite its fluid meandering and variability we cannot understand the surrounding geography without it.

5

LET'S STOP FOR A MOMENT . . .

We have been tramping through the woods for some time now. Catching our breath, perhaps it is time to look around—not only to *experience* where we are, because maybe the view is memorable, but also at a more practical level, to orient ourselves, to make sure we know where we are and where we are going. We shall review the journey thus far, reconstructing the path we have taken, and I intend to do that briefly, but more importantly what I shall encourage you to do with me is to simply look at our surroundings. What do you see from this vista? Do you know how to describe it? Can you put it to use?

Folk wisdom tells us that moss grows on the north side of trees. This information comes in handy if we become disoriented and need to establish direction. Perhaps we should examine the trunks of particular trees. Is all the moss growing on one side? Yes? The technique may not be foolproof, but it offers to keep us from becoming lost.

In the same manner, when a person reaches a particular stage in an argument, he or she can easily become lost. It is not uncommon for readers of the classic philosophy texts to find themselves entirely lost—a predicament most readers repair by shutting the book and going to something else. I do not want to lose you, however. I want you to be able to say that you completed the hike. And in my wilder fantasies, I even want you to enjoy it.[1]

Since by now the issue is one of motivation, it might be useful to list three reasons to study an argument. The first reason is probably the most basic: a person will study an argument in order to put it to use in his or her life. Most of us want to apply what we learn. That purpose fits the pragmatist in each of us. Sadly, this motive also pushes us to arrive at a destination, quickly. "What's the upshot?" "Cut to the chase." A second reason to study an argument is that it often shows what a particular person once thought, in a kind of historical sense. What did this guy say about that? How did she work herself through her dilemma? It is not so much that you agree with what that person wrote, as it is that you want to understand what was going through his or her mind. In this manner, historians go back to explain what some author tried to do. The most immediate example is probably the teacher's interest in assigning a book. "What am I supposed to be learning here?"

There is in addition a third reason to study an argument that often goes unstated. And it takes some explaining.

The third reason to experience the argument is aesthetic. It is to have had the intellectual pleasure, so to speak, of a well-crafted line of reasoning. All arguments have architecture, a structure, that the human mind judges as better or worse—as tight or loose, for instance. Some arguments can be regarded as elaborate. Others might be regarded as neat and clean. One of the highest compliments would be that an argument is elegant. So, yes, it is my hope that the arguments you encounter in this particular book strike you as somehow pleasing, a gratifying exercise. A well-crafted argument cleanses the mind. It has a way of making you feel good.

Look, sometimes you walk somewhere in order to arrive at a destination. Well and good. Sometimes you walk somewhere because you are curious where it will take you. But sometimes you take a walk just to have the experience of taking a walk. And of course, to be thorough, it is not uncommon for a person to have more than one reason for taking that walk. Now might be a good time to ask *yourself* why you have made it this far. Remembering why you set out might encourage you to keep going.

So . . . here we are, having stumbled around definitions, symbols, theories, and images—without having arrived yet at a destination. Where exactly are we? We considered the possibility that leadership is really just an interpretation people give to social events. They experience life and try to communicate about it using language. From centuries of such usage, we now come into possession of symbolization for something we call leadership. Leadership exists where people infer that one person brought about change in another person or persons in a specific direction. Apparently, they find it useful to think this way and talk this way. Can this interpretation known as "leadership" be studied scientifically?

We have to be careful. There at least four aspects to the problem. Part of what we would be doing is studying the past, which makes us historians. Part of what we would be doing is observing and measuring present behavior, in a systematic way, which makes us social scientists. Part of what we would be doing is thinking rigorously at a theoretical level, and this makes us philosophers. But perhaps most importantly, we would be trying to understand the role of the imagination, which makes us psychologists.

With all of these hats to wear—historian, scientist, philosopher, and psychologist—we find that each one presents us with choices of vocabulary, method, and even purpose. No wonder that by now the field of leadership studies is (as they say) all over the map, in a state of confusion. This predicament led us to contemplate the advantages of pragmatism, which gives us a method for bringing some kind of order to leadership studies. A person lost in the woods might come across numerous trails, so that what she needs more than anything else is a plan for choosing which trail to take, as choices arise. Pragmatism advises us to adopt theories that work, that stand up to tests of intrasystematic consistency and harmony with our impressions for the sake of practical effectiveness in the world so long as we retain sufficient humility—humility about the limits of our own powers and about the vast and perplexing flux of human experience. We have to remain open and adaptable.

In our attempt to find the simplest and most basic feature of leadership, we found instead a complex relationship of experience-theory-symbol, and delicately mediating that relationship is the imagination, which is, as it were, the narrowest point of our journey. Leadership rests on imagery, of two kinds: *Urbilder* and *Denkbilder*. As William James observed, "The intellectual life of man consists almost wholly in his substitution of a conceptual order [*Denkbilder*] for the [impressions] in which his experience originally comes [*Urbilder*]" (quoted in Hitt, 1992, p. 40). Part of our job in leadership studies is to bring some kind of coherence to these images, although complicating matters is the tendency of differentiation, which multiplies symbols as it divides compact experience. We will find ourselves operating between *Urbilder* and *Denkbilder*, securing our researches on the shifting ground of impressions that ordinary people use and attending to the seemliness of our symbolizations, which constantly threaten to overwhelm our existing schemata. That would be the nature of our collective task as leadership studies. And that's how we got here.

In the woods, one should be able to hike downhill toward ravines and creek beds, to the very bottom of the valley, to reach the river that flows out eventually onto human habitation and rescue. Down is the way out. That is the direction we have taken thus far, toward the bottom of the valley, the imagination, the flux of life that leaves compact impressions. Rather than hike our way out of the forest, however, the next part of our task is to climb again to the highest level, to the peaks, to see the forest from a special vantage point, from a vista. To understand the valley, sometimes it helps to see it from the mountain tops. I am not saying this perspective is *better* than moving about in the valley itself. The two perspectives complement each other. In the same manner also, sometimes it helps to see the mountain from the valley. What we must learn to do is move comfortably between complementary perspectives when it comes to leadership. We can label this ability to shuttle back and forth quickly an "elasticity" of our critical powers. Not everyone in the valley wants to climb mountains. Not everyone on the heights wants to mingle in the valley. A true student will learn to move comfortably at either altitude.

The movement from the valley to the peak, which justifies the rest of this book, illustrates what is known as the hermeneutic circle. We shall be moving conceptually from the most basic unit, the experience of the primal image, to the most complex unit, known (pretentiously) as the meaning of life. What constitutes leadership and what does it constitute? The hermeneutic circle is a broad concept or conceptual tool, going back centuries. It is stated repeatedly in the literature, in diverse ways, and even codified in 1972 by Emilio Betti, who calls it the principle of totality. He wrote:

> [T]he meaning of the whole has to be derived from its individual elements, and an individual element has to be understood by reference to the comprehensive, penetrating whole of which it is a part. (Quoted in Ormiston & Schrift, 1990, p. 165; see also pp. 43, 45, 108, 113)

The hermeneutic circle between the whole and its parts can be used any number of ways in leadership studies. When William James urged the pragmatist to integrate new ideas and beliefs into the vast storehouse of residual beliefs, for example, he was urging a turn on the hermeneutic circle.

Very briefly, let us give several more examples of the utility of this thing called the hermeneutic circle.

1. Whenever a scholar compares a particular individual to the class of all leaders, she uses the hermeneutic circle. "Was Eleanor Roosevelt a leader?" Remove the classification of leader, and all you have are a bunch of unrelated people doing all sorts of unrelated things. Remove the individual leaders from the class, and the class becomes empty. You understand one by means of the other.

2. The hermeneutic circle also allows the observer to compare a single leadership episode with the entire relationship between the leader and follower over time. Each makes more sense from the perspective of the other. What

happens once between two people will have meaning in the context of their entire history together, just as the relationship is not really a relationship without a string of episodes.

3. In the same manner, leadership forms a part of someone's life. "Leader" is a role she plays. As such, one can understand the leadership as part of her story, her biography. Of course, her life is better understood once we understand such things as her participation in this leadership.

4. Just to illustrate the utility of the hermeneutic circle one more time: leadership studies is only one instance of the social sciences. The philosophical quandaries of the social sciences pertain to leadership studies. Leadership studies is hardly immune. Thus, to understand leadership studies completely, one must appreciate the standing of the social sciences generally. The same holds true in reverse. Social sciences encounter and work through their quandaries within distinct fields of study, such as leadership. Imagine someone who claims to know the social sciences without the least knowledge of sociology, economics, and so on.

Individual to class, episode to relationship, role to biography, leadership studies to the social sciences—all of these comparisons illustrate the hermeneutic circle.

This book revisits the hermeneutic circle elsewhere more than once (without mentioning it by name), especially during the forthcoming discussion of the *dimensions* of leadership. It seemed worthwhile to emphasize the hermeneutic circle once, in and of itself, as we have done here.

The old joke is that philosophy textbooks cannot be much good, since the answers do not appear in the back of the book. True to form, this book has no definitive answers. We might be more familiar now with the terrain, but we do not seem to have arrived anywhere. Consider however the extent to which the path we have been following makes it virtually *impossible* to arrive at any one place. Primal images are not immediately available for study because they are mediated through symbols largely derived from ordinary usage, and these symbols suffer from the problems of all first-degree constructs. Primal images and symbolizations also change over time. Not only does one image or symbol replace another, they also differentiate, so that we are confronted with more and more of them, all ostensibly related to the same phenomenon. In working through this project, we have at our disposal a variety of incommensurate intellectual tools from history, science, philosophy, and psychology. Such a deep, impenetrable forest can make one feel hopeless.

It was not just the German philosopher Heidegger (whom we quoted in the preface) who used the metaphor of the pathway through a forest. José Ortega y Gasset used it in his lecture on the *Mission of the University* (1930/1944). He wrote:

> Life is a chaos, a tangled and confused jungle in which man is lost. But his mind reacts against the sensation of bewilderment: he labors to find "roads," "ways" through the woods, in the form of clear, firm ideas concerning the universe, positive convictions about the nature of things. (p. 37)

Ortega traces the imagery back to the ancient Greek, Chinese, and Indian languages (ibid., p. 37, n. 10).

> That metaphor of ideas as paths or roads (*méthodoi*) is as old as culture itself. Its origin is evident. When we find ourselves in a perplexing, confused situation, it is as though we stood before a dense forest, through whose tangles we cannot advance without being lost. Someone explains the situation, with a happy idea, and we experience a sudden illumination—the "light" of understanding. The thicket immediately appears ordered, and the lines of its structure seem like paths opening through it. (ibid., p. 74)

This book was intended to "light the understanding." But now let me as the author confess that my intentions have included the perverse desire simply to show you the depth of the forest. You have heard it said that a person cannot see the forest for the trees. In the study of leadership generally, that is often the case. Other writers are so keen to illumine their one or two trees that they fail to explain the surrounding wooded area. Readers could easily come to believe that the study of leadership is a matter of a small thicket, a stand of trees and nothing more. What I have tried to show is just how *thick* the forest is. No point fixating on one or two trees, in isolation.

In a series of lectures he delivered in Buenos Aires, Ortega went so far as to say that "it is essential man lose his way" (1984, p. 15). So I guess in one sense I led you deep into the forest to get you lost, to leave you so far in that you appreciate its magnitude. In my opinion, students of leadership have to respect the forest if they are ever to make their way through it. And I have tried to give you some of the landmarks and some of the techniques for orienting yourself.

At one point, I intimated that we have always lived among the trees. This is our habitat as thinking beings. In leadership studies, to my regret, we seem lost within our habitat. I go further (and this is a metaphysical claim): *It is all forest.* We cannot wish it away. We cannot work it away. And why should we want to?

It has taken me some time personally to feel at home in the woods and make my way around in it—even though the surname "Harter" originated in the Black Forest and means "deer-hunter"!

But as I say, far better to acknowledge our condition than to pretend that we can end up somewhere else. Besides, the forest possesses a richly textured majesty I have learned to revere.

Come, shall we continue? It is time for us to climb.

6

LEADERSHIP AS FORM (PART I)

A prior chapter emphasized the importance to leadership studies of the images people have of one another. We say that I have an image of you, and you have an image of me. *People also have images of their relationships.* I have an image of you, but I also have an image of my relationship with you: we are friends, for example, neighbors, or enemies. That image of the relationship, that *Denkbild*, we can refer to as the "form" of our relationship. It is a *sociological* form, to be precise. That form is an object of study appropriate to leadership. It is the purpose of this chapter to explain sociological forms and begin to show what they contribute to our understanding of leadership.

A. PERSPECTIVES ON THE MOUNTAIN

It might be helpful to look around one more time before we ascend.

1. A view from the valley. We experience each other as primal images or impressions. Over time, we learn to put these images to use, to think about them in different ways. At this point in our exploration of leadership, near the base of the valley, so to speak, we could take any one of several paths. The goal for most people in ordinary life would be to fit those impressions together, in the imagination, like elements into some kind of unity with a discernible order. That will be our goal as well. But how is it to be done? We have choices. We could in other words slice the apple at different angles. It is not my intention to insist that there is only one way to do this. As in life, however, we are fated to choose one path at a time, which is why I have chosen to imagine leadership as a sociological form.

What we are doing in this part of the book is climbing up from the valley floor of impressions to a relatively simple *Denkbild*, a synthesis of elements, which in turn becomes an element in a larger, more complex *Denkbild*, higher and higher until we reach the peaks. As we move up from the valley, we move away from the primal images that give us our experiential base, so it is important always to remember that. We have more discretion the further removed we get from human experience and reality, but reliability suffers and the temptation to "misplaced concreteness" intensifies. Thankfully, in the words of Voegelin, to keep us honest "[r]eality has a way of asserting itself." Nonetheless, we have to rise, to arrive at a serviceable image of leadership per se, and then to place leadership within a meaningful context. In rough terms, then, impressions fit into forms, forms fit into organizations and societies, and organizations and societies fit into the sweep of human history.[1] That is the pattern for the rest of this book. As your guide, I am pointing up toward the summit and telling you we plan to get there.

We mentioned previously that usually we accumulate impressions to form a composite of types, of which "leader" is one. Then, as we differentiate further, we notice types of leaders. For purposes of science, however, types pose problems. They are attempts at generalizing, when science often needs to differentiate ruthlessly. They are approximations, concessions to our inability to regard every other person we meet as unique. It is not always advisable in ordinary affairs to regard every other person as unique, anyway. There is much wisdom in detecting patterns and learning to anticipate something about the people we encounter. That is practical life.[2] Nonetheless, as science confronts the task of categorizing types, it runs into unavoidable difficulties.

The empirical fact is that different people use the symbolization of leadership in different ways for different settings, so that taking the whole sweep of historical examples, at all levels of society and organization, we are easily bewildered how to make sense of them all as a single object of study. Pragmatism told us to adopt that which works best. Phenomenology sent us looking at the root images that people have when they use the symbolization of leadership. From these two traditions, we should now move toward a third tradition before attempting to ascend from the valley floor. Previously, this book was blending pragmatism and phenomenology—two conventional, philosophical traditions. The first philosopher to blend them found it necessary to complete his work by introducing something called perspectivism. We can think of them as the three p's:

- Pragmatism
- Phenomenology
- Perspectivism

How should we understand perspectivism?

2. Perspectivism. In his magisterial work *From Dawn to Decadence* (2000), the historian Jacques Barzun had reason to state that "an object or idea is rarely seen in the round. Like a mountain, it presents a variety of faces. Moved by an ulterior purpose, observers take a few of these for the whole. This is a cultural generality" (p. 47). Barzun was actually articulating a version of perspectivism, which A. J. Ayer attributes originally to two philosophers, one of whom was José Ortega y Gasset (Dobson, 1989, p. 144). It is Ortega's version that we adopt.

Ortega used the familiar properties of visual perspective to make the more general assertion that we can know reality only from conceptual perspectives (or "points of view") and never entire—at one glance, as it were. Hilary Putnam later declared that "no theory or picture is complete for *all* purposes" (quoted, with emphasis supplied, in Menand, 1997, p. 359). This is significant, because it reminds us there is always a complementary relationship between the knower (subject) and the known (object). Knowledge emerges from this encounter. Ortega wrote: "All knowledge is knowledge from a definite point of view" (1923/1961, p. 90; see also James, 1880, p. 442). There is no authentic perspective separate from human experience (Dobson, 1989, p. 146). Instead, "The whole truth can only be obtained by joining up what I see with what my neighbour sees and so on. . . . The absolute all-embracing truth is arrived at by weaving together everyone's partial viewpoints" (Dobson, 1989, p. 152, quoting *Obras completas* 3:202).

Some perspectives are better than others, though none is complete. Better still is the sum of all perspectives, for a divergence among them does not have to mean contradiction (1923/1961, p. 95; 1914/1961, p. 170). Differing perspectives can complement each other (1923/1961, p. 91). It is possible for there to be many perspectives, all "veracious and authentic." What we require is bringing them together in some way.

Alfred Schütz has added in his work that we already tend to assume that our perspectives are interchangeable and congruent. They are interchangeable in the sense that if you were similarly situated, you would have an equivalent experience to the one I am having. They are congruent in the sense that our different perspectives of the same object will fit together to represent a single paramount reality, even if it is not readily apparent how that will be so. These beliefs contribute to the possibility of communication about the world we share, because if our perspectives are not interchangeable and congruent, we have little reason to bother trying to communicate (1955/1962, pp. 315–316; see also Boulding, 1956).[3]

In leadership studies, assuredly we detect divergences and often wonder which theory, definition, or model is correct, when (according to perspectivism) we should *expect* divergences and integrate them as best we can. We are in the business of reconciling apparent contradictions. That is part of the chore of conceptual housekeeping. Then, in our own research and teaching—as scholars—we would have to remember at all times the relevant point of view. "In this or that situation, who wants to know? Why? What is the context for asking?" And at the conclusion of our private studies, we find someone else has a different take. So we have to talk with each other and explain our various perspectives.

When Peirce the pragmatist presupposed a "critical community of inquirers" and when James tried to fit new theories into existing beliefs and when Voegelin recited two tests for the adequacy of a *Denkbild*, they were all contributing to a perspectivist approach. No thought, idea, hypothesis, or creed persists on its own, like a scrap. It belongs to a larger complex, and for the sake of conceptual hygiene has to embed itself. So that when a writer tries to claim that "leadership is an art" (just to take one popular example), the rest of the academic community should respond in part by determining what kind of art it might be and how it would be assessed as art. In other words, we all bear responsibility to the larger enterprise, which entails finding a place among our studies for the new perspective . . . if that is at all possible. Professor Levine wrote the following: "To rescue our scholarly integrity, an effort to articulate new principles for mapping our intellectual universe is mandated" (1995, p. 293). And to do that, in my opinion, we can use the pragmatist's method.

As a practical matter, perspectivism requires extraordinary humility, because it reminds us that no matter how valid, true, or useful our current beliefs—even after long years of experience or study—we still do not possess the one encompassing vision of leadership. Our only hope is a community of voices—voices from the past and from the present, voices from different disciplines and different cultures, erudite voices and voices that are barely articulate. We must become *perspicuous*.

If the imagery of multiple perspectives does not seem adequate, perhaps the reader might consider another image. Richard Bernstein (1992) once depicted the strength of arguments to be more like a cable of fibers than a chain of links. A chain, as we all know, is only as strong as its weakest link, which is why critics look for that weakness and attack it. If they succeed—and usually they can—then the chain lies broken on the floor. It did not work. A cable of fibers, on the other hand, offers "numerous, intimately connected" slender supports, so that the weakness of any one is compensated by the strength of others. To build that kind of cable requires weaving or knitting them together, and it takes a village to do that.

It was also Bernstein (1992) who gave a useful taxonomy for understanding the demands of perspectivism, since in effect perspectivism is an acknowledgment of the pluralistic universe we had reason to mention earlier. When confronted by a multitude of theories about leadership, as we are today, we might misconstrue perspectivism to mean that we are free to go our separate ways and never speak to each other. That is one of the extreme manifestations of postmodernism, and Bernstein refers to it as "fragmenting pluralism," characterized by the centrifugal force of new ideas. This is not what we want. That is not what perspectivism intends. We are instead supposed to engage each other. A second misconstruction of perspectivism is what he calls "flabby pluralism" by which writers feel free to roam around in the literature in a lazy manner, picking and choosing whatever argument or definition suits them at the moment, heedless of incongruity, without trying to integrate them. "If it's all true, then what do you care?" They are more like lawyers gone in search of dicta to lend respectability to their case. That is also not what we want. "Polemical pluralism" allows a person to use perspectivism to justify any old assertion he wants to make, as though all claims are equal and equally deserving of respect. "I can say whatever I want." Similarly, "defensive pluralism" allows a writer (or teacher or student) to dismiss the claims of other people as irrelevant to me—not because they are mistaken or injurious, but because in a perspectival environment, no one can possibly incorporate everything, so I choose not to incorporate yours. "I don't have to listen to you" (quoted in Menand, 1997, p. 397).

Perspectivism does not have to entail these four postures or misconstructions.

- Fragmenting pluralism
- Flabby pluralism
- Polemical pluralism
- Defensive pluralism

It is imperative that we notice this.

Perspectivism and its imagery are not unheard of, by the way, in the managerial sciences. The approach of this book finds such intimate parallels with the approach of Gareth Morgan in *Images of Organization* (1986) that a thorough accounting would prove tedious. Though not about leadership per se, his book is especially applicable on this point in its introduction and last two chapters. For purposes of illustration, we can read that

Morgan recognized that a "complex, ambiguous, and paradoxical" reality frustrates our ability to think simply, directly, and clearly, since any one point of view fails to incorporate others. He also found it useful to ground his analysis in imagery. By using alternative imagery of one and the same thing, from different points of view, a person comes to understand it more completely and figures out how best to deal with it. His book is in my opinion an excellent companion to this one.[4]

3. Perspectivism and the contingency approach. Joseph Rost has remarked, "All leadership . . . has to be effective because leadership does not exist unless it is effective" (1993, p. 77). Leadership is by definition effective, or it is not leadership. It is something else. And Rost is correct to say this, even though it makes sense to speak of leader effectiveness as a matter of degree, in that there is such a thing as being more or less effective. The goal is usually to be more effective. Thus, the practical purpose for leadership studies is to determine how to lead more effectively. That is its real world mission, as we had reason to acknowledge previously.

It is also true that according to the contingency approach to leadership, there is no one right way to lead effectively. Rather, effectiveness will depend on certain contingencies, on certain unrelated factors, such as the nature of the follower, the nature of the task, and the nature of the relationship between leader and led. The contingency approach proceeds on the assumption "that leadership effectiveness is maximized when leaders correctly make their behaviors *contingent* on certain situational and follower characteristics" (Hughes, Ginnett, & Curphy, 1996, p. 488). Machiavelli was really the first thinker of any stature to have insisted on this approach (e.g., 1532/1991, chap. XXV), and it dominates the literature today. Chemers has observed, "One would be hard put to find an empirical theory of leadership which holds that one style of leadership is appropriate for all situations" (Wren, 1995, p. 96).

By expanding perspectives, one sees alternatives. A limited or narrow perspective restricts the ability to see, which in turn leads a person to find few alternatives. By expanding perspectives, one becomes more comfortable with the contingency approach, because different situations call for different responses. In this way, perspectivism serves the contingency approach and ultimately serves the leader who needs a range of choices for leading. To be useful, however, perspectivism has to permit some kind of order among perspectives so that the leader knows why to choose one alternative or another. The goal is not simply to amass choices, so much as it is to align choices with purpose. "If a, then b. If c, then d." A man with only one perspective has only one response. As the saying goes: to a man with a hammer, everything is a nail. A man with many perspectives, on the other hand, has too many possible responses, and he is likely to freeze, unless he also knows which perspective fits each situation.

Thus, in order to draw lessons with practical appeal, in order to conclude with confidence that any one style of leadership will have the desired effect, we must first classify the various types of leadership and explain which contingencies matter. Then we can prescribe the right type for the right contingencies. Otherwise, we are left with the practically useless observation that "there is no one right way to lead effectively" (Wren, 1995, p. 420).

One of the most familiar projects in leadership studies still is the identification of types. People tend to want to classify leaders, to break them out into groupings or subsets. Earlier, we mentioned Heinemann, Steyrer, Gladwell, and Plato. John Gardner said simply, "Leaders come in many forms, with many styles and diverse qualities. . . . The diversity is almost without limit" (1990, p. 5). What it comes down to is that observers find it helpful to make distinctions. Distinctions begin to give a contingency approach structure and meaning.

As scholars have turned away from studying leaders *per se* to studying leadership as a process, the tendency to identify types has not changed. Instead of types of leaders, we now have types of leader*ship*. There is the classic contrast between being task-oriented and being people-oriented, which many theorists have accepted in one form or another (e.g., Hughes, Ginnett, & Curphy cite the following: Blake & Mouton, 1964; Hersey & Blanchard, 1969; Fiedler, 1982; see generally Bass, 1990, chap. 23). Bass includes a table of twenty-nine studies between 1938 and 1985 trying to distinguish autocratic leadership from democratic leadership (1990, table 21.1; see generally chap. 21). Bass devotes the very next chapter to the difference between directive and participative leadership (1990, chap. 22). James MacGregor Burns (1978) is famous for his distinction between transactional leadership and transforming leadership. Simmel found it helpful to contrast leadership by authority with leadership by prestige (1908/1950, pp. 183–185). Back in 1987, John Keegan made an interesting argument for at least four kinds of military leadership, which he labeled Heroic, Anti-Heroic, Un-Heroic, and False Heroic. In other words, writers believed that it was an improvement on the delineation of ideal *types* to come up with a delineation of *styles* of leadership, based on the leaders' behaviors (e.g., Robbins, 2003, pp. 314–319). Frankly, the difference between types of leaders and types of leadership behavior is barely detectable and less than useful. Whether (a) a type of leader uses a distinctive style or (b) a type of leadership behavior is embodied in the image of a particular leader, the project to come up with types can be helpful, but it has its limits.

Types we have aplenty. I prefer sociological forms. They are the first conceptual tool we shall be using as we leave the valley floor, rather than using types of leaders or types of leadership. A sociological form has numerous advantages for purposes of synthesis, some of which leadership studies has uncovered on its own. One of the most obvious advantages is the fact that leadership includes more than the leader and the leader's behaviors: there is always a follower and there is always a relationship.

Please understand this: by choosing to study forms, we have not completely discarded the study of types. For one thing, ideal types of individuals still make up the imagery on which participants rely; it is part of the reality we must come to understand. In addition, we will begin to look at a different kind of type: types of forms. What we are purposefully setting aside for now are types of individuals and types of behavior. Participants themselves might readily appreciate the extent to which they rely on their impressions of each other, and they might protest that they do not use sociological forms in their own imaginations. We could argue that contention. Even so, at this point, we must leave behind the way participants in leadership think and establish a more scientific method that is abstract and frankly independent of individual experience. By doing so, we have not betrayed our commitment to pragmatism or phenomenology, which is to say we have not betrayed our radical empiricism. If anything, we are more radically empirical, more objective, by moving away from individual experiences in isolation and moving toward shared experiences, which leadership always is.

Lewis Coser described the situation this way: "[C]oncrete phenomena could be studied from a variety of perspectives and . . . analysis of the limited number of forms which could be extracted from the bewildering multiplicity of social contents might contribute insights into social life denied those who limit themselves to descriptions of the concrete" (1971, p. 180). Given the insurmountable diversity of perspectives out there and our need to organize them in a meaningful way, I prefer the sociological form. Let me explain further.

B. WHAT IS A SOCIOLOGICAL FORM?

A leader without a follower is like a married bachelor. It is a contradiction. You cannot have one without the other. The study of leadership has to include the relationship between leader and follower. In fact, leadership is commonly understood to be a relationship, a kind of relationship, shared by the participants. Together, they participate in it. It is not something one of them is or does in isolation from the other. Leadership has to be inter-personal, or we are talking about two different things. That is usually how people use the term (Drath, 2001, pp. xvf, 61, 165; contra Manz & Sims, 1989, p. xviii, chap. 1).

The study of leadership is the study of a relationship, a particular type of relationship. It is a relationship with a distinctive form or shape. We can distinguish leadership from other types of relationship by its form. The form of the relationship matters a great deal. What exactly is the nature of that relationship? How did it emerge? What does it do? By answering these questions, we go a long way toward understanding leadership. In addition, as we differentiate various types of leadership, we now have a tool for un-derstanding what makes them distinctive. How does the form of *this* type of leadership differ from the form of *that* type?

The recognition and study of forms is something that happens in the mind, something the mind uses to make sense of the content in the world. Lots of things happen out there in the real world. The world goes by in a blur. How do we organize these experiences in our minds? You and I might do this differently. What you call music, such as Charlie Parker's jazz, I might dismiss as noise. What I approach as a competitive sport, such as pick-up basketball, you might approach as play. Perspectivism and the plu-ralistic universe already acknowledged the possibility of such diversity.

Specifically with regard to leadership, we might say that, at one ex-treme, each incident of leadership is altogether unique, *sui generis*, in a class by itself. And that may be true, in a sense, because even if the very same persons do the exact same thing a second time, some amount of time will have passed, and they have the prior experience as background for the new episode—something that was not true that last time. Saying that each lead-ership episode is unique is one extreme available to leadership studies, and it serves as a corrective to those who would over-generalize that "all charis-matic leaders" would do thus-and-so. We cannot afford to over-generalize. The problem as we had reason to mention earlier is that if leadership stud-ies remains stuck on this approach, to the effect that no two leadership episodes are alike, then precious few conclusions of any use will be reached. Understanding requires *some* groupings or types. That is primarily what Max Weber helped us realize.

Lewis Coser explained it this way.

> Weber argued that no scientific system is ever capable of reproducing all concrete reality, nor can any conceptual apparatus ever do full justice to the infinite diversity of particular phenomena. . . . When his concepts are very general . . . he is likely to leave out what is most distinctive to them. When, on the other hand, he . . . particularizes the phenomenon under

discussion, he allows no room for comparison with related phenomena. (1971, p. 223; see also Fontrodona, 2002, p. 65; Schütz, 1953/1962, p. 36)

If everything is completely unique, then there is no basis for comparison. If everything is the same, then there is no reason to compare. Ordinary experience tells us that some things are alike and others are different. Or, more accurately, even two things that are alike will be different. "[P]articular historical events are unique, [although] one need not concern himself with the uniqueness of these events but, rather, with their underlying uniformities" (Coser, 1971, p. 179; see also Schütz, 1953/1962, p. 36).

For this reason, we might persuade ourselves on occasion that we have done a good deed when we refute a claim by naming a counter example. When another person claims that men tend to be more overtly active in group settings than women are, we might be tempted to give examples of overtly active women and of passive men, as though we have thereby completely demolished the claim, but that is not correct. There is no basis for smug satisfaction, let alone triumph. Counter-examples are useful, as I said, in preventing over-generalizations and sweeping dogma, but they do not disprove the usual claims of social scientists, which are based on tendencies, generalizations, correlations, so that even if we could name a hundred overtly active women, the original claim might still be true overall, and therefore still useful. Both the generalization and the counter examples contribute to arriving at a nuanced understanding.

Don Levine, one of the world's foremost interpreters of the work of Georg Simmel, has gone a long way toward explaining what is meant by a sociological form. Forms can be thought of, he writes, as the result when a person selects "elements from the raw stuff of experience and shape[s] them into determinate unities" (Levine, 1971, p. xv). More specifically, with regard to *sociological* forms such as leadership, Levine explains the important distinction between contents and form. It is worth quoting in full.

> "Contents" . . . are the needs, drives, and purposes which lead individuals to enter into continuing association with one another. Forms are the synthesizing processes by which individuals combine into supraindividual unities, stable or transient, solidary or antagonistic, as the case may be. (ibid., p. xxiv)

I find myself lost in a city, let us say, and encounter a man in uniform who appears to be headed in a specific direction. I enter into some kind of relationship with him in order to find my way home. Or suppose I need a large splinter removed from my foot, so I ride to the doctor to have it extracted and treated. In each case, I experience a need and approach another person in order to satisfy the need (Levine, 1971, p. 23). People fall together for any number of possible motives, and as they start to interact, their behavior assumes a specific character or shape. (When I arrived at the doctor's office, I became a patient to the doctor, as well as a customer to his business office.) People convert their needs into some kind of relationship, however brief or hostile. That relationship has a discernible form. Georg Simmel once wrote about an interpersonal relationship as "the *form* around which the interests of human beings crystallize" (quoted in Frisby, 1992, p. 12).

Ortega was to use the term "structure," rather than "form," yet he intended the same thing (see Coser, 1971, p. 181). A structure is the combination of elements into some kind of order. Ortega even wrote it as a formula: "elements + order = structure" (Marías, 1961, p. 177, n. 13; Ortega 1914/1961, p. 87). Interpersonal reality as humans experience it takes on a structure. In leadership studies, we are simply trying to figure out one of these recurring structures. And we do this over time by examining the order among elements. In other words, the images we have of other persons become elements in leadership only to the extent they participate in some social structure. The simplest social structure would be the form.[5] Coser put it this way: "In formal analysis, certain features of concrete phenomena . . . are extracted from reality . . . to compare phenomena that may be radically different in concrete content yet essentially similar in structural arrangement" (1971, p. 180).

Sometimes the easiest way to see a form is to see it concretely, like fossils you can touch and measure at your leisure, without all the squirming of a live specimen. Forms do fossilize, in a manner of speaking, and that is when they take on a life of their own, a degree of permanence. These sociological forms take on a life of their own in two ways, adds Levine (1971, p. xxvi). One way is by hardening or solidifying into "institutionalized structures"—sort of like lovers who then marry or like antagonists who settle into a feud. The relationship becomes more explicit and enduring. We tend to say that it becomes more "formal" and increasingly ritualized. The other way forms take on a life of their own is when the form detaches from the original contents (or purposes). Here is an illustration. Military training has a very practical purpose pertaining to combat, but today literally thousands of men undergo quasi-military training for the sole purpose of participating in battle reenactments, such as Gettysburg or Antietam. The purpose is no longer winning or losing. It's a diversion for them, a kind of adult play.

Leadership can be studied as a sociological form, which is why we should keep in mind that as a form it might exist among us with a kind of autonomy no longer serving the needs that first brought it into existence. Using Levine's first example, leadership can become institutionalized, such as when an entrepreneur becomes so successful he must formalize his relationship with employees by means of policies, articles of incorporation, and so forth. For a leader to assume a title, whether as captain, chief, boss, or rabbi, is one clue that the sociological form is becoming institutionalized. One can picture this process as the *congealing* of leadership. (We will see this process again when we consider elites.) For this reason, people refer to the "leadership" of a corporation or of a political party when they want to refer to the institutionalized form of the leadership process. The nominal leader in such instances might in fact be leading nobody. As for Levine's second example of forms taking on a life of their own, one can see this start to happen when a business hires various mid-level managers whose primary objective has nothing to do with leadership *per se* and everything to do with career advancement, perks, and ego gratification. Likewise, when a candidate for political office wants to win an election as a stepping-stone to higher office later, but not to do anything substantive for the commonweal once in office, that candidate seeks leadership for reasons having little or nothing to do with the original reason the community created the office and decided to hold elections. Again, the form takes on a life of its own, and alien contents fill it.

Participants create the form for themselves, as an expression of their liberty, but then the form places demands on them, circumscribing their liberty.

The same form can be filled by very different contents, just as the same content can find its way into multiple forms (Levine, 1971, p. 26). It works both ways. Leadership as a form can serve different contents; there is no reason to believe that all leaders (and all followers, for that matter) enter into that form for the same purposes. Burns was one of the first to examine this possibility up close with regard to leadership (1978, chap. 3). McClelland was another (Hughes, Ginnett, & Curphy, 1996, pp. 132–135). One leader seeks recognition, but the next seeks the feeling of dominance over others. The form is still the same. Lenin, Stalin, and Khrushchev held essentially the same political office in Soviet Russia, but they were there for radically different purposes. And just to round this out: the contents that bring some people together into the leader/follower relationship might bring other people together into a different kind of relationship.[6]

Sociological form is an abstraction, a response to "the urge to disregard the features that lie on the surface of things, in hopes of finding the kernel within that does not change and is therefore felt to be *the* reality" (Barzun, 2000, p. 196). Abstraction "enables one to deal with large groups of things or ideas on the basis of their common features" (p. 213). Admittedly, this thing called abstraction "is a calculated departure from experience, from what is seen and felt as the real" (p. 213; Simmel, 1908/1950, p. 200). And that would appear to contradict earlier strictures in this very book to pay more serious attention to the concrete experiences that we call leadership, were it not for the admonition to move *between* the abstract and the concrete, to see the one from the vantage of the other. Neither can disclose as much as they can together in the hermeneutic circle. This requires what had been referred to as an elasticity of our critical powers. So, yes, the sociological form is an abstraction, a departure of sorts from the concrete, but that alone should not disqualify it as an instrument for understanding.[7] No less an authority on pragmatism than Charles Sanders Peirce insisted abstraction "really does represent a step in sound reasoning" (1997, pp. 133–137, quoting from p. 133). As I said earlier, therefore, we must leave the valley.

Here then is the message of this chapter: leadership studies would do well to study leadership as a form, regardless of its content. Levine lays out a plan to conduct that study.

> [Scholars] are directed to identify and classify the different forms of social interaction; to analyze their subtypes; to study the conditions under which they emerge, develop, flourish, and dissolve; and to investigate their structural properties. (1971, p. xxviii)

Simmel was explicit back in 1908 in calling for this very thing. He wrote, "What is needed is the study of specific kinds of superordination and subordination, and of the specific forms in which they are realized" (1971, p. 28). Leadership studies is suited to the task.

7

LEADERSHIP AS FORM (PART II)

A. THE STRUCTURE OF FORMS

There are three key features to a sociological form: reciprocity, distance, and tensions. We should introduce each of these in turn.

To start, first, nothing about leadership has any meaning outside of a relationship, so it is just as we said, no leader is a leader without a follower. And the relationship involves some kind of reciprocity, even if the terms of exchange are unequal (Levine, 1971, pp. xxxiii–xxxiv; e.g., Simmel, 1971, p. 43). Each participant becomes involved in order to get something out of it. They might end up being vague or mistaken, but that is a separate matter. People enter relationships for some reason, to get something or achieve something. Leadership is no exception. The first feature of leadership is *reciprocity*.[1]

Second, participants keep a certain psychological distance from each other, in the same way that two Italian men talk to each other on the street. That distance is a part of what determines the form (Levine, 1971, pp. xxxiv–xxxv). When participants keep a great distance between each other, that would be a different form than when they are psychologically much closer. And leadership occupies an interesting middle range when it comes to distance, because the follower is unlikely to respond to a leader who seems too remote, alien, or aloof, yet the follower has to have some sense that the leader is sufficiently different or higher for there to be any reason to follow him. There is a range of *social distance* within which leadership falls. More precisely, within that range, one might notice different types of leadership, depending on the distance (see Bailey, 1988, pp. 6f).

Third, forms can be understood as the product of dualisms, tensions between seemingly contrary parts. Leadership implies the dualism of leader and led, for example, as well as the dualism between the present state of affairs and the desired future or objective. These dualisms pop up everywhere, because they give shape to the relationship (Levine, 1971, pp. xxxv–xxxvii). For purposes of illustration, consider another example of a dualism or tension: leadership falls somewhere between absolutely determining what the follower does, such as flinging him through a plate glass window, and having no impact whatsoever on the follower. At both extremes (total control and no influence) leadership cannot be said to exist, but the specific form of leadership takes into account just how strong the leader's influence has been. Soon, we shall have reason to itemize some of the *dualisms* or *tensions* in leadership.

Many of the most vivid distinctions split leaders or leadership into only two types. This would seem to illustrate the dualisms inherent in leadership. We already mentioned the distinctions between being task-oriented and being people-oriented, and between transactional leadership and transforming leadership. These distinctions often give the impression that all leaders fall into one of these two categories. They set up an "either/or" decision. What they describe are mutually exclusive alternatives. A leader is either A or B, but never both. Simmel sometimes meant dualism this way, as we saw in the previous chapter, but only sometimes did he mean it this way. A more sophisticated schema represents the two types as polar extremes on a continuum. Rather than a simple "either/or," the continuum provides for the possibility that a leader tends toward one extreme or perhaps the other, without being completely at the extreme altogether. Leaders can be situated between the two extremes on a gradient. It becomes a matter of degree, and that schema turns out to bear a closer resemblance to reality, just as the colors black and white rarely exist in their pure form, but instead appear in shades of gray, even in a supposedly black and white film!

Either/Or might look like this.

The bipolar schema might
look like this.

By way of illustration, in American politics with its system of two dominant parties, people often speak as though a person must be ideologically conservative or liberal, right-wing or left-wing. That's it, as though there were only two possibilities. "He who is not with us is against us." Obviously, many people object that these two "wings" have their extreme (or radical) factions and their moderate factions, while a huge number of voters fall somewhere in the middle and think of themselves as moderates. Others object to the right/left dichotomy altogether by arguing that there are other ways to slice the apple: the populace is made up of those who are engaged in politics and those who are not, for instance, or libertarian and totalitarian, true believer or cynic. (See, generally, Bobbio, 1994/1996.) Just imagine an infinite variety of distinctions, and within each distinction an infinite degree of gradients.

All of this talk about gradients on a continuum could obscure the utility of these dimensions. There is something to gain by thinking in terms of bipolar dimensions, even when we recognize the shades that lie between them. Here is another example to demonstrate what I mean. One way to divide instances of leadership is between relationships in which the participants are legally committed to each other and relationships in which they are not. It is true that actual relationships fall somewhere between these two extremes, as we were just saying. Nonetheless, as "polarizations," they help us to classify types of leadership (Weber, 1913/1990, p. 116). Relationships in which the participants are legally committed to each other would occur in the military, in education, and in employment relationships. Relationships in which they are not would include (in Western cultures) partisan political and sectarian religious relationships. Participants in the latter type of relationship involve themselves "at will," with only unofficial sanctions for resistance to leadership or outright termination of the relationship (Weber, 1913/1990, p. 119; see Bass, 1990, p. 575). From project to project and from task to task, the participants are free as to not only *how* they will participate, but also *whether* to participate at all. In ordinary language, we call them volunteers. Leadership in one kind of relationship will be very different from the leadership in the other kind. Mixing them together conceptually could be a mistake.

We have been talking about dualisms, whether we imagine them as strict either/or dichotomies or as bipolar continua. Simmel meant something more by dualisms. Yes, some of these dualisms allow us to describe polar opposites and then orient ourselves by these extremes to find some mean or midpoint between them. There is also a more perplexing kind of dualism. Levine refers to "the coexistence of a diametrically opposed element" (1971, p. xxxv). The polar opposites are often both present in a relationship. Coser refers to "harmony *and* conflict, attraction *and* repulsion, love *and* hatred" (1971, p. 184; emphasis supplied). It is not either/or. It is not somewhere between. It is both/and. A leader can be psychologically close and distant. Some followers are passive/aggressive. In certain circumstances, the more powerful participant in a relationship can be more vulnerable. Sometimes, a leader must be cruel to be kind. According to Freud, the sons of the primal father admire and fear him and seek to destroy him, horrifying themselves. What Simmel does is open the door to paradox, a paradox familiar to leadership studies in the various two-dimensional models that allow seemingly opposed measures to coexist: both task-oriented *and* people-oriented, both assertive *and* accommodating, both directive *and* supportive. Perhaps scholars with a tolerance for paradox will continue to become more attuned to these both/and dualisms in leadership and help the rest of us appreciate them.

Kenneth Thompson made paradox the centerpiece of an article on leadership in 1984. As an expert on the American presidency, he noticed "a series of contradictions, tensions, and antinomies" (p. 9). The article offered nearly a dozen examples. Leaders are expected to be sufficiently different from followers, for example, distinguishable—better in fact—yet it helps if they seem "close to the people." Leaders are unique, but not unique in such a way that followers should ever despair of modeling themselves after the leader. Leaders dominate the situation, however subtly, yet they are expected to downplay and even hide their influence. Leaders harmonize, on the one hand, and galvanize opposition, emphasizing disharmony, on the other. Leaders are decisive without being rash, and hopeful without being naïve. They exhibit enthusiasm and passion, yet they must remain detached and objective. They possess a vision, while at the same time they should appreciate the real-world obstacles they face. Leaders who don't want to be confused by the facts can come across as dreamers or utopians. A leader simplifies complex problems for followers, but avoids trivializing and even falsifying the situation. Thompson lends credence to the proposition that leadership is *inherently* tensional. (I think that it is.)

At least for now we can say there is already a program for studying leadership as a sociological form. We can investigate the structural properties of leadership, especially with regard to reciprocity, psychological distance, and various tensions, as we have just begun to do here. This would be the *statics* of leadership. We can study the conditions under which leadership emerges, develops, flourishes, and dissolves. This would be the *dynamics* of leadership. Finally, we can analyze the subtypes of leadership, as we had reason to call for previously. (The third task is actually the ongoing process of differentiation we addressed at some length in the chapter on the imagination.) This program suggests three overarching psychological dimensions of space (statics), time (dynamics), and variation (subtypes).

B. WHAT, THEN, ARE THE CONDITIONS UNDER WHICH LEADERSHIP EMERGES?

Levine gave as one of the tasks of studying a sociological form trying to determine the conditions under which the form emerges. Process models, like flow charts, frequently begin here. It is my contention that leadership emerges under at least two conditions. The first condition to discuss would be a prospective follower who is not already pursuing the leader's goal. The second condition is that a would-be leader must bring to the relationship some notion of what he wants to happen. Leadership can be depicted as a convergence of these two conditions.[2]

1. A Follower. The first condition out of which leadership arises would be a follower who is not already achieving the leader's goal, or at least seemingly not achieving it in the desired manner. The follower has to be the locus of impending change.

When delineating what makes a follower, it helps to remember at the outset that not all followers are created equal. What works with one person will not work with another (Aron, 1964/1986, p. 260). Campbell was right to caution that "subordinates are not passive organisms but are purposive and active participants in [leadership]" (1977, p. 227). Rost makes the same assertion in these words: "passive people are not in a relationship" (1993, p. 109). Therefore, passive people cannot be said to participate in leadership, by definition.[3] Rather than catalogue innumerable types of followers (even though that has been a worthwhile project), we are here to ask what is constant. What do they share?

By specifying conditions for leadership, we are in effect trying to give a name to something that has not yet revealed itself. Just as a lump of coal is perceived to be an object with certain properties—right now, in actuality, as it sits there—nonetheless under the right conditions, that lump of coal can be converted into energy, heat, and light. Until that happens, however, it remains just a lump of coal. In other words, the task is to regard the circumstances prospectively, looking ahead to the moment of leadership. There has to be in the follower a *potential* to follow. Carnall refers to it as "energy for change" (Carnall, 1990, pp. 98–101). It has also been called the follower's "development level" (Northouse, 1977, p. 56).[4] There are two necessary potentials: competence or ability is one potential; willingness or susceptibility is the other. Without them both, leadership is impossible. On this, I agree completely with Hersey and Blanchard (in Wren, 1995, pp. 207–211).

a. Competence/Ability. The first potential might be termed the potential to act, to do what the leader wants done. Often it is referred to as one's competence or capability. Marx understood this as "labor-power" (Carver, 1982, pp. 59, 91). A follower has to be able to attempt what the leader requires. If the follower is unable to follow, then the leader is unable to lead. It is that simple. A mute cannot be "led" to sing, and a pig cannot be "led" to fly. Leadership won't change that. Situational leadership envisioned by Hersey and Blanchard has explained that leadership depends in part on the follower's ability (Shriberg et al., 1997, p. 175; Northouse, 1997, chap. 4).

Hersey and Blanchard go on to emphasize that concomitant with ability is the follower's confidence in that ability, because a follower who does not believe she can do a task will not do it. No less an authority than Aristotle asserted that human behavior is never intentionally futile (*Nicomachean Ethics*, I:1 [1094a1], III:3 [1112b25]). As we said earlier, followers enter into the relationship for some reason. When a follower feels incompetent, that poses a problem for leadership, so the leader has two choices. The leader can try to convince the follower she can do the task, or the leader can try to make it possible for the follower to do the task by removing barriers, offering tools, and the like. These two choices are not mutually exclusive. Neither are they altogether distinct. Sometimes by seeming to empower the follower, what he is really doing is building confidence, as in, for example, the Disney cartoon when Timothy Mouse persuades Dumbo to fly by giving him a "magic feather." The feather had nothing to do with Dumbo's capability and everything to do with his confidence. The feather works in the same manner as a placebo. So, even when the follower is without the potential to do a task, leadership is not inconceivable. It just adds a step for the leader to have to alter the conditions before attempting to lead. In other words, the leader can attempt some combination of encouragement and empowerment to establish follower competence—although strictly speaking encouragement and empowerment are preliminary to the phenomenon we are studying. (See generally Conger & Kanungo, 1988.)

The follower must be able, and believe herself to be able, to follow. It goes without saying that just because a follower is able to do a task, that does not mean she will. This is because of the other variable in Hersey and Blanchard, willingness, which correlates with potential number two.

b. Willingness/Susceptibility. What Hersey and Blanchard refer to as "willingness" can be thought of as a susceptibility of the will to defer, and apparently different people possess this susceptibility in different degrees. Some followers successfully resist the blandishments over which others swoon—although with increasing intensity they might also eventually succumb. (We mean this when we say that every man has his price.) Susceptibility is not just a matter of more or less. Rather, people are susceptible to different things—different combinations of circumstance, task, and trait—so that from person to person the particular range of possibilities will vary. For this one, it is money. For that one, it is fame. And so forth. Need-based theories of motivation of the kind Maslow made famous were developed to catalog these susceptibilities. Why is one man impervious to another man's charisma? What makes some women at a rock concert throw their unmentionables to the band onstage?

Despite the variety of possibilities, however, there is considerable overlap in the population. It is a kind of formula, like the genetic code, which in most respects everyone shares, but which in the particular allows for a rich variety. Faces all have two eyes, two ears, one nose, etc., yet faces are thoroughly individual, unique.

Two fundamental reasons a follower might be willing to follow: either she does not know what to do or she does not care. The act of following originates in anxiety or apathy—even though one might have thought these were polar opposites. (Here, for instance, contrary contents fill the same form.) One comes from caring too intensely, even worrying, whereas the other comes from caring very little, if at all. A person who knows what to do and cares enough to do it will need no leadership and frankly will not want leadership (Bardwick, 1996, p. 131).

Apathy is easy to understand. If it really does not matter where you are going, then it does not matter who leads. "[I]n the masses the readiness to yield to leaders who claim to get things done is a reflection of their own apathetic anxiety and the disinclination or inability to do anything effective themselves" (Ginsberg, 1936/1965, p. 98; Carnall, 1990, pp. 98–101). An apathetic follower is easily led about (Michels, 1915/1949, pp. 49–59). Some decisions are really too small, trivial, beneath notice. Where does a customer stand at a bank? At the end of an existing line. On which side of the road does one drive? In the United States, on the right. To be sure, we are free in a metaphysical sense to stand elsewhere and drive elsewhere, but that would be stupid. Conformity is such a small price to pay for simple, everyday order. Convention makes little decisions easier, since it would be a burden all day long to re-think every social usage. So, yes, let someone else make a few decisions. I am indifferent why they chose X or Y, so long as they pick one of them.

Simmel portrayed this in different terms when he wrote that domination is easier for a single leader when followers contribute proportionately less of their "personality" to the relationship than when they contribute more (1908/1950, p. 203). The less they "invest" in someone else's leadership, the less they will feel compelled to resist. "No big deal." Apathy suggests an absence of resistance.

This willingness to be led that is rooted in apathy is what alarms so many about indifferent citizens: political power will flow to the few who do care, such as the activists and the ambitious, who will fill the vacuum left by a heedless electorate. Management consultant Peter Block once wrote the following: "Our search for strong leadership in others expresses a desire for others to assume the ownership and responsibility for our group, our organization, our society. The effect is to localize power, purpose, and privilege in the one we call leader" (1993, p. 13; see Oakeshott, 1961/1991, pp. 363–383). It is for this reason pundits remind us that the price of liberty is eternal vigilance and that the only thing permitting evil to prevail is for good men to do nothing. They are right, to a point. Apathy does leave room for someone else's aggression. The existentialist philosopher Jean-Paul Sartre has been understood to make a comparable argument (Olson, 1962, pp. 54, 89). He is represented as having said that motivation originates with a realization of the possibility that things could be better. Particular exemplars demonstrate what is possible. Visionaries paint a picture of the future. The rest of us become aware of the existence of choices, maybe better choices. This alone might impel a person to act.

It is just as possible that the prospect of choosing becomes a burden. A person might choose to defer to someone else, even though to defer to a leader is, in the philosophy of Sartre, to be unethical. On questions of ethics, Sartre could be pretty hard on followers, urging them to assume more responsibility for their lives, but the British political philosopher Michael Oakeshott went much further, attributing followership to some "combination of debility, ignorance, timidity, poverty or mischance" (Oakeshott, 1961/1991, p. 371). The follower is inadequate, weak, barbaric, and derivative, a shadow of a man.

With this series of criticism, we lapse into measuring leadership, which would be premature. It remains only to observe that there is a flip side to their argument. An indifferent, even cynical mass is unwieldy; the quality of their response to leadership will be very poor. They bring no passion, no loyalty, no sacrifice. So really, what good is such a populace to any leader? "If I don't care, then why should I follow you?" Apathetic followers might be quick to comply, but they are also quick to quit trying. Easy come, easy go.

Thus, there are those who complain that relinquishing autonomy is an abdication of one's responsibility as a free-thinking, fully human being. The decision to follow is a choice not to render life "authentic." This deference to leadership is little more than an escape from duty, they say. Followers surrender the right to call themselves free. Leadership signifies unfreedom for the follower.

For present purposes, most of us would acknowledge that leadership in small matters actually helps us lead our lives; the pursuit of excellence in this world rarely permits agonizing over petty details. In any society, everyone but the tyrant has to defer to others, to some degree. In a complex civilization, with extraordinary access to expertise on just about every question, it might come easy not to care, easy to become passive and indifferent—some might say gullible—yet by the same token there is a hazard in caring too much about too many things. We are finite creatures. The system overloads. Something has to give. We can take this heroic drive to autonomy only so far. Authenticity can be exhausting. Besides, on a multitude of life's tasks, some people know more than others—how to drive a nail, how to bake a cake, how to import graphics from one computer software into your particular word processing file, and so forth. We all need teachers for us to learn how to operate our world effectively; we all need rulers to order the community; we all need exemplars to show us what is possible. This is, as I say, especially true in times of specialization (Michels, 1915/1949, p. 89). For this reason, leadership has the potential to facilitate life's purpose.

Now, just as there are decisions too small to make, there are also decisions too great. Some moments in life are overwhelming. Some issues are too complicated. People often let someone else lead them in order to become unburdened even when they care intensely. Oakeshott noted that "the art . . . of leading [entails] the offer of release from the burden of making choices" (1961/1991, p. 380). In these cases, the condition out of which leadership emerges is the follower's anxiety (Lipman-Blumen, 2001). What do I mean by anxiety? This is not the place for a treatise on existential angst or psychopathologies attributable to discordant inner values or chemical imbalances in the brain. The matter is fairly simple. The person who becomes the follower (a) comes to doubt him/herself and (b) in response to another person alters behavior in order to conform in some way with the apparent wishes or example of that other person, whom we call the leader.[5,6]

The leader is meant to show the way, to alleviate anxiety (Hummel, 1994, pp. 125–128; Block, 1993, pp. 13–17; Oakeshott, 1961/1991, pp. 373–380). Lipman-Blumen explains: "When our angst drives us to seek certainty and security, we turn . . . eventually to leaders. We hold fast to leaders who take control, who can provide us with a sense of certainty—real or imagined—that we don't feel within ourselves" (2001, p. 128). In support of this understanding, briefly consider two apparent counter-examples. These are likely objections to the point I am trying to make, yet they actually make the point for me. In the first counter-example, a leader-to-be imposes anxiety, perhaps through fear and intimidation. This would seem to refute the notion that the follower looks to the leader to alleviate anxiety, yet the leader has seen to it that that is precisely what the follower must believe: that compliance removes the source of fear and intimidation. "Obey me or suffer the consequences!" (contra Northouse, 1997, p. 7; Rost, 1993, pp. 157–160).

The leader does not have to be overt and heavy-handed. Novelist Joseph Conrad provided a vivid example of "leadership by anxiety" in the character of the General Manager in *Heart of Darkness*. Here was a nondescript man without discernible gifts supervising a far-flung operation of considerable value in the wilds of central Africa. The story's narrator searches for an adequate explanation.

> [T]here was only an indefinable, faint expression of his lips, something stealthy—a smile—not a smile—I remember it, but I cannot explain. It was unconscious, this smile was, though just after he said something it got intensified for an instant. . . . He was obeyed, yet he inspired neither love nor fear, nor even respect. He inspired uneasiness. That was it! Uneasiness. Not a definite mistrust—just uneasiness—nothing more. You have no idea how effective such a . . . a . . . faculty can be. He had no genius for organizing, for initiative, or for order even. . . . He had no learning, and no intelligence. . . . He originated nothing, he could keep the routine going—that's all. But he was great. He was great by this little thing that it was impossible to tell what could control such a man. He never gave that secret away. (1910, pp. 87f)

In the second counter-example, the leader confronts a complacent follower, a person who feels no anxiety whatsoever. The leader exhorts, challenges, provokes the follower to undertake a risky course of action, just as a king urges his knights to the quest and an athletic coach fires the imagination of the players to undertake an extraordinary training regimen for the sake of a championship. The leader draws the follower toward peril. "When such charismatic personalities succeed in seizing Power (*Pouvoir*) then humanity trembles both in anguish and in hope" (Aron, 1964/1986, p. 274). In this case, again, the leader can be said to impose anxiety, or at least to induce the follower to put herself into a situation rife with anxiety. Leadership sometimes puts followers in harm's way. As with the first counter-example, this scenario does not contradict the assertion that followers must pass through anxiety. A leader would not be sought or heeded until the follower experiences anxiety, so the leader might arrange to implant the anxiety as a precondition to leadership. Itinerant evangelists open tent-meeting revivals by preaching hellfire and damnation in order to soften up resistance to the message of grace. It is classic salesmanship to create a need first for what you are selling. If a leader cannot lead without the follower's anxiety, then the leader might have to create it. It would be a preparatory step, a step preliminary to leadership itself.

Another reason it is no contradiction to say that leaders both alleviate and instill anxiety is that in many instances the leader makes the follower aware of reasons to become anxious so the leader might then be able to lead her toward a less perilous course of action (Carnall, 1990, pp. 98–101). The physician has to explain that the patient has cancer before explaining the risks of various treatments. The leader exposes, discloses, reveals the cause for alarm, so that even when the leader prescribes a risky solution, that solution would have to be contrasted with a far riskier choice to do nothing. The leader is not necessarily the source of anxiety. The leader draws attention to the source. Lipman-Blumen characterized it this way: "[W]hat does the good leader do but dispel our illusions, or at least make us aware of them, thereby opening our eyes and heightening our tension?" (2001, p. 129). Then, although the proposed response imposes risks on the follower, it imposes fewer or less severe risks than the alternative.

Again, regardless of whether the follower is already anxious or becomes anxious, the follower does not follow without *passing through* anxiety. It is part of the process.

In gnomic terms, anxiety accompanies liberation that is without direction. If there is no choice, says the wise man, then there is no problem. Once there is a choice, if the choice is clear, then again there is no problem. Suppose I do not get to elect between X and Y. Instead, you impose X. In those instances, I am unlikely to become anxious. I might be resentful, but not anxious. Suppose I do get to select, and I prefer X. Again, anxiety is unlikely. If I do get to select, however, and I do care to choose rightly, yet I cannot tell whether X or Y is better, then anxiety has an opportunity to trouble me. At such moments, I am likely to appreciate guidance from somebody else. I shall have become susceptible to leadership.

We end with the notion that the follower, being in a state or condition of apathy or anxiety, decides that someone else has a better understanding of the way. What way is that? This question introduces our second precondition.

2. Direction. We now turn to the second precondition for leadership. Would-be leaders bring to the relationship some notion of what they want to happen. Burns wrote that by definition "[l]eadership brings about

real change that leaders *intend*" (p. 414; emphasis supplied). Call it the leader's goal, vision, objective, or plan; it really does not matter (Kouzes & Posner, 1987, pp. 23, 91–120; Gardner, 1990, pp. 11–13; cf. Rost, 1993, p. 119). I use the term "direction"—as in the phrase "this leader is taking us in a whole new direction." The leader does not even need to have a very definite goal in mind, so long as it has some content, that is, a discernible direction. "Work smarter, be nice, walk this way." In fact, it does no violence to the concept of a leader that all he wants is to be perceived by the follower as the leader, and nothing more.[7]

In any event, the end might be noble or base, trivial or profound, easy or impossible to achieve (Davis, 1996, pp. 121–131, 133; Cronin, in Wren, 1995, p. 27; Harter, 1992).[8]

According to Heidegger, Aristotle grounds change in an experienced need that yields an idea, or *eidos* (εἶδος). This idea serves as the origin, or *arche* (ἀρχή), of change. In order to be disclosed as action, an idea shall have had to become purpose, or *telos* (τέλος), expressed in "oriented striving." Thus, a need yields an idea that becomes purpose, and from this sequence we derive the origin of change (Heidegger, 1981/1995, pp. 60–62, 85, 118, 129). It is the leader who bears or generates this idea and transfers his purpose to the follower.

Take this to its logical extreme. Suppose as you prepare to leave this room and turn left down the hall, somebody you know calls over to you from the right, "please come here," so you turn right instead of left in order to go over and greet her. All you have done is go out of your way briefly to hear what she has to say.

Now hold on to your hat. I say that *even this is leadership*. I am biting the bullet. Leadership can be such a slight and inconsequential moment. The word embraces everything from flirting to commanding troops in battle. Most colleagues do not follow me to this expansive position, I should confess, but I do not see how they can avoid it. I am taking things to their logical conclusion looking at the form itself. All of it is leadership. I should think the burden is on them to draw the line and clarify at what point it becomes leadership. In all likelihood, they are concerning themselves with a sub-type of leadership, one kind among many, so that people can talk about leadership in very different ways without contradicting each other. That simple device of expanding the meaning of leadership to include such transitory moments makes it possible to embrace most understandings of leadership without having to choose among them as to which is the real thing.

Not incidentally, it is worth remembering that leaders are not required to disclose their true objectives, so long as they make some headway; the followers might not know where they are going or why, and in fact they are often misled, but their understanding of the situation is secondary to the existence of the sociological form (Machiavelli, 1532/1988, chap. XVIII; Davis, 1996, p. 126; contra Rost, 1993, pp. 118–123). Jennings conceded that leaders "can become so skillful in disguising their direction . . . that even their so-called intimate friends are without the means of judging them accurately" (1960, p. 110; Blake & Mouton, 1964, chap. 8). Which is not to say that a leader disregards the needs or values of the follower as irrelevant to the task, for it is the very stuff a leader uses.

In short, the direction does not have to be entirely clear to the follower or even to the leader, even though it would undoubtedly help.[9]

C. CHAPTER SUMMARY

These last two chapters began the process of synthesis, which has been characterized as an ascent from the valley floor. Rather than emphasize the perfectly legitimate pathway toward ideal types, we turned instead toward something known as a sociological form. It was largely to explain why it would be permissible to choose one path as opposed to another that the previous chapter had to introduce perspectivism. Perspectivism derives from two traditions appearing in this book previously, namely pragmatism and phenomenology, and it tries to include as many authentic points of view as possible, so that the end result is a composite of perspectives— some better than others, but all of them better than one.

Perspectivism encourages humility, since each perspective is limited and only part of the truth. In order to accumulate and make sense of all of these various perspectives, a scholar is compelled to confer with others—in person or in print—and remain open to alternative viewpoints. None of which is to suggest that perspectivism is the same thing as dreaded relativism, as though I have my truth and you have yours. There is one paramount reality out there. We must collaborate in order to understand it better.

The analytical unit of the sociological form, introduced by Georg Simmel, promises to assist in leadership studies as one way to organize our various perspectives into some coherence. The contents of life assume different forms, many of which resemble each other across human experience, so that by abstraction we may show the similarities. Leadership will be seen to possess a distinctive structure.

Don Levine advises that the proper study of any sociological form would trace its lifespan, from origins to dissolution, and investigate its structural properties—specifically the properties of reciprocity, distance, and tensions. The end of this chapter suggested some of the conditions under which leadership emerges. First, there is a follower who must be *able* to follow and *willing* to follow. The ability to follow includes the confidence that one has the ability. Sometimes, preliminary to leadership itself, the prospective leader has to encourage or empower the prospective follower, so she is able and *knows* that she is able to follow. The willingness to follow derives from apathy or anxiety: the follower must care too little to resist or care too much to take action without leadership. Again, preliminary to leadership itself, the prospective leader might have to cultivate that willingness, before proceeding further. This explains why it is often noted that the task of leaders is to comfort the afflicted and afflict the comfortable.

The second condition under which leadership emerges is a prospective leader who has in mind some direction for the follower to take. On this point, I took a strong stance to the effect that any intended influence, no matter how slight, is leadership, even if all you do is get me to alter my walk home. It is certainly not the purpose of this section to have delivered the complete and exhaustive description of those conditions under which leadership emerges, so much as it was to begin working through the process.

And now, I have to escort you through an excursus. Our interest in the birth of forms should be matched by an interest in their death, inasmuch as leadership has a life cycle. Leadership also comes to an end. In many instances, the very purpose for leadership had been the moment it was no longer necessary. Followers are graduated, turned loose, even pushed out of the nest (e.g., Hersey & Blanchard, in Wren, 1995, chap. 32; Manz & Sims, 1989). That moment might come once the follower proves worthy, and for many types of leadership the final test is a struggle against the leader. This is not to be confused with ending leadership by destroying the leader, by supplanting or obliterating the one who led (Harter, 2001). This "turning against" the leader also brings leadership to an end, though this was not its purpose. If anything, it shows that something in the relationship went terribly wrong. Which is not the only way that leadership ends badly, however. Sometimes, the follower so internalizes the wishes and visions and methods of the leader that further supervision becomes unnecessary. The follower is more like a wind-up toy, ready to be released, an embodied extension of the leader's will, so that the relationship itself ends yet the follower continues to follow on his own, indefinitely. Leadership can end in other ways. Sometimes, external forces or authorities interfere. Sometimes, the parties agree to a limited duration, say, by contract. Sometimes, one or the other party walks away, quits, without resolution. The point is that a thorough treatment of the sociological form would study not only the way leadership begins, but also the way it ends. And as for perpetual leadership of the sort which never dies, that makes no sense. Aside from the eventuality of physical death, after a certain point, leadership that persists becomes something else—a kind of permanent dependence that falls outside the scope of leadership studies. Water can be cold, but below freezing, it is no longer water at all. It is ice. There is another way to say this: If leadership expresses human freedom, as the parties enter into it for their individual need satisfaction, then any perduring dependency renounces freedom. Whatever it is (e.g., slavery), it ain't leadership.

In any case, just as this chapter does no more than outline the study of the dynamics of leadership as a form, without giving all of the details, the following chapter is not meant to give a complete and exhaustive description of the structural properties of leadership. It does start to sketch some of the dimensions, including two that frequently puzzle the best students of leadership, namely power and morality. In other words, the next chapter continues our discussion of leadership as a sociological form.

8

SLICING THE APPLE

I have a suggestion. Picture leadership as a large apple. You can slice the apple in almost any direction, at any angle, in thin slices or thick. There is no one-right-way to slice it. The analogy is meant to suggest that selecting types of leadership or tensions within leadership as a sociological form is a job that can be done any number of ways. In effect, what we shall be doing in the words of Voegelin is offering possible differentiations. Plenty of work has already begun along several dimensions. There is no reason to reproduce it all here. To be honest, in actual practice there is no way to exhaust the possibilities. (Bernard Bass has probably come the closest.) The permutations are endless. As a result, the literature is a sweep through many of the permutations. One might examine the leadership styles of women in eighteenth-century France, or the optimal age difference between a mentor and protégé. As the studies proliferate, they threaten to overwhelm us unless we are able to bring order to them, as we said earlier. One objective therefore would be to schematize all of these studies according to *dimension*. Such a project would gather similar studies together for ease of use and to achieve some coalescence of method and vocabulary, and it would expose the gaps where new studies might be overdue, showing a new scholar where to make her mark. After one person studies the leadership styles of women in eighteenth-century France, let us say, another writer might wonder whether it mattered then how old the women were, or she might wonder whether the same findings apply to French colonies and so forth.

Is there some way to organize these dimensions?

A. BASIC DIMENSIONS

The structure of a sociological form has multiple dimensions. It might help to classify some of the basic dimensions. Ernst Cassirer explains that the most basic dimension would be *spatial,* between me here and you (or that) there. For purposes of communication, the center is constant: wherever I am. The periphery however contains numerous things that vary in relation to each other: some are closer to me than others, and they occupy a field in an array that has height, width, and depth, so that we can speak intelligibly of things present and things absent, things higher and things lower, things larger and things smaller, and so forth (Cassirer, 1921/1953, chap. 3, §1). He wrote, "It is only when a content is determined in space, when it is distinguished by fixed boundaries from the undifferentiated totality of space, that it gains its own real form" (ibid., p. 204). You might ask, "What does all this have to do with leadership?" Quite a lot, surprisingly. (See generally Bass, 1990, pp. 658–670.)

When students are asked to draw leadership, to depict it on a blank sheet of paper, they frequently use spatial imagery. They draw arrows, for example. They show the leader as higher than the follower or larger than the follower. Organizational charts are real-world applications of the imagery of hierarchy as it relates to positions we associate with leadership. Ordinary language about leadership frequently uses spatial imagery. We speak, for example, of an overseer or supervisor, both of which denote the same exact thing, namely watching from above. Leaders are often said to be "over" or "above" their followers. One person has power "over" another.[1] Leaders also seem "larger than life," "grand," the "big" man, so that the closer one gets to preeminence he is said to be "growing" or "living large." Leaders do not just take up space. They move, figuratively, as they "point the way" and themselves move to the front toward something. They give direction, in other words, and they move like the figure to the ground against a backdrop of relative permanence. So whether they are situated differently from followers or on the move, leaders can be represented in spatial imagery.

These are spatial images, metaphors for psychological phenomena, yet the dimension of actual space affects leadership. Historically, leaders occupied places of preeminence such as capital cities, palaces, and thrones. Today, they get the corner office. Leaders not only use physical space to seem preeminent, by standing higher and waiting behind secretaries and closed doors while you fidget, they often change the physical space by their presence. Wherever they are located is the center. Whatever aircraft is transporting the President of the United States is known as Air Force One and assumes preeminence. More memorable leaders sometimes change a place just by having once been there. "George Washington slept here." People orient themselves by location with regard to their leaders: the top floor, the home office, even the gravesite.[2] Proximity to power is itself a kind of power. Space, psychological and physical, is a relevant dimension for studying leadership.

One of the most fruitful dimensions of leadership derived from spatial imagery has to do with the "distance" between the leader and follower, as we had reason to mention earlier briefly. Berger and Luckmann refer to a classic dimension that runs from intimacy in a relationship to distance (1966, p. 33). They were not the first, of course.[3] Neither were they the last.[4] Berger and Luckmann (ibid., p. 31) also detect a correlation between this dimension of *intimacy/distance,* on the one hand, and the dimension of magnitude, which we shall consider shortly, because magnitude is also a spatial image.

There is the dimension of *span of control,* signifying differences related to the sheer number of followers. What you can do with one size group you cannot do so well with another. "In sociological cases," wrote Simmel, "increasing quantity results in entirely new phenomena which, in a smaller number, seem to be absent even in a slighter proportion" (1908/1950, p. 116).

Like the dimension of space, there is the dimension of *time,* which subdivides roughly as follows.

- Leadership by era, as we saw in the section on historical studies
- Succession planning, in which one relationship succeeds another[5]
- Leadership development, such as tracing the personal history of leaders
- Duration of relationship, as for example in Hersey & Blanchard's situational leadership (1969, 1977, 1982)
- Sequence within a single episode, which itself varies according to the urgency of the task, that is, according to the *perception* of time

Alfred North Whitehead explained that when trying to describe a person, we could mean any one of three ways to understand that person. Do we mean that person at a specific moment, such as Caesar at the Rubicon? This is the most concrete. Do we mean the person as a completed history, from birth to death, in the form of a biography? Or do we mean that which is constant, essential to that person (1927/1955, pp. 27–29)? We face a similar choice when talking about leaders. Ron Heifetz will study the leader at a moment of crisis, when it becomes necessary to do what he calls "adaptive work" (1994). This is like studying Caesar at the Rubicon. Warren Bennis will study *On Becoming a Leader* (1989). This is like studying Caesar as a biography, with a history. (These two ways of study correspond to the classic difference between static and dynamic models, which we had reason to describe earlier.) What interests us primarily in this book is the most abstract level of all: that which is constant, essential to leadership. This is like studying why Caesar was Caesar: what was it about him that made his name a title for all subsequent emperors, including the Tsars and Kaiser? Each of these three ways of study has its place: the momentary, the historical, and the timeless.

There are also the dimensions of gender, ethnicity, race, religion, age, and perhaps other categories identified by *legally protected classes* (e.g., Bass, 1990, chaps. 32–33). Related to this are the dimensions of *jurisdiction* and *culture,* both societal and organizational.[6] Simmel also notes the importance of *similarity/dissimilarity* between persons (1971, p. 9), as well as the *degree of discord* that exists between them (1971, chap. 6). Mazlish differentiates by *intensity of devotion* to the leader, "between immediate followers—disciples— and general supporters" (1976, p. 40). The disciples suffer a "boundless love," whereas mere supporters have "ambivalent feelings" (1976, p. 126). We mentioned earlier that Kenneth Thompson found a dozen or so dimensions in the American presidency (1984). Anytime someone makes a distinction about types of leadership or degrees of leader effectiveness, they are talking about dimensions. Taken together, wrote Simmel, these dimensions "form a sort of coordinate system, through which, as it were, the locus of every part and content of our life may be identified" (1971, p. 354).

B. POWER

Another dimension basic to the sociological form of leadership is the dimension of power. Power has been a tricky topic for leadership studies. It probably deserves closer scrutiny. As before, by looking around at ordinary usage, we begin the process of analysis. Therefore, we can start by asking ourselves what kind of leadership will be found in books with the following titles:

- Leadership Secrets of Attila the Hun
- The Art of War for Managers
- How to Swim with the Sharks
- Looking Out for Number One
- Warrior Politics: Why Leadership Demands a Pagan Ethos
- Buck Up, Suck Up . . . and Come Back When You Foul Up: How to Fight and Win . . . in Business, in Politics and in Life
- Patton's One-Minute Messages: Tactical Leadership Skills for Business Management
- Winning Through Intimidation

Books with titles such as these appear to celebrate, or at least recommend using, power. To some people, the word "power" suggests violence and the threat of violence to enforce a command. One hears the word and easily imagines intimidation, domination, coercion, aggression, and force. At an interpersonal level, one thinks of weapons and hostile gestures, whereas at the societal level, one thinks of the military and police. In those guises, power has existed since the dawn of recorded time. John Gardner refers to coercion as "[p]robably the oldest source of power" (1990, p. 59). There is also little reason to believe it will ever go away. A number of psychologists for example believe that aggression is innate (see Rapoport, 1974, chap. 10). Georg Simmel declared flatly that "coercion is necessary for social organization" (1908/1950, p. 298). If this is leadership, it is a leadership grounded in fear.

Studies of leadership that neglect this kind of influence are either naïve or they have defined it away by saying that coercion cannot be leadership, so they are not required to include it. Power connotes coercion, and there is no question that coercion bears a family resemblance to leadership. They are both methods of interpersonal influence. Often, when a study about leadership defines coercion away, insisting without further explanation that they are incompatible, it actually presents leadership as an alternative, so that even when coercion gets set aside, it looms in the foreground (as it were) as the undesirable choice. Leadership is meant to be understood only in reference to coercion, as some kind of anti-coercion. For this reason, if for no other, coercion as the use of power belongs at the front of the study, naked and explicit. If it turns out we are to choose one path (leadership) over another (coercion), we should first investigate our choices.

Upon closer examination, leadership appears to seek the same basic outcome as coercion, which is a positive response to direction. The purpose seems to be the same. Both are types of influence. To the extent coercion can be said to be direct and honest, leadership as an alternative can appear to be indirect and manipulative, a set of techniques to get from point A to point B without incurring resistance. Not a few critics of leadership attack it on those grounds, specifically that it hides the brutal fact that one person is trying to get another person to do something in particular. How much better, they argue, for us to say what we mean and mean what we say. Leadership looks too much like cunning.

More than one person has declared that the use of power is incompatible with leadership (e.g., Rost, 1993, pp. 105f), in direct opposition to those who hold that without the use of power, leadership cannot even take place. James MacGregor Burns, for example, wrote, "Leaders are a particular kind of power holder" (1978, p. 18). John Gardner was more emphatic: "To say a leader is preoccupied with power is like saying that a tennis player is preoccupied with making shots an opponent cannot return. Of course leaders are preoccupied with power!" (1990, p. 57). Is power incompatible with leadership, as some like Rost believe, or is it essential? Somewhere between these two diametrically opposed positions, Max DePree wrote a book entitled *Leading Without Power* in 1997—claiming that the use of power is compatible with leadership without being necessary. Here, then, are our choices so far:

1. Power is incompatible with leadership

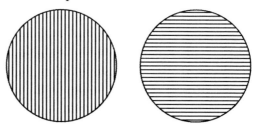

2. Power is not necessary for leadership, but it is compatible

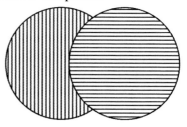

3. Power is necessary but not sufficient for leadership (it requires something more)

4. Power is necessary and sufficient for leadership (they are the same thing)

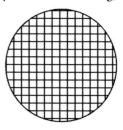

This whole question about the relationship between power and leadership hinges on the meaning of the word "power," and in ordinary usage the word "power" in English tries to do too much.[7] Other languages use several different words to do the job. Ancient Greek, to name one language, used *dynamis, energia, ergon, kinesis*. German uses *Kraft, Gewalt, Macht*, and so forth.[8] The English word often refers to coercion, as we have suggested. Violence and its threat—whatever we choose to call them—certainly do exist as one basis for power. In their famous article, French and Raven (1959) referred to them together as coercion and listed coercion as one of five bases of power, but they also mentioned four others (i.e. reward, legitimacy, expertise, and referent power), so there is a variety. Robert Dahl once wrote:

> Power terms evidently cover a very broad category of human relations. Considerable effort and ingenuity have gone into schemes for classifying these relations into various types, labeled power, influence, authority, persuasion, dissuasion, inducement, coercion, compulsion, force, and so on. . . . (1968/1986, p. 40)

Behind all of these labels, regardless, power is something that emerges out of a relationship, since one does not have power unless it is in relation to a thing being changed. Power, in the sense of interpersonal power, exists between people. I do not own or possess power as an attribute. What one finds, then, at the very least, are the following elements:

- It is an interpersonal phenomenon, as we have been saying,
- that involves change in one person
- attributable somehow to the other person.

These are three of the four core elements of a definition of leadership from the very beginning of this book. The distinction between coercion, on the one hand, and leadership, on the other, as though they are entirely separate or even antithetical phenomena, is frankly inadequate, and this is the reason: the word power comes from the same root as for the words "potential" and "possible." Power is what might be latent, undisclosed. I say, "might be," because nobody knows, when it comes to interpersonal power, whether one has power until one attempts to use it. Then of course it may be too late.

The usual meaning of "power" is "power over" someone else. And in many instances that is an appropriate way to think about it. However, power can also be "power with" or "power to." We are not restricted to relationships of domination when we talk about power.

What we are really talking about is causation; that is, how does one person cause another to behave in a way they otherwise would not have behaved? The secret, known since before the time of Aristotle, is that very little behavior is *caused*. The person being affected almost always has a choice. That is why it is better to use the term "influence." One person can certainly "influence" another. *Power is nothing more mysterious than the capacity to influence* (Baron & Greenberg, 1986, p. 411, citing Cobb, 1984).

And because the person being affected has some choice, even if only to refuse, it makes sense to speak of power as the potential one person has to influence the choices that another person might make. So, to round this out, power—interpersonal power—can be thought of as a product of one's perceptions, because if I believe you will hurt me when I do something, even if in truth you cannot, then I am likely to alter my behavior accordingly. Thus, leadership can be defined as the use of power toward desired goals and objectives. (See Baron & Greenberg, 1986, p. 374, citing Hollander, 1985.)

Clearly, more could be said on the topic of power (e.g., Bass, 1990, chap. 13). Our purpose here was to emphasize the importance and nature of power to leadership studies, as one dimension of the sociological form.

C. THE *MORAL* DIMENSION

If any use of power can be construed as leadership, then qualms swarm around us about the implications of power for measuring leadership according to morality, because superficially morality and power seem opposed to each other. In other words, talk of power implicates morals.

We can regard leadership as a sociological form with reciprocity, distance, and tensions, according to a number of basic dimensions, such as space and time. Some dimensions are more problematic than others. Power is one of these. It varies by intensity, proportion to the follower's power, the power of third parties, and base of power. In this section, we must also consider the problematic dimension of morality, even though, like the previous section on power, we cannot presume to exhaust the topic.

1. Must leaders be moral? So much has already been written on the morality of leadership that there is no way to exhaust the topic in one chapter.[9] By the same token, because of the vast literature, there is no way to ignore the topic either. For many people, morality fits the very definition of leadership. Here in this book we include it as one of the dimensions of the sociological form—important, yes, but hardly more important for understanding leadership than other dimensions.

When scholars try to define the word "leadership," they often insist that leadership is "good" or "moral" or "positive." Otherwise, they say, it is not leadership. Rather than list examples, I would simply cite again Joseph Rost, who not only reproduces a number of these definitions but also ends up disagreeing with them for cogent reasons. He writes, "Including a moral requirement in . . . the definition of leadership . . . is too limiting, and thus unacceptable" (1993, p. 124; see also pp. 165–177). Michels went further. He wrote, "Leadership is a necessary phenomenon in every social form of social life. Consequently it is not the task of science to inquire whether this phenomenon is good or evil, or predominantly one or the other" (1915/1949, p. 400). Definitions notwithstanding, the whole question of right and wrong frequently arises in considerations of leadership. Whether it appears in the definition of leadership or not, it is still a legitimate project to appreciate the moral dimension of leadership. Rather than debate whether the *definition* calls for a moral or ethical requirement, let us proceed to consider the moral *dimension* of leadership.[10]

One has to identify what something is before deciding whether it is bad or good (Davis, 1996, pp. 2, 153–160). Otherwise, how could you know whether it is bad or good? A bad novel might be an excellent paperweight.

Once successfully defined, leadership can be measured according to more than one standard or dimension, which is why it helps to identify that standard when passing judgment. If by good leadership one person means "efficient" and another means "morally just," folks will misunderstand each other. Does an "effective" leader benefit (a) society as a whole, (b) his specific organization, (c) the leader personally, or (d) the follower? One should probably identify the stakeholders and assess the impact of leadership on each of them before rendering a final judgment. Unfortunately, writers in the discipline of leadership studies risk miscommunicating, confounding each other and achieving little. The standard for measurement ought to be explicit. *What is meant by good leadership?*

The question arises with the assertion that a leader must be moral, or "principled" (e.g., Panichas, 1996, p. 311; Grob, 1984, p. 269). Now, first, if it means anything at all, the assertion is empirically false. Immoral leaders exist. Labeling them something else such as "tyrant" or "quasi-leader" in order to set them aside only hinders analysis. In this way, wrote Jacob Heilbrunn (quoting this for the second time), "the science of leadership has devoted too little attention to what might be called the darker side of the question" (1996, p. 10; Born, 1996, p. 59; see also Johnson, 1996, p. 13). There is a further complication trying to determine what it even means for a leader to be moral. The Reverend Martin Luther King, Jr. was an exemplary leader of the civil rights movement, notwithstanding several documented defects of character. Questions naturally arise: to what degree moral? in what specific pursuits? and for that matter, whose morals?[11]

It is not inconsistent (a) to say that immoral leaders exist and (b) still personally to hope for moral leaders. Morality is just not part of the definition. I wish every oil painting were beautiful and every quiz answer true. They are not.

Often, when people argue for "principled" leadership, they come back with another empirically weak assertion that unethical leaders will be found out, that they ultimately fail. The argument seems to be that leadership is proven by long-term success and that long-term success is possible only if the leader has been moral. Again, there are problems with the argument, not least of which is defining "long term," since Josef Stalin and Mao Zedong governed quite a long period of time and died natural deaths. There are bosses at the workplace who are jerks until the day they retire. The followers of Jim Jones and David Koresch presumably never lost their faith. To what extent can it be said these leaders were "found out"? How long is "long-term"? More significant, however, is another confusion. Instead of arguing that leaders are moral, we are now arguing that leaders are effective, and that being moral is merely a precondition for success, not a good in and of itself. In other words, what the argument really means to say is that there seems to be a correlation between being ethical and being effective. People may debate whether this is true (and how anyone can even prove it one way or the other), but at least now the proposition is clarified.

It has been something of a parlor game in leadership studies to ask whether Adolph Hitler was a leader. In light of recent events, we might choose to ask whether Osama bin Laden is our leader, inasmuch as we attribute to him certain changes in the way we do things after the terrorist attack on New York City on September 11, 2001. He financed and orchestrated the attack, which means that he fits some of the usual definitions of leadership. He was oriented to us in the West, since it was our horrified reaction that he desired, and he took actions to influence us toward that end. After the attack, we became oriented to him and to the prospect that he might attack us again, so we did many of the things he wanted us to do, such as increase security at home and lash out with violence abroad. But most people recoil from the possibility of calling a terrorist our leader, which is much the same thing as calling prison guards, enemies at war, and rapists leaders. Are we required to include terrorism within leadership studies?

I am willing to entertain the possibility. I am biting the bullet, as they say, by holding to a more expansive interpretation of what leadership includes. For one thing, we cannot alter our definition of leadership to keep out persons we do not like. Referring to someone as a leader is not the same thing as bestowing an honorific. We are not in the business of rewarding those we like with this label. If that were the case, we would have different definitions for every nation-state, ethnic group, and political party, because Nazis make sure to include Hitler and we make sure to exclude him. A scholarly definition cannot depend on our favor, which varies from culture to culture and even within a culture over time. Are we saying that Hitler was a leader at one moment, and then he was not? Whether a scholar approves of the person he is studying is irrelevant to problems of definition. Osama bin Laden, a man whose historical significance will fade quickly, presents us with a methodological problem that will never fade, and it has to do with the detachment of our scholarship.

None of which is to suggest that our repugnance is in any way invalid. We are free to castigate, criticize, calumniate, and otherwise condemn bad guys. We *should* do so. In my opinion, leadership studies is the perfect place to study bad guys in particular, to dissect their methods and inoculate the public against them. And to the extent we disagree about which ones are the bad guys—and it is inevitable that we will—we can have that debate without closing off discussion through some definitional sleight of hand.

A scholar is expected to examine leadership in a detached manner, leaving prejudice aside. Regardless of the scholar's detached judgment, it does seem to matter whether the follower *perceives* the leader to be moral, even though that is a separate matter from whether the leader is in fact moral (Baron & Greenberg, 1986, chap. 4).[12]

An understanding of leadership is served by making ourselves absolutely clear what standard we are using to measure leadership. And again, prior even to that, we must distinguish between (a) defining leadership and (b) measuring it according to any standard. Thus, I agree with Rost, who wrote that we "should not confuse the nature of leadership with what [we] think good leadership is. The two are not the same" (1993, pp. 127, 144, 148).

2. Thinking about morality. Aristotle is always a solid place to begin any philosophical inquiry. When it comes to the topic known as Ethics, he certainly set the standard. Aristotle opened his *Nicomachean Ethics* with the observation that all voluntary behavior is directed toward something that the person believes to be good. Every action aims at "the Good." What Aristotle wanted was knowledge of the Good: What is good? Are some "goods" better than others? Is there a supreme good against which we can measure all human behavior? It was his belief that we could pursue a science dedicated to just this sort of question (I:1f [1094a]). And so we have: We call it "Ethics."

Rather than present a full-blown theory of leadership ethics here, I am simply drawing attention to the ethical dimension of leadership and suggesting a couple of ways to think about it. There will be more to say in the next chapter.

Perhaps the best way to begin is for us to contrast two beliefs. One belief is that leaders not only ought to be moral, but in order to be effective *must* be moral. The other contrasting belief is that leaders ought to be willing to behave immorally if they truly want to be effective as leaders. The first belief enjoys a long and venerable tradition in both religion and philosophy. The second arises from only a few voices.

One of those bold, dissenting voices was Niccolò Machiavelli. Scholars will never agree entirely about the messages in Machiavelli, though one thing is sure: he clearly wrote that a ruler's effectiveness sometimes requires immoral behavior. He premised his argument on the historical record, on what actually happens in the real world (Strauss, 1987, p. 300). This was very important to Machiavelli. What he set out to show was that in fact immoral behavior in the past, such as fraud and murder, did preserve and even increase a ruler's effectiveness. We would say he tried to prove his point by empirical evidence. The issue is not whether morality *ought* to be effective, but whether it has been. And he offers numerous examples to the effect that it hasn't always.

What he concludes from the historical record is that immorality sometimes helps. Anyone desiring to be effective has to take this into account, or he is a fool, just as an acrobat who wishes away the laws of gravity will surely stumble. This is not to say that a leader is necessarily evil. He still aims toward the good, which for the leader has to be effectiveness. A leader *unwilling* to be effective guarantees he will soon no longer be a leader. The whole purpose of leadership is to lead. That alone makes it "good."

Machiavelli used a subtle argument. He argued that judgments of what is moral or immoral are made after the fact, *ex post facto*, based on outcomes. Did things turn out fine? If so, then, "all's well that ends well." People withhold judgment until they experience the consequences, at which time they condemn failure and praise success (*Discourses* I:9). Thus, the ends *do* justify the means, but only in the sense that the outcome (the end) determines whether folks will look back with gratitude or contempt. In other words, morality in public affairs is nothing more than public acclaim.

What Machiavelli did was to strip from leadership the notion that there exists an independent, objective morality, separate from the judgment of history. Machiavelli renounced the moral claims of disembodied reason and revelation. People do not live their lives that way. They do respond to results. Thus, there really is not a moral dimension to leadership, according to Machiavelli, except this:

a. The leader must strive to be effective. That alone is good leadership.

b. The people will reject a leader they believe to be unethical, if it turns out they do not like what the leader has accomplished, so whether the leader is moral or not turns out to be secondary to how moral he seems.

What then did Machiavelli advise? Do whatever it takes to succeed, but cultivate in the people the impression that you are entirely moral. In other words, deceive them when necessary, albeit for their own good.

In fairness, other interpretations of Machiavelli abound. One scholar argues that for Machiavelli, in the absence of civic order there is no such thing as morality, so whatever he does to impose order will be permitted (de Sanctis, 1956/1960, p. 25). It cannot be immoral if there is no such thing as morality! Another scholar argues that Machiavelli fully believed that immoral behavior is immoral and deserves damnation, which is why a leader to be effective must consent to going to hell for the sake of others (deGrazia, 1989). Yet another scholar rejects Machiavelli, saying that he was a teacher of evil, without any affinity for the Good, except to the extent it serves his evil purposes (Strauss, 1987). And then there are the scholars who believe Machiavelli was being disingenuous when he wrote all of this, whether because he was lying to get a job or because he was writing satire.

Until now, we were assuming for the sake of discussion that we knew what is moral and immoral, so that it was just a matter of choosing. In point of fact, today folks do not agree with each other on what is moral, and in some instances they have to admit they do not know themselves. "I'm not sure what is right or wrong in this situation." Because this is so, how are we supposed to assess the morality in leadership without a cogent and universal basis? This is a fair question. For all the pleas on behalf of moral leadership, we are left with a bewildering array of understandings about what it means to be moral. At the very least, exponents of moral leadership should make their understanding explicit.

Due to the importance of this topic, we shall take a side trip into the next chapter to take a closer look at the ethics of leadership. Then, we should plan to resume our ascent.

D. CHAPTER SUMMARY

Just as the prior chapter began to sketch the conditions under which leadership emerges, this chapter began to sketch its structural properties. It did this by reference to various "dimensions"—of which there is (or are) a multitude.

Among the more basic dimensions are space and time, but the list quickly exceeded the space and time available to write this book. Much work—seemingly unrelated in the literature—elucidates many of these dimensions. More work is required.

More problematic are two topics not often depicted as dimensions of a relationship, namely power and morality. Power, the capacity to influence, emerges out of the relationship and rests on several bases—including perhaps coercion. At some point, too much power disparity removes the relationship out of the category of leadership and renders it something else. Of course, there has to be *some* power disparity for there to be leadership at all, so it comes within a range that requires further definition.

As for the moral dimension, plenty of writers have weighed in (as it were) and left it inconclusive. Even so, leadership studies must continue to wrestle with it, if for no other reason than the overwhelming importance of values and morality to the participants and their assessment of leaders. Any implication of interpersonal power implicates issues of morality, as well. They are intimately connected and famously fuzzy.

9

TREAD A THORNY PATH

What follows is an excursus on the ethics of leadership, which by nearly any standard is a thorny topic. In part I, we will turn in fairly rapid succession to three ways of thinking about ethics—ways that have implications for the formation of elites—a topic that will return in the next chapter. In part II, we will consider the meditations of an aging Eric Voegelin, for the purpose of contemplating a completely different way to think about our supposed predicament—a way to think about ethics that will be found to fit the precepts of pragmatism. In most debates over ethics and morality, Voegelin's path is rarely used.

PART I: FROM MORALITY TO ELITE FORMATION

A. ALASDAIR MACINTYRE

MacIntyre explored the problem of conflicting moral standards in a book titled *After Virtue*. As a professor of philosophy, he could not help but notice that our society is engaged in a debate with no apparent way to resolve who is right and who is wrong, and the reason we cannot resolve the debate is that we share no standard of what constitutes right and wrong. Nonetheless, we talk to each other as though there were. When a person says, "That was the wrong thing to do," he makes an appeal to some standard he wants the other person to recognize. MacIntyre simplifies what has happened, in three stages.

- Society not only believed in objective morality, it also tended to agree on its basic content.

- Then society experienced a breakdown, a crisis (or series of crises) that cast doubt on the prevailing morality.

- In an attempt to substitute something in its place, society has settled on Emotivism.

What is emotivism? Emotivism holds that moral judgments are really "*nothing but* expressions of preference[,] attitude or feeling [*emphasis supplied*]" (1984, p. 12). Whereas we tend to believe that facts are either true or false, we tend to believe that moral judgments or "values" are neither true nor false. Instead, moral judgments are now thought to do only two things. They express one's preferences, and they attempt to create similar preferences in the other person (ibid., p. 12). In all instances of leadership where a moral judgment arises—as it will—we could very easily regard these moral judgments as attempts to manipulate others into adopting the leader's preferences, with the consequence that we likely resent them.

MacIntyre connects emotivism with two trends in the popular mind, trends for which we see some evidence today. One is the trend toward the private self, where I retreat to what I think and leave you to what you think. This is one kind of pluralism—a pluralism Bernstein had reason to reject, as we saw earlier in this book. The private self knows better than to try and justify its moral judgments, because there is no standard the other person must recognize. So by tacit agreement everyone quits talking about morals, except to assert oneself in a pinch and perhaps on occasion to get someone else to yield. This trend toward the private self—a self that comes out of hiding only in order to manipulate (or even coerce) others—leads to chaos, as society and its organizations fragment further and further into tribes and into individuals contented with their (idiosyncratic) positions, in isolation. We are little more than atoms bouncing against each other.

The other trend "oscillates" with this one (ibid., p. 35). That second trend is a kind of lowest common denominator (LCD) collectivism. LCD collectivism is a crude insistence on simple rules of the game, rhetorically justified as the common good—rules such as free speech, mass popular elections, and the like. In other words, to bring order to the chaotic swirl in society and its organizations, where no one agrees on basic morality, we feel the need to establish a bare consensus and empower an agency in our collective name (the People, the Firm, the Community) to enforce it. We want to enjoy our private autonomy, yet we apprehend what widespread autonomy will bring about. "That would be crazy! You can't have folks going around doing whatever they feel like doing at the time." This trend toward a collective lowest common denominator agency, MacIntyre fears, establishes the conditions for authoritarian and perhaps even totalitarian regimes, as Thomas Hobbes once predicted. We need a Leviathan.

What MacIntyre detects is a strong (increasing?) sentiment in the populace not to be told what to do, which puts prospective leaders on notice. MacIntyre also detects a strong (increasing?) willingness, if not an impatient expectation, that someone fix things that go wrong.[1] Now the stage is set for leadership promising to remove those barriers to autonomy that we increasingly notice and resent. If a leader promises to enhance your private welfare by ruthlessly wielding power, then that leader positions herself to succeed. Put another way, the leader (representing the state or party) creates the cohesiveness and *is* the cohesiveness that permits society to break apart, seemingly without consequence, since our unity resides in the leader, as we then go our separate ways. She is the one constant in a state of flux.

Sadly, both trends—private selves and Leviathan—conspire to bring ruin. What we want out of life cannot happen . . . certainly not this way. MacIntyre undertook to explain why it cannot happen and then to point toward a possible remedy, but the obvious thing should not go unsaid, which is that the more I empower a leader, the more I disempower my neighbors, because I want the leader to bust some heads. Just not mine. The two sentiments encourage both withdrawal and hostility.

B. MICHAEL OAKESHOTT

This British conservative built a similar argument, less directly tied to the subject of ethics and more directly tied to the subject of leadership, in an essay titled "The Masses in Representative Democracy" (1961/1991). His interpretation is that with the collapse of a binding authority—largely understood to be the *ancien régime*—individuals were set free. Conventional views and traditional institutions fell by the wayside over time, leaving a vast number of people (who had always been dependent on that system) loose, untended, and insecure. The more-capable individuals flourished, in science, technology, commerce, and art, but the rest could not bear the weight of their freedom. They had adapted nicely to the old system. The emerging system forced them into roles for which they were not suited, roles such as entrepreneur, voter, and "the priesthood of all believers."

Imagine, if you will, a bouquet of balloons. (The image is mine and not Oakeshott's.) Some balloons contain helium. Most do not. The balloons tend to cluster until someone cuts the strings that hold them together. Helium balloons rise quickly, dramatically, while the rest of them float helplessly to the ground.

Oakeshott described these listless balloons as the masses who now found themselves alone responsible for themselves. They cannot overlook the increasing disparity between the winners in life and themselves, the losers. "The rich get richer, and the poor get poorer." Their inadequacy in the new way of doing things has become obvious. They "just don't get it." And the prevailing ethos, championed by the freedom-loving winners, is that the losers *deserve* their fate. This is the ethos of rugged individualism or social Darwinism: struggle or die. Quite a lot of people chafe under this ethos, so they counter with a different ethos, one that emphasizes not freedom but equality, not self-help but social obligation, not achievement but security—in effect, a reasonable facsimile of the feudal ethos . . . without the religion and (they hope) without the oppression. The practical problem however is that the masses cannot impose their ethos from below, as it were, partly because they rely on the creativity and hard work of the new elites and partly because they really do not have what it takes to orchestrate social change. The masses are numerous, yes, but they lack unity and direction.

Enter the leader. Oakeshott actually despises the leader and says he is without a soul. At the Great Liberation of the Balloons, the "winners" in life all soared off in different directions, exploring and experimenting. A winner would not stay behind to make a point of championing the cause of losers. That would be self-defeating. The leader, by way of contrast, is not a winner in his own right. Neither is he a despondent loser. His identity depends on having followers, who are the dependent masses. He will promise them, as we said earlier, to remove their stigma, harness the power of the elite, and make all of those awkward decisions in freedom they could not bear to make on their own behalf. What the masses gladly surrender to him, the leader, is that very freedom they never really wanted and the winners worked so hard to get and use for themselves.

In this sense, Oakeshott can be understood (unlike MacIntyre) to mean that individuals going off in different, even uncoordinated directions can be thought of as a good thing. But only for certain individuals (the elite). Likewise, he can be understood (unlike MacIntyre) to mean that the strict use of authority can be thought of as a good thing as well. But only for certain individuals (the masses).

We arrive at a moral condemnation of leaders as enablers, making it easier for the weak to remain weak and making it easier for the weak to weaken the strong. MacIntyre, if you recall, was not so contemptuous of leadership *per se*. He did wonder about the tendency of people to accept manipulation, but he did not make the sort of sweeping generalization Oakeshott did. Nonetheless, both men find that in today's moral climate, leadership is fraught with peril, difficult to generate and dangerous to society.

These are by no means the only ways to schematize social structure. They do illustrate the kind of schemas that accompany ethical analysis. A distinction between elites and masses, like any social distinction (of race, gender, etc.), automatically raises the issue of fairness, whether the two classes deserve their standing, for example, and what we owe one class that we do not owe the other (e.g., Harter & Evanecky, 2002). Is one class, the elites, meant to be in charge of the other? Why? Does that mean the elites should enjoy greater autonomy and greater responsibility? What exactly do the elites owe the masses, as a class or as individuals? What do the masses owe the elites, as a class or as individuals? So much moral consternation surrounding this deceptively simple schema of elites and masses! (The next chapter will approach the topic again.)

C. GEORG SIMMEL

By way of contrast, if only to illustrate the diversity of schemas and their implications for a science of ethics, let us revisit briefly the contribution of Simmel about the consequences of the contents of life assuming form, as we had reason to explain previously. After describing the interplay of content and form, then we can look anew at moral considerations.

One of the central lessons in Simmel is the gradual separation in "which life 'becomes more and more thing-like and impersonal" (Habermas, 1991, citing Horkheimer and Adorno, p. 532). The forces or impulses that bubble up in us—what Simmel elsewhere referred to as "contents" and "perplexed urges"—express themselves in forms external to ourselves. In crude terms, love solidifies into marriage, an idea solidifies into an assertion, ambition solidifies into a career. The content of our lives takes discernible shape, and these shapes become part of our reality, they "take on a life of their own." We end up surrounded by these forms, the objectification (if you'll pardon the term) of subjective initiative, for that is the way of culture.

Let us be more direct. Two persons with private needs and private values encounter each other. Rather than simply influencing each other, they might "solidify" their encounter into a relationship. The relationship might be informal, like friendship, or formal, like an employment contract. The point is that the encounter takes on a shape or form independent of the ongoing, spontaneous drives of the two people, like spring water, cast from the earth onto a frozen mountain side, that becomes ice. The two participants develop habits and expectations, and they drag into the relationship their memories of similar relationships, since to their way of thinking their past informs them and tells them how to behave in the current relationship. They also struggle sometimes to come up with a name for their relationship. "Are we going steady or just dating?" "I dunno. What's the difference?" However it happens, together they *create* something that belongs to neither of them; to some extent, now *they* belong to *it*.

The tendency in society is for these forms to persevere and become the models for subsequent forms. With time, the various forms become ordered and shaped into larger, more complex forms, just as the relatively simple employment contract becomes part of an intricate and massive network of formal (and informal) relationships known as bureaucracy. There are people, and then there are all the forms into which they pour out their lives. There is the worker, for instance, and there is the firm, such as Nabisco or IBM. There is the voter, and there is the nation-state. There is the priest, and there is the community of saints. We create and are created by these objective forms. As Habermas put it: "personal and societal systems build *environments* for each other" (Habermas, 1991; emphasis supplied). The environment for leadership is usually an organization. Plus, forms proliferate and differentiate into a fantastic array.

This way of looking at social forms helps to explain MacIntyre's fear of the trend to radical autonomy, on the one hand, and totalitarian collectivism, on the other. Over time, less and less of our selves remain free from the pre-existence of forms. These forms surround us and mold us and burden us with expectations. As a child, you are expected to pledge allegiance to the flag, adopt the faith of your fathers, marry one of your own kind, and prepare yourself at school for an existing job to sustain you throughout adulthood. "Where in all this lies freedom, man?" So of course the few realms of autonomy left to you become precious and are held purposely private, to keep them from becoming just another form. (See, e.g., Ortega, 1943/1985.)

The skeptic quits going to church. The divorcee swears off the institution of marriage. The disgruntled worker fantasizes about owning his own business. And why not? There is a certain logic to preserving one's own creative powers. Even so, we all become dependent, by an inexorable process, upon increasingly complex systems. Each discrete step toward objectification makes rational sense, in and of itself, yet with the passage of time the accumulation of these steps creates an oppressive environment: omnipresent, omnipotent, and highly impersonal. We flee the protection of clans to embrace the municipal police. We scorn individual classroom teachers and learn about our world from television networks. That sort of thing.

One word for the process from the subjective "perplexed urges" to the objective "forms" is Alienation—to sense the other as Other, over against ourselves. There is me. And then there is this thing I helped create. I have taken something from within myself and put it out there, beyond me, like the dead cells of my hair. I do this to satisfy my drives, to increase my potency, though in the very process of alienation I realize that I have lost control. If I do this often enough (and I shall), I come to live among forms, to the extent that I become like a prisoner of my own weapons, of my own treasure. The irony is complete. That which I help to devise in order to enhance autonomy ends up controlling me.

An unpleasant image that vivifies this lesson is the crab that surrounds itself with a hard, protective covering that it secretes from its own body for the purpose of survival. The "form" enables the living thing to move around unmolested, until the living tissue grows to the point that it becomes cramped in its own shell. The throbbing pink flesh has nowhere to go, so it begins to curl in upon itself, destroying itself, putrefying within its casement, unless its living force shatters the outer covering to permit it to grow again, unencumbered. Having shed its shell, the tissue may grow freely, yet the new problem is that it has become naked to the elements, exposed once again to predation. In response, the crab secretes a new, larger shell, which of course accommodates the new dimensions . . . until further growth presses into it and the sequence begins all over again. The crab's shell is very much like a social form.

Here is the kicker: the same pattern applies to leadership. Leadership can be understood as a social form, produced by the parties for intended gain. The encounter "solidifies" into a relationship, a special kind of relationship we call Leadership. If the parties are not careful, the intended gain will be offset by loss. Many are the times a feeble request for direction from one person to another becomes a mandate, a barely detectable slide toward being dominated. (And I hasten to add that leadership can emburden *both* parties, and not just the follower.) Leadership itself "solidifies" into the formation of an elite.

And so we arrive at one explanation for the elites/masses distinction that exercised MacIntyre and Oakeshott (and a lot of other writers to boot). It was the French political scientist Bertrand de Jouvenel who went to great lengths demonstrating that power congeals. The Italian socialist Roberto Michels tried to show that every group or society, no matter how egalitarian, eventually gives way to an elite. The Spanish philosopher José Ortega y Gasset, in the now famous *Revolt of the Masses*, diagnosed the consequences of a civilization that relinquishes power to the masses. (It isn't pretty.) All of these writers can be read profitably as a part of leadership studies . . . and especially of the moral dimension of leadership.

In our present predicament, without universal standards, we become frustrated and likely will cry out for ethical leadership. Where, oh where, is the leader or elite to rescue us? We desire freedom for ourselves and seek some kind of social order. The tension is uncomfortable. Is there someone out there willing and able to answer our cry?

D. SUMMARY OF PART I

Many thinkers have considered the predicament of a pluralistic, even global, society that is without any universal ethical standards. In the vacuum of authority, ethics would appear to have deteriorated. At the very least, ethics are problematic. The predicament seems connected to the formation and authority of society's elites. It seems that our uncertainty, our anxiety, disposes us to follow. Is there perhaps another way to characterize the predicament?

PART II: THE CRY FOR ETHICAL LEADERSHIP

A. OUR PREDICAMENT

The cry for ethical leadership is a response to the perception that something is wrong—usually, that something is wrong with existing leaders. People have no reason to cry out when everything is fine. Even when something is wrong, people have no reason to cry out when a remedy lies close at hand. You do not call for a Band-Aid when you already hold one. The cry for ethical leadership is evidence that many of us sense that something is wrong, yet we do not know how to fix it.

The experience of crisis sends us in search of answers. In this case, the search for answers reveals that we have plenty to choose from. It will not be necessary to invent ethical leadership out of nothing. Our predicament is different. We have uncovered too many answers, too many different ways to respond. How do we know which answer is the best? Judeo-Christian, Moslem, Hindu, Deontological, Utilitarian—a guy can become bewildered. Even if we are not personally bewildered by the choices and know perfectly well what to believe, we also know that other people make different choices. Some of these choices are incompatible with our own. We live in a pluralistic society, where reasonable people disagree. What are we to do about the apparent lack of a shared authority? That would seem to be the threshold question.

We live in a pluralistic society at a time when our differences are magnified by the access we have to each other by means of travel and the media. We are not isolated from alternatives. Organizations operate in a global environment and straddle cultures. We have become aware of multiple religious traditions, even if our knowledge is superficial. We know, for example, that Christians are divided among themselves on many issues of the day. We are increasingly cautioned not to think of Islam as a monolith, as though all devout Moslems endorse the practices of Moslem terrorists. And for centuries, philosophers have conducted a search for one, universal, non-sectarian ethic, though in vain. As a result of these pluralistic pressures, we all turn in different directions.

Where do people look? There are already plenty of books on ethics. That is not the problem. There are trainers and gurus. More and more schools are adopting character-building curricula, partly in response to the perception of parents that it would be better to teach their children at home, away from the relativistic values of public education and away from the kids who would corrupt them or shoot them outright in the classroom. Churches still offer Sunday School. The persons and institutions we look to for moral authority, however, cannot agree among themselves. We have tried religion, education, and government. For about a hundred years, we relied on psychologists, represented lately by televised talk show therapists.

In this ethical disarray, upsetting as it is, we also suspect that a number of people are using the confusion as cover to do wrong and, when confronted, justify their behavior. Unscrupulous people frequently take advantage of confusion. They will reply to our rebukes with disdain. "You are simply being judgmental, narrow-minded, bigoted, trapped in a limited worldview. Really, who is to say what is right or wrong?" If the malefactor cannot quickly snatch an argument from the many that are readily available ("Society made me this way . . ."), he can at least cast doubt on our position. He can insist that we are hypocrites, or that ethics are really a matter of power and rules, and therefore a means of oppression. He can challenge us to cite chapter and verse: "Where does it say I cannot do this, in particular?"

In other words, he exploits the possibility that we lack confidence in our own position. Whether we are personally confident is immaterial when the rest of a community cannot bring itself to reinforce ethics anyway. If the community were confident, it would reinforce its values. In light of this, there are in reality two leadership tasks. Ethical leadership promises to bridge our differences and authorizes taking action against the bad guys. That is apparently what we want when we cry for ethical leadership.

Making the situation worse, as everyone knows, are the persons with moral authority who let us down, who betray our trust. We hear stories about crooked televangelists, radical college professors, slimy politicians, and shoddy journalists. We get thrown back, in other words, away from the notion there is such a thing as a moral authority. We tend to give up on ever finding the one person or the one institution that can answer the problem that prompted us to cry for ethical leadership in the first place. Nonetheless, we do cry out for someone to step forward. We call for a volunteer.

What would that noble volunteer do? The volunteer either holds himself out as an ethical leader, riding on a white horse to rescue a fallen world, or the volunteer devises a plan to locate and develop ethical leaders. "I may not be one. But I know where to find them."

The cry for ethical leadership sounds like a cry of wounded faith. We are uncertain now. We are tempted to despair. There are too many theories and not enough living models. All leaders are flawed. We become skeptical at the very time we are most desperate. Perhaps the cry for ethical leadership is not the beginning of a search for answers. Maybe it is the last yelp before completely giving up, the sound idealism makes when it has been punctured.

B. ERIC VOEGELIN

If the foregoing section adequately describes our predicament, then someone in my position has to explain why there is still a purpose in writing about ethical leadership. If it is not (a) to urge once again a familiar code ("Back to the Bible!") or (b) to disclose to the world a new code or (c) to entice the reader to quit looking, then what is the point?

It is the purpose of this section of the chapter to suggest an alternative way of thinking about the problem altogether, and this alternative way of thinking appears thoroughly in the work of Eric Voegelin.[2] Voegelin crafted a response to the terrors of the twentieth century—a response that promises to help us in our time, since the underlying experiences are equivalent.

The experience behind this cry for ethical leadership is an experience of disorder. That is one way to characterize it. We prefer order. So where is it? We go in search of order. *In Search of Order* (1987) is actually the title of Voegelin's last book, uncompleted on his deathbed (OH-5). In that book and in essays he completed toward the end of his career, he struggled to explain the response it took him decades to understand—a response to fascists, communists, and all sorts of ideologists, in person and in print.

What did he say? And how can it help?

C. THE CHALLENGE FOR ETHICAL LEADERS

First, we might assure ourselves that Voegelin would have appreciated the nature of our problem. He was responding to the same tension. Voegelin understood how we are dissatisfied with our personal and social existence. He agrees that "there is ample reason to be dissatisfied with the order of existence" (OH-5, p. 36). We are motivated by the "prevalent disorder" to find answers and restore order—not just in our personal lives, but also in our society, so that if we eventually do uncover the answer, we must persuade others of its truth and form some kind of durable organization to bring about social change (OH-5, p. 25). Ethical leaders presumably have answers and agree to use or create a durable organization to restore order. That would seem to be the meaning of a cry for ethical leadership.

If a leader were to start making headway, he and his followers must contend with four types of people. We met them earlier, as you will recall: (a) The old guard, of course, wants to preserve the status quo. They will resist any change. (b) Rival leaders prefer their answers and their organizations. They will resist this particular leader. (c) Skeptics will challenge any new leader. And, as the number of alternative leaders grows and as they jostle for position, skepticism will spread: when two or more factions preaching absolute truth squabble among themselves, their mutual cause suffers. (d) Finally, many people simply cannot invest in the movement, because they do not care or they do not understand. They resist only by their dullness. They are dead weight to the cause (OH-5, p. 25).

These four types were mentioned previously. Voegelin noticed a fifth type of person, and it is the type that will be of primary interest to us here. A person could experience disorder, as we have, and somewhere get "the idea that this present imperfect world is to be followed by a more perfect phase" (CW 11, p. 244). Such a person could conclude that rather than looking to God or luck to intervene, humans must bring this about. It is up to us. What is required would be "knowledge of the recipe for bringing about the more perfect realm" (ibid.). This was, after all, the objective, was it not: to restore order? This is also, according to Voegelin, where good hearted people can go wrong.

D. WHAT DO WE EXPECT?

Frequently, we tend to regard the truth as a thing capable of assuming a particular form. We might imagine it as a proposition, a plan, an answer, or ethical theory, in which case we experience what Voegelin called a metastatic faith that truth can intervene in a concrete way, embodied in a leader or a group. We expect ethical leadership to bring about social reform. "Otherwise," we ask rhetorically, "what would be the point?"

Suppose a person were to adopt "the belief that the truth of existence is a set of propositions concerning the right order of man in society and history, the propositions to be demonstrably true and therefore acceptable to everybody" (CW 12, p. 117). This belief is not uncommon. Nonetheless, in actual practice, that person will find no such thing. Such truth does not exist. In his frustration, he might cry out for ethical leadership, as we have, but "we shall hardly blame him if in the end he decides that skepticism is the better part of wisdom" (ibid.). He could easily come to realize that his questions "cannot be answered through propositions concerning right order, or through a catalog of permanent values" (ibid., p. 119). In that case, he might lose heart.

Instead of expecting concrete answers, maybe we should characterize the "answer" as more of a search or quest, rather than as a final or conclusive proposition. It is not so much that we finally get to stop looking for a solution and arrive at results (OH-5, p. 32). Truth is never some *thing* we reach or possess (ibid., p. 37). It is what we seek. It is more of a horizon or direction than a destination (ibid., p. 40). Voegelin also called it an "erotic tension," a "love that never seems to reach its object, this indefinite process that never comes to an end" (ibid., p. 54). To expect more is to expect too much.

The possibility that truth is a receding horizon we never actually reach unfortunately leaves us in the predicament that we are never to be satisfied. Disheartening though it might be, is that realization not closer to lived experience? This possibility matches the empirical evidence. Over and over, people have placed their faith in some particular leader, group, or plan. Nevertheless, here we find ourselves in the same basic frustration. We experience dissatisfaction. Maybe we always will. It would be tempting in that case to swing to the other extreme and give up faith altogether. What would be the point of ethical leadership? Maybe the skeptics were right. We could adopt a more fatalistic or defeatist attitude, like so many who went before us. Is that what Voegelin recommends? Not at all (OH-5, p. 33).

E. WANTING TO ESCAPE THE TENSION

We can imagine it this way—a way that purposefully resembles the pragmatist's oscillations between doubt and belief that we had occasion to explain in the second chapter.

Let experience be our guide. What we experience is a tension. That tension is uncomfortable. We would prefer to escape the tension, one way or the other. Ideally, we would escape by locating the truth, because all that would remain to be done is gather sufficient power to impose order in the name of that truth (OH-5, p. 38). This is the metastatic faith Voegelin referred to. If we cannot escape the tension by resolving it, then we prefer to escape the tension by pretending it does not exist and by surrendering hope. Metastatic faith or despair? That would seem to be our choice.

Escaping the tension might be what we *prefer*, but within that tension human experience has been a dynamic process. Humankind has been changing. It continues to change in a creative process. To abort the process and claim that any theory, plan, or person is the ultimate solution requires what Voegelin refers to as imaginative oblivion—willfully neglecting or ignoring aspects of reality for the sake of our comfort in believing the search is finally at an end (ibid., p. 41). We want so badly "to finish the story" (ibid., p. 69). To use his vocabulary, metastatic faith requires imaginative oblivion: fixing on one answer or one person excludes all of the rest. Instead, we need to abide within the tension and participate in the never ending process.

Voegelin's reasoning is not unfamiliar to management theorists and leadership studies. In fact, it captures quite well the usual pattern. Managers experience dissatisfaction and go in search of solutions to their organizational problems, latching on to scientific management, human relations, systems theory, in a series of breakthroughs that never eliminate, once and for all, the manager's troubles. Most managers understand they will never find the magic formula, the secret of the ages, even though they continue to attend seminars, buy bestsellers, and gossip among themselves. Managers persist. Success is a receding horizon for them, yet they cannot bring themselves to despair.

Voegelin offers words of caution about "deformative reification" (OH-5, p. 80) as a warning against identifying too closely with any one guru or method. What is deformative reification? It is the course of action taken by someone with metastatic faith. It is the attempt to make the false answer real. Perhaps it can be explained best by an example. When TQM (or Total Quality Management) becomes a religion, and all past practices must yield, a manager commits the error of a metastatic faith in one thing and imaginative oblivion for all the rest. The latest flavor-of-the-month fad assumes great importance. Managers usually know better than to enshrine any one of these fads and stop learning. Maybe there is a kind of experimental wisdom in the rhythms of fads. That is certainly how managerial thought tends to progress in actual practice.

Even if that accurately describes the evolution of management theory as a never ending rotation of fads, people do expect ethics to be made of sterner stuff. They want to believe that back of their managerial practices are certain imperatives, absolutes. They want their ethics to be *grounded*, in other words. Because of this desire, they might misunderstand Voegelin to be saying there is no such thing, that either (1) truth does not exist or (2) it is all relative. He was saying neither of these things (e.g., CW 12, p. 121).

F. OPENNESS TO THE GROUND

After decades of exhaustive research, Voegelin had come to the conclusion that all communities engage in a search for the ground. This is a constant (CW 11, p. 225). They represent their answers with symbols of all kinds, such as God and Reason, to explain what they consider to be their ultimate purpose (ibid., p. 227). Even if they do not participate in the search itself, they act as though they had a purpose (ibid., p. 228). It is not as though people are drifting around without a goal or purpose. As we mentioned earlier, there are almost too many answers. That raises the question how we can find the right answer. (Obviously, there are wrong answers. Otherwise, we would not feel the need to cry for ethical leadership.) How then do we know our ultimate purpose? What standards do we use to determine this?

How is a person to live within the tension? Voegelin worked conscientiously to understand this question (OH-5, chap. 2). All of the various answers humans have historically come up with around the globe refer to something we cannot entirely comprehend, even if individuals repeatedly report having experienced it. It affects them deeply. For want of a better term, Voegelin sometimes called it "the divine ground." And he had every reason to believe in it. Just because we never reach it does not mean it does not exist. *It* often reaches *us*. It draws us into that tension, toward the truth, leaving us to operate with love, hope, and faith (CW 11, p. 230). We participate in it. There would be no tension if we did not experience the draw or pull toward the divine ground. But if we never do reach it and cannot possess it, even while at the same time we cannot ignore it, what should be our approach, our attitude? Voegelin preferred the imagery of openness and closure. Imaginative oblivion, as we described it before, is a posture of being closed (OH-5, p. 47). The objective, therefore, is to remain open.

Openness suggests that leaders and followers talk with each other about their expectations and ethics. The literature on management, for example, should probably continue to include topics of spirituality, religion, and faith. Another method for encouraging openness would be to devote more space to research on leaders who did precisely what Voegelin warns against: devise case studies of zealots, monomaniacs, and petty tyrants, to determine the consequences empirically and to consider the subtle costs of their questionable heroism. At the sharp end a scholar might establish whether leadership entails a degree of righteous energy. Is that the price of leadership, that leaders necessarily suffer from a metastatic faith? According to Voegelin's historical studies, there does appear to be a correlation. The more you are convinced that you are right, the more you would be eager to stick up for your convictions and act on them.

The conditions that have led to a cry for ethical leadership present us with an opportunity. The familiar symbols do not work. Paraphrasing Voegelin, they are like candles burning out. As we recognize the predicament, we get to go in search of the truth for ourselves. Some among us, maybe all of us, could seek an encounter with the divine ground. (The literature on spirituality in organizations has exploded recently for this very reason.) When that does happen, we might call it a religious experience, a revelation, even "a state of ecstasy or mania" (CW 12, p. 125). Sadly, "the enthusiasm of renewal and discovery can be so intense that it will transfigure the new truth into absolute Truth—an ultimate Truth that relegates all previous truth to the status of *pseudos*, of lie" (ibid.). That is the grave temptation.

G. DEFORMING THE TRUTH

It matters a great deal, in other words, how a person responds to an experience of tension. He or she would have been right to detect and deplore disorder. He or she would have been blessed to experience the divine ground. Still, things can go terribly wrong. "As far as society is concerned, the spiritually sensitive revolt against its unsatisfactory state is conducted by existentially deficient men who add themselves as a new source of disorder to troubles which are bad enough without them" (CW 12, p. 218). Elsewhere, Voegelin continued the sad story, as "the social scene fills up with little emperors who each claim to be the possessor of the one and only truth; and it becomes lethal when some of them take themselves seriously enough to engage in mass murder of everyone who dares to disagree" (CW 12, p. 285). Once in power, this "ethical leader" must take actions to impose order, yet the tension persists, a number of subordinates will refuse to yield, the best laid plans go awry. What devices might the leader use? Even if we set aside talking about heads of state who command armies and the police, the leader of any group can forbid questions and demand faith in his leadership. The leader can pass over criticism in silence or defame the critic, in what has since come to be known as the politics of personal destruction. The leader can punish dissent or build walls to outsiders (CW 12, p. 287)—in an atmosphere not unlike groupthink. Under the guise of ethical leadership, as a result, we get the exact opposite.

Some of the most heinous episodes in history originated in the desire to impose order, when the perpetrators had, for all we know, the loftiest intentions. One has only to mention the Crusades, the Inquisition, the Thirty Years' War, and the agrarian reforms of Stalin, Mao Zedong, and Pol Pot. Closer to home, corporate managers took paternalism to new heights at the turn of the last century, and for some time after they have been accused of making decisions detrimental to women for the sake of a chivalrous code. Today, critics are right to notice the same self-righteous tendency in political correctness.

In his lectures on Hitler, Voegelin made a startling announcement to his German audience back in 1964: "Whoever has a fixed idea and wants this to be carried into effect, that is to say, whoever interprets freedom of speech and freedom of conscience to the effect that the society should behave in the way that he considers right, is not qualified to be citizen of a democracy" (CW 31, p. 85).

It might be fair to say that leaders must perpetually sacrifice the comfort of certainty and resist the temptation to put the world to rights. (See also Lipman-Blumen, 2001.) Perhaps the most ethical leaders proceed with fear and trembling. At the very least, a leader might adopt the dictum of Hippocrates: first, do no harm.

H. CONCLUSION TO PART II

It is important to point out that on more than one occasion, Voegelin stated there are worse things than being closed in this manner (e.g., OH-5, p. 53). Being obtuse to the tension in the first place for example is pretty bad. Using the tension consciously to perpetrate evil is worse. Closure is more of an understandable mistake. Those who cry for ethical leadership are on the right track, but they come to expect the wrong thing, which then distorts their judgment.

The cry for ethical leadership could be an appeal for someone to set us free from an unsatisfactory reality, in which case Voegelin objects. That cannot be done . . . not without disastrous consequences. There is another possibility, however, which is that the cry for ethical leadership calls us back to the never-ending quest, to rise up and open ourselves again, to that hardest of all ethical tasks: pursuing order without imposing it. Voegelin invites us to consider that "[n]obody can heal the spiritual disorder of an 'age.' [A person] can do no more than work himself free from the rubble [which] threatens to cripple and bury him; and he can hope that the example of his effort will be of help to others who find themselves in the same situation and experience the same desire to gain their humanity under God" (CW 12, pp. 231f).

In the meantime, we are not completely lost, bereft of guidance. By and large, we know what to do. Life is not a perpetual crisis. "Most of the problems you have to handle," wrote Voegelin, "are commonsense problems on the pragmatic level within contexts about which you perfectly well know what pragmatically can be done" (CW 11, p. 250). At such times, we probably do not need a leader, ethical or otherwise. Things are better than they might seem.

The following summary embeds Voegelin's argument into the decision process familiar to any leader. The decision process begins with an experience of ethical disorder. For the sake of order, we look for a solution, only to discover a multitude of prospective answers. Because of the disorder, we feel obliged to choose an answer, and once we choose an answer, we feel obliged to impose it—whether that answer is a creed or a leader. We should expect resistance to our imposition, of course, but if we truly believe in the answer, as well as in the order it promises to deliver, then we probably will feel obliged to overcome resistance, even to the extent of using coercion.

Ethics, what mischief is perpetrated in thy name!

Voegelin interrupts the decision process by changing the expectation. Once the so-called "answer" appears to be more of a search, an openness, then we are *unable* to impose it. Instead, we move away from the disorder and, by our example, show others around us what can be done about it. For most decisions, the ethical path is clear. People tend to appreciate ordinary ethical choices. These are not so mysterious. Nonetheless, the cry for ethical leadership arises from extraordinary circumstances, to which we owe, as our first obligation, the humility—and courage—of self-doubt. At such times, we have to embrace the uncertainty

Voegelin's contribution to the process of making ethical decisions resembles the *daemon* of Socrates, a guardian angel of sorts who never told Socrates what to do. It intervened on occasion only to tell him what *not* to do. That is probably enough of a contribution to the decision process: to guard against making mistakes based on a desire for certainty one can never possess.

.

10
WEBS OF INFLUENCE

As we make our way up from the valley floor, we become involved in abstractions. We move further from concrete experiences and contemplate a more idealized version of events. At the same time, we will have to synthesize elements, piecing leadership together into its context.

In the abstract, a leader is the only one who leads. The follower follows, and there is nobody else to worry about. That is the simplicity of the sociological form: it plucks out essential elements for a limited purpose and freezes them in the act, encasing them in amber while holding them up to the light for a closer look. "This is leadership." We all recognize however that reality is far more complex and fluid. It was necessary for a time to distil leadership, to pay attention to it and not to everything else. That part of the study continues in the literature, which it is not our burden to replicate. Instead, the time has come to unfreeze the elements, to set the film back into motion, to release leadership into the wild.

This chapter does that conceptually in three ways.

First, it places leadership within the more realistic setting where various leaders exert their influence, in concert and opposed, and where leadership episodes take place among multiple leaders. Just as the gravitational pull between two objects can be affected by the presence of a third, so interpersonal influence between two persons will be affected by the influence of a third. And at any given moment, there are multiple leaders exerting different kinds of leadership. That is to say, leadership occurs within the context of many interlocking and overlapping webs or fields of influence—an image provided by Simmel (1922/1955).

Second, in a section I refer to as an "excursus" or side trip, this chapter begins to elaborate on the counter-influence of followers within the form itself. The leader is not the only one who leads. Neither are all of the other leaders in the webs of influence the only ones who lead. In reality, followers and beneficiaries exert some influence. And there is another class or category of person, someone we might have to call the phantom leader—a person imagined by the follower to be leading when in fact no one is. This happens too frequently in the real world to ignore.

Third, this chapter takes up a topic already begun in the previous chapter, namely the part leadership plays in the formation of elites. Elites serve as part of the structure of society; they enjoy their webs of influence. What then is the relationship of leadership to elites? Is an elite the larger, calcified form of leadership, over time? In effect, in this third section of the chapter we rise further from the valley floor to begin placing leadership within the context of organizations and entire societies.

Once again it becomes important to emphasize that any one stage of the journey passes through regions that it is not our burden to explore in depth. This hike covers a lot of territory in a few steps. The literature exists out there to help anyone learn more about each region, such that entire monographs have been written on topics we can mention only in passing. There is no way to avoid this. All we are doing is taking a walk in the woods, finding our way around. The reader who expects more expects too much or expects the wrong thing. Citations appear frequently in this book to guide the interested reader toward selected paths that might give access to the literature, and beyond that we dare not go.

In the lingo of tour guides everywhere, I have to remind you to "stay with the group."

A. MULTIPLE LEADERS

Simple dimensions present themselves in simple leadership relationships. In the project to differentiate forms of leadership, several *complex* dimensions present themselves in the consideration of multiple leaders, since in those cases there are complications arising from the web of influence within which leadership actually takes place.

Leadership takes place within a social context. That social context influences leadership. What works in one context will not work in another, just as different flowers thrive in different climates. The effectiveness of leadership varies, depending on the circumstances (see Bass, 1990, chap. 26). Social context is, in other words, one of the contingencies to leadership. In this section, we are using the image of a web of influence.

That web of influence frequently assumes the complex form of organizations. In many instances, leadership takes place in organizations, which serve as the larger context for leadership. Thus, to understand leadership fully, we have to appreciate its organizational contexts, just as zoologists came to understand the zebra only after studying its habitat (Gardner, 1990, p. 81).

1. *Magnitudes* of leadership.[1] A group, organization, or society can enjoy multiple leaders. There is not necessarily only one leader. Even when we study the traits, styles, and behaviors of a single leader, or even of a single *type* of leader, we have to remember that in reality, there are often multiple leaders, and this fact could make a difference in how individual leaders lead. In ordinary speech, people refer to multiple leaders collectively as the "leadership" of a firm or community. What does it mean, therefore, to say that there can be multiple leaders?

The most obvious way to recognize that there could be many leaders is to distinguish the overall task—whatever it is—from its smaller tasks. There is on the one hand the encompassing project, such as running a corporation or prosecuting a war, and then on the other hand there are a bunch of component pieces to that project. When coming to appreciate the existence of multiple leaders, it would be a question of *magnitude* (e.g., Hughes, Ginnett, Curphy, 1996, pp. 19–22). We might say that a general "led" his troops to victory in a battle, but we also realize that a battle is comprised of various, barely coordinated tasks. One unit holds a key position, another storms a hill on the flank, while a third cuts off an escape route. We then say that individual officers "led" their troops in these limited tasks. Leadership would seem to apply to both the battle as an event and the various tasks that were part of the execution of that battle. Leadership takes place at both levels. Burns refers to this dimension as "the *size* of the *arena* in which power is exercised" (1978, p. 16; emphasis supplied). It only makes sense to acknowledge this distinction at the outset, rather than assign credit (or blame) out of proportion to the events themselves. Thus, one way to delineate the variety of leaders for any enterprise is to describe a hierarchy based on the scope of responsibility, similar to any organizational chart.[2]

As you will recall from an earlier chapter, the primal images of what it means to be human originate in exemplary persons. Their example influences others, who in turn influence others, in a network of relationships over time, at each level of society. Such a schema serves ably as a schema for the distribution of leadership, with varying types and degrees of influence. We can speak intelligibly of great leaders, leaders of world-historical importance, such as Caesar, as well as leaders on a small scale, in an army platoon or at a factory. The key distinction would be the *magnitude* of leadership.

> Traditional conceptions of leadership tend to be so dominated by images of presidents and prime ministers speaking to the masses from on high that we may forget that the vast preponderance of personal influence is exerted quietly and subtly in everyday relationships. (Burns, 1978, p. 442; cf. p. 16)

McGill and Slocum (1997) note that in the literature on leadership we tend to read about large problems requiring dramatic effort by outsized characters and call it leadership, when the real need is usually little acts by ordinary people. They conclude: "A little leadership has what followers want and what leaders can do. Moreover, it can be learned. No less important, it is exactly the amount and kind of leadership that most organizations need" (see also Pruyne, 2002, pp. 16f).

Even within a single magnitude, however, there is not necessarily just one leader. It would be a mistake to restrict ourselves to such a simplistic model or *Denkbild*. Often in collective enterprises the group or team has multiple leaders.

2. Usually, it is easier to understand what I am saying by reference to *the chronological shifting of leadership* from one person to another; the most vivid way to illustrate multiple leadership, in other words, is by laying out a sequence of different moments in which first one member and then another leads the rest of the people. We witness the ebb and flow of leadership from person-to-person, depending on the task at hand. The senator works to pass legislation, for the president's signature, but her moments of leadership follow in time the visioning of the academic who first thought up the idea for the legislation. All three—the intellectual, president, and senator—exhibit leadership at different stages in a sequence.

3. Another way to understand a multiplicity of leaders is to identify *sub-groups of leaders,* such as an executive committee or an officer's staff, so that the multiple leaders comprise a subgroup that in turn leads the larger group. Simmel examines this phenomenon under the heading of "subordination under a plurality" (1908/1950, part 3; chap. 3; see Harter & Evanecky, 2002).

4. The example of the organizational chart illustrates *the division of labor* among leaders who might be of equal rank, in which one leader might be responsible for one facet of the project, while another leader has a different responsibility (Weber, 1922/1958, chap. 8). Each is a leader with regard to a different aspect of the project, simultaneously.

Thus, we can identify within a single magnitude three ways right off the bat to explain what it means to say that there might be multiple leaders:

* Leadership can shift from person-to-person over time
* Sub-groups can lead the group
* Leadership can be apportioned in a division of labor

Further delineations would include other configurations of power. For instance, the leader in one activity might be competing with the leader in another activity for the follower's time and energy: the pastor of your local congregation might complain that your boss keeps scheduling you to work on Sunday mornings. A student might feel pressure to complete homework for a classroom teacher on the same night her coach scheduled a game far away. Another scenario with multiple leaders would be the competition within a single context between rivals, such as candidates for political office. Then there are instances in which established authorities vie with rebels. The list could go on.

Further study of leadership could go through the various permutations and examine leadership as it pertains to them.

B. EXCURSUS ON THE LEADERSHIP OF FOLLOWERS, BENEFICIARIES, AND NONEXISTENT LEADERS

1. Often, leaders are thought to accomplish their task by means of other people. This is a surprisingly common way to think about leadership (Rost, 1993, p. 59, citing Plachy, 1978, p. 16). It is also potentially insulting, as well as being incomplete. The leader is definitely affected by the followers. Their influence is mutual. There has to be some kind of reciprocity in a relationship, as stated earlier (Simmel, 1908/1950, pp. 181–183, pp. 185f). To some extent, one might say that the followers lead the leader (Rost, 1993, p. 105; Wren, 1995, part 6; Hughes, Ginnett, & Curphy, 1996, p. 68; Bass, 1990, chap. 18).

It would be a mistake to assume that the followers themselves were nothing but passive, inert material for the agency of others, even though this is often the model that behavioral scientists use when they think they are following in the footsteps of the venerable Aristotle. What they are trying to do in such cases is apply a theory of interpersonal causation . . . wrongly.

When Aristotle explained the four causes of production—the material, the formal, the efficient, and the final—he understood they were all complicit in the process. One does not achieve the desired end without each of them. And within this model or schema, he gave considerable weight to the influence that the material has on the outcome.[3] Thus, the material (that is, the follower) is not without its importance. Nonetheless, this insight will have to be metaphorical, because when Aristotle introduced his whole schema of causation, he was referring to the production of *things*, i.e., human artifacts. He was talking about physics. He, better than most, knew that the study of *interpersonal* causation is a separate kind of undertaking.

None of which is to suggest that leader and follower are indistinguishable. The distinction between them has its uses analytically, if only because ordinary usage draws a bright line between them. They are different roles within a relationship in which the participants mutually influence each other to give shape to their interactions. Just because they both participate does not mean that they are the same thing. The reason for mentioning that followers can be said to lead the leader is two-fold. First, we have to recognize that there is some influence flowing back toward the leader from the follower, no matter how slight (Simmel, 1908/1950, pp. 181–183; Coser, 1971, p. 185; Peirce, 1997, pp. 155f). Second, in the course of many relationships, the follower and leader swap roles. I lead you now. Then you lead me. Leader and follower are separate roles that we exchange periodically (Simmel, 1908/1950, pp. 283–291).

2. Now let me try in this brief excursus to take this a step further. I want to point out that the person for whom the leader and followers work together, whether we understand that person as the customer, beneficiary, shareholder, or a subsequent generation, also leads. Such a person or persons might not even exist at the time of the leadership. The participants within the leader-follower relationship might not know this person directly.

The influence of the beneficiary is complex, and it goes to the heart of interpersonal influence. In this I follow the work of Bruce Mazlish (1984b & 1981), who, as we saw earlier, held that any person forms an image of others, and it is in response to that image that a person will engage in social behavior. For example, I do not have to have ever met the person, yet I carry with me an image of him and take certain actions in anticipation of him. When that is the case (and for scholars such as Mazlish, that is always the case), we can find ourselves saying that the person responding to the image is "following" it. Leadership can be understood to be made up of such responses (Harter, 1998). It follows logically that everyone engaged in doing something for someone else was responding to their (admittedly vague and shifting) image of the ones who would be benefiting. In other words, the beneficiary can be said to be part of the leadership.

The pragmatist would interject by saying, "So what? What difference does it make to think of the influence of beneficiaries? What is the cash value of that notion?" In politics, it is not uncommon for office holders to plead on behalf of future generations or, more concretely, "the children." They know support would dwindle if they were to urge some course of action for the sake of keeping themselves in office or as a pay-off to some corporate contributor (Burnham, 1987, p. 219). There are few occasions that a leader is likely to succeed when she impresses on the followers that they would be doing it for her (although it does happen on occasion). Let us think instead of the many times that leadership looks to a beneficiary. A number of leaders have learned as a tactic to personalize and "put a face" on the beneficiary. Manufacturing firms sometimes send employees to a customer firm in order to fix in their mind the end user of their products. Think especially of charities and philanthropy. Much work gets done in volunteer organizations for the sake of the destitute and the sick, especially if the donors can see pictures of the starving infants or know the victims personally. At one time, Roman Catholics from all over Europe truly hoped to liberate loved ones from purgatory by funding St. Peter's Basilica in Rome—regardless of the surrounding venality. I would go so far as to say that the grandest purpose of leadership is to serve non-participants. It stands as a useful question, therefore, in the study of leadership to inquire "for whom" it is being done. More importantly, in actual practice, leaders interested in success might consider identifying and communicating better with followers "for whom" they are to follow. So, in a manner of speaking, beneficiaries lead.

3. Finally, there is an extension of this excursus that is worthy of a comment. We have already seen how it might be possible for a person one has never met to influence him. It is just as possible to be influenced by a person *who does not exist*. Three quick illustrations should suffice.

- I take precautions against the possibility of there being burglars.
- My child eats a particular breakfast cereal because a cartoon character told him to.
- Someone else continues to obey the wishes of a parent long after the parent has died.

We might resist the notion of referring to leadership exercised by non-existent persons, but once we accept the role of imagination into our study, we should at least consider the possibility. To what extent does leadership occur *without the existence of a leader?*

A follower follows an image. That image is more important to understanding leadership than the "real" person of the leader, because it is the image that the follower follows. Images are at best partial representations of reality, perspectives, often attributed with traits and characteristics for which there is no basis in fact. (Most familiar would be the so-called halo effect.) It is a short leap to the possibility that the entire image has no correspondence with reality whatsoever. *No one* wears the mask. After all, the image operates within the follower's imagination, which is also the repository of the *imaginary*. People can be said to take action based on the leadership of someone who exists only in their imagination.

The movies present variations on this theme. The wizard in *The Wizard of Oz* materially existed behind the curtain, though hardly in the guise presented to the denizens of the Emerald City. He was in his own words a humbug. In *El Cid,* the commander of the Spanish forces dies on the eve of battle, so unbeknownst to the troops of both sides, the next morning his coterie props his corpse upon his horse and rides out with it to inspire one side and intimidate the other. There was no Cid any longer but the one they imagined. They followed a corpse into battle. *1984* never discloses whether Big Brother really even ever existed, because it does not really matter. He is ubiquitous and beloved, regardless. Woody Allen spoofs the idea in *Sleeper* by showing a futuristic regime that broadcasts soothing photos of a leader, even though all that remains of him is a nose in the laboratory, which it becomes Woody's task to clone back into a complete human being. I could go on, but this is fiction.

One of the best illustrations of non-existent or phantom leadership in the real world appears in a *Reader's Digest* article by Jon Franklin (1996), where he explains how strenuously he worked to satisfy an editor he had come to admire, only to discover that the editor had actually done nothing. It was Franklin's imagination that had created a persona of the omnicompetent editor, exacting and scrupulous, when in fact the man he ascribed this to admitted he was nothing of the kind. "[T]he corundum I held you against," said the older man, "was yourself." The editor was not above fostering the impression that he knew more than he did, but the follower, Jon Franklin, concocted the perfect editor in his head and then struggled through the years to please him. The old man was just the face he put on this creation. It was the image, and not the man, who led him throughout his career. Franklin just didn't know it.

The possibility of phantom leadership upsets a number of assumptions. For leadership to take place, there would not need to be a leader, so there would not have to be a relationship; neither would it be a precondition in leadership for there to be some direction one person wants another to take, since it all happens in one person's imagination. By the same token, phantom leadership explains a lot of human behavior and in some ways is truer to the underlying experience of all leadership. Georg Simmel once examined a comparable situation in which there could be leaders without followers. He wrote: "The fact that one is the ruler presupposes an object of one's domination; yet the psychological reality can, to a certain extent, evade this conceptual necessity" (1908/1950, pp. 269f). This whole question of followers without leaders and leaders without followers is, in my opinion, provocative, but the pragmatist would be right to wonder how it pertains to the prescriptive mission of leadership studies. There we shall have to leave it, maybe to take this path some other day. We have to climb.

C. ELITES

We have considered some of the implications of multiple leaders as a complex web of influence that can be understood to include even followers and beneficiaries, for the purpose of illustrating the many dimensions at work in any one sociological form. In order to get a sense of the scale of complexity, this section of the chapter takes a macro perspective. Toward that end, we shall examine the relationship between leadership, on the one hand, and the presence of elites, on the other.

1. *Elite theory.* Elite theory begins with ruminations about the inescapable differences among individual human beings. Simmel said it once and for all: "equality in people is impossible because of their different natures, life contents, and destinies" (1971, p. 18). Simple observation demonstrates that some individuals are better equipped for one task and some are better equipped for another. This variation is without debate. Elite theory derives from thinking about these differences (Bobbio, 1994/1996).

More specifically, elite theory as a coherent intellectual problem considers the tendency for societies to separate within themselves into layers or strata.[4] This is not to say that the dividing line between one stratum and another is altogether distinct, like an impenetrable boundary. Nonetheless, a neutral observer should be able to abstract from any community the presence of two or more strata, even when a certain amount of interpenetration does take place. It does not have to have been so formal as a caste system or apartheid.

Even more specifically, elite theory reflects on the tendency of certain strata to amass a disproportion of goods, including power, wealth, fame, and leisure. Members of this stratum can be said to constitute the elite.

With few, if any, exceptions, every society has its elite, if not more than one. An elite stands opposed conceptually to another stratum, defined by its exclusion from the elite: namely, the masses.[5] It is the relative share of these goods that determines who belongs to which stratum . . . and vice versa.

According to Professor Don Levine of the University of Chicago (1995), elite theory has been one notable strand in the sociological tradition, a strand reaching from Aristotle toward a series of Italian sociologists, chiefly Vilfredo Pareto and Gaetano Mosca. Of course, the strand existed in some form long before Aristotle, and it has wound its way through many different traditions. Today, the emerging discipline of leadership studies represents one of its threads, and also serves as my own professional interest.

Grandiose sentiments about the importance of elites seem unrelated to the persons we might actually think of as elite: the spoiled athlete, the blue-haired heiress, the rock star, the glib politician, the chubby set at the country club. Which is precisely the point. Elite theorists do not restrict themselves to describing the actual means by which people join the elite. On the contrary, they are just as likely to observe a privileged group squandering its opportunities, an elite undeserving of its place. We find elite theorists critical of elites. True, these theorists are just as capable of despising or pitying the masses as well, hoping to abuse the prevailing elite by classifying them as no better than the masses (and in at least one sense worse, since the elite is without excuse).

We can now divide the two broad categories into four. (a) There are the masses, the *hoi polloi*. This is the largest number. (b) There are elites who for one reason or another belong with the masses. This is the next-largest number. (c) And there are elites who deserve their status, many of whom, it turns out, emerge from among the masses. (d) Finally, let us not overlook the thinkers whose place it is to study and teach the elites, the small number who lead the leaders, including many of the writers cited for this book. In *A Defense of Poetry*, Percy Shelley called this group of ultra-elite visionaries "the unacknowledged legislators of the world" (1966, pp. 415–448).

Of this last group, it could be said that, in the lives of their disciples, philosophers, prophets, and poets do mean to rule the world, as Marx has been quoted as claiming, for example, when he wrote that "it is the philosopher in whose brain the revolution is beginning" (1947/1932). Startling to contemplate, perhaps, but leadership studies presumes to serve as that ultra-elite, the leaders of the leaders, those who shape the future by shaping the minds of the young. If anyone aspires to become the highest elite, it might be the writer and teacher of leadership.

2. Leadership and elites. The question has been raised as to how these two so-ciological phenomena, namely leadership and the elite, are related (Heilbrunn, 1996, pp. 9f.). This subsection begins to respond to that question.

We have begun with primal images of individual persons and moved to the images we have of their relationships, which we called sociological forms. Now we take a further step to find an image of the relationship be-tween sociological forms, i.e. leadership and elites. In other words, after taking hold of one little strand in the great ball of reality, we shall have iso-lated the role of imagination—a nearly transparent moment in human ex-perience—and placed it in larger and larger contexts, by a process of synthesis, until very nearly reaching world-historical patterns of continuity and change. We went through a narrowing of the subject matter to primal images in the first part and then by stages greatly expanded what we are talking about.

As for the relationship of leadership, as a sociological form, to elites: leadership seems to occur on a smaller scale for a shorter period of time; the elite is an entrenched part of the structure of an entire society. Leadership describes the process, directed outward, of changing followers; elite theory describes the influx of goods to a privileged minority. Leadership suggests direct, even face-to-face involvement, which means specific behaviors in mutual orientation, whereas the elite progressively distances itself from the masses and employs indirect techniques for channeling resources. We rarely think of active leaders in terms of silent partners and passive in-vestors—living in gated communities, flying first class, and sending their children to private schools. Leadership is about closing a gap. The elite re-inforces the gap.

For all their differences, the two phenomena are related, however. An elite engages in leadership in order to establish and maintain itself. And leadership tends to consolidate itself in the conservation of power (e.g., Michels, 1915/1949, p. 366). It is undoubtedly true that simple leadership does occur all the time among the masses (Michels, 1927/1949, p. 80), and it is also true that many among the elite lead scarcely anyone at all, but over time these facts contribute to the famous circulation of elites, as leaders from among the masses emerge to challenge the established elite and as the lethargic or incompetent elite tumble from their place of privilege. Leadership can be thought of as the movement in a thousand associa-tions—creating, sustaining, and ultimately destroying an elite—in a man-ner similar to boiling water sending bubbles to the surface. Leadership is the means whereby elites constitute themselves, the micro-phenomenon; having an elite is the eventual consequence of patterns of leadership, the macro-phenomenon. Maybe leadership forms an elite. One recent book on elite theory even refers to elites as "leadership groups" and "leadership cadres" (Lerner, Nagai, & Rothman, 1996, p. ix). This is a particularly useful way to understand the relationship.

Leadership is a form that takes place in a context, a web of influence, among multiple leaders, some of whom cluster together—consciously or not—into an elite (Simmel, 1950/1908, pp. 209f). The elite is, in this sense, a complex of forms.

3. Democracy and elites. One objection has been raised against elite theory to the effect that it is anti-democratic (e.g., Tolson, 1995). When a society commits itself to democratic principles such as equality and participation, the whole notion of an elite seems contrary. Citizens of democracy tend not to like to think of themselves as governed in any sense by an elite. Democracy means that the people govern; the presence of an elite suggests an oligarchy.

Democracies openly tolerate *nonpolitical* elites, such as entertainers and entrepreneurs. Due to the conservation of power highlighted by Michels, an elite of any kind does tend to coalesce and create political power (cf. Michels, 1927/1949, pp. 52, 72, 92, 108; Machiavelli, *Discourses* I:35). Movie actors and celebrities frequently become influential and sometimes stand for election. More importantly, however, in every historical example elite theorists could find democracies experience some kind of political class, whether by this we mean (a) an official elite, such as an upper chamber in the legislature and a supreme judiciary, which means that an elite is built right in to the system, or (b) an unofficial elite, such as party bosses or rich lobbyists. Rousseau has been quoted in support of this view: "To take the term in its fully rigorous meaning, there has never existed a true democracy and one will never exist. It is against the natural order of things that the great number governs" (Michels, 1927/1949, p. 89, citing *The Social Contract*).[6]

Democracies might abhor elites, yet empirically they tolerate them. What is going on? Since elite theorists disagree among themselves, there are several possible answers.

> a. A cry for leadership can be thought of as a cry for ballast, for countervailing power, to balance against a ruling class, so it does not get too comfortable and monopolize the franchise. Gramsci, for example, suggested that Machiavelli revealed the secrets of wielding power to make it public, so no one could use them on a populace that is caught unawares (Gramsci, 1957/1992, p. 142). It is a move toward democracy to foster leadership, be-

cause the rising leaders offset the tendency of the prevailing elite to convert democracy into an oligarchy.

b. The cry for leadership can be thought of as a cry for a more competent and more principled elite—not so much to counter the ruling class from outside as to improve it from within. Society needs leaders, but only if they are competent (Levine, 1995, p. 233). Even a democracy wants competent leadership.

c. Then again, the cry for leadership could be a cry for discrete relationships and episodic moments of leadership, calling for something less than an elite. At such times, people prefer a sense of proportion. Asking for leadership and getting an elite is like asking for a drink of water and getting a flood. According to this way of thinking, leadership is good up to a point.

d. Of course, some who cry for leadership would not mind the idea of an elite in the first place and are willing to give up on democracy as a pure, egalitarian ideal. Mosca noted that trying to repair democracy with even more democracy frequently makes matters worse (Bellamy, 1987, p. 41). For many elite theorists, democracy is problematical. Leadership helps to soften or nullify the ill effects of democracy.

e. Bentley saw no contradiction. "Democracy, to justify itself, must *include* aristocracy. . . . Aristocracy is one of the goals of democracy" (1957/1944, pp. 264f). It is in other words a mistake to imagine these as opposing concepts. Democracy is the manner by which we determine who becomes the elite. Leadership is in this case the way that happens.

f. By way of contrast, some theorists argue that democracy and leadership are simply incompatible (e.g., Burnham, 1987, pp. 160, 186, 266), whereas others argue that democracy and *elites* are incompatible (Nye, 1977). For these to coexist at any one time is a contradiction that will result in tensions. Therefore, according to this view, elite theory and leadership studies are inherently anti-democratic.

Rather than rejecting leadership studies and elite theory as anti-democratic, however, perhaps it is especially important in democracies to study leadership and the elite, to measure its size, impact, and overall direction.

Democracies tolerate non-political elites, and in every case institutionalize some kind of political elite, whether formal or informal. But I would offer a third response to the objection that democracies abhor an elite. Abhorrence for an elite does not seem to carry over in the popular mind to leadership. No one seems to be crying out specifically for an elite, but there does seem to be a cry for leadership. D. H. Lawrence was most emphatic: "Leaders—this is what mankind is craving for" (quoted in Bentley, 1944/1957, p. 231). Leadership is thought to be a good thing, a thing to be done even better. Yet if leadership seems necessary, then an elite would surely follow. To empower leaders is to risk enabling an elite. How can a person favor leadership *without* accepting an elite? That is the question to be answered (DeMott, 1993; Block, 1993, pp. 13–17).

D. CHAPTER SUMMARY

Leadership takes place within a context. It is an event within a vast and surging complex of influence and counter-influence. We have depicted that complex as a web. Part of what makes the web confusing is the presence of multiple leaders. And let it not go unsaid that followers and beneficiaries also exert influence. The prospect of non-existent or phantom leaders, based on the role of the imagination in human behavior, has to be included in the web of influences. Despite the simplicity of a leadership dyad in which influence flows in one direction, reality is far more complicated. The one-way influence of leadership is part of a larger, multi-directional web, with competing influences and counter-influences, some of which are purely imaginary and no less real!

To illustrate how the form of leadership might be understood in relation to other social and political forms—forms that are more solid, as it were—this chapter referred to elites and to democracy. We could have chosen other forms. In the study of leadership, we should be meditating on these larger themes and frequently ask one another, in the spirit of pragmatism, how our findings and our advice implicate them as institutions. Do we in leadership studies empower elites, in some way? Would that be so terrible? And are we undermining or strengthening democracy, directly or indirectly?

"The challenge," writes Thomas Cronin, "is to seek ways to reconcile these concepts—leadership and democracy" (quoted in Wren, 1995, pp. 304f). I concur.

11
TIME TO CATCH OUR BREATH

Once again, as we make our ascent, perhaps we should pause for a moment in order to assess where we have come and where we plan to go next. It is not uncommon during a laborious climb to take breaks occasionally, partly to rest, but more importantly to orient ourselves. It was the purpose of this entire survey to orient ourselves in the forest. Since the last pause, we have come a long way. Things will look different from here.

The valley floor gave us one perspective of the forest, where it is dark, wet, and thick. We understood there must be other perspectives. Familiarity with the forest, as with anything, involves multiple perspectives, so we resolved to climb. Climb to where? There are a number of hiking trails leading up from the valley, so I chose one for you, and I explained its advantages.

Leadership can be understood as a sociological form. Sociological forms are units of understanding that were extensively mapped already by Georg Simmel and his successors. The objective was to learn what a sociological form is, why it would assist leadership studies, and how leadership as a sociological form might be studied.

One way to study a form is to determine reciprocity, social distance, and myriad dualisms or tensions. This static model shows the structure of a form. Another way to study a form is to identify the conditions under which it emerges, as well as its trajectory, until it finally ossifies or dissolves. This dynamic model shows the lifespan of a form. We spent a lot of time, if you will remember, outlining each of these models.

Two dimensions of leadership seem especially important and problematic, as well as interrelated, and they are power and ethics. Much has already been written on each of these dimensions, separately and combined, so we looked briefly at several writers who rarely appear in the literature on leadership, to find out what they had to say.

Even as we tried to describe the sociological form of leadership, we also recognized that leadership takes place within a context. It is not enough to see leadership in the abstract—useful though that is. We must synthesize further by examining the web of influence surrounding the participants, including some of the competing and countervailing influences, real and imagined. A number of these influences are centered in larger, more complex forms, such as elites. In fact, leadership studies should, in my opinion, reclaim its place alongside elite theory as a complementary study.

Let me put this another way. Leadership arises within an existing order. It is frequently a reaction to some existing order. And leadership can be said to alter the existing order or even inaugurate a new order. A thorough study of leadership would discover how it is embedded in the structures and dynamics of social order, up to and including the political order, such as democracy.

As we moved up from psychology, we reached the realms of sociology and political science, where work is presently also being done on leadership. What you and I have been doing, in a manner of speaking, is taking a survey of the literature, connecting these realms, in the hope that by gaining all of these perspectives, we have a better, more comprehensive understanding of leadership studies as a distinct pursuit. As we quickly discover, different realms have different issues, different tools, and different intellectual heroes, yet they all work in the same forest, without necessarily being aware of each other.

What I have found in my own studies is that a small cluster of intellectual heroes deserves more notice. (Academics also need their exemplars, their leaders.) More students of leadership would benefit from reading William James, Georg Simmel, José Ortega y Gasset, and Eric Voegelin, and to a lesser extent perhaps Charles Sanders Peirce, Vilfredo Pareto, Alfred Schütz, Bruce Mazlish, and James Hillman. When our tour ends, you are invited to return to the paths that interest you most, and if as a result of your own studies these particular names gain currency in leadership studies, then I have been successful.

All that being said, it remains for us to assault the summit. We are not done. We have not exhausted the realms where leadership studies can be said to apply—as, for example, history. Before gathering up to go, however, we should preview the rest of the journey.

Part of what we have been doing is conceptual housekeeping, consistent with pragmatism. At present, we are juggling in our minds sociological forms at different levels or magnitudes, all the way from simple dyads to the hurly-burly of democracies, trying to determine how they might be connected into one grand schema. Maybe that cannot be done. Pragmatism advises caution. Nonetheless, we are right to try. Is there some way to schematize all of these abstractions so that they make sense in relationship with each other? In the next chapter, we consider one unifying schema known as systems and systems theory. This is probably one of the more rigorous and coherent alternatives, having been developed in a number of realms, from biology to cybernetics, so that the most we can expect to cover on our particular journey is a bare introduction to systems thinking. According to the tenets of pragmatism, systems theory is a working hypothesis, a handy way to conceptualize webs of influence, so long as we resist the temptation to deviate in the direction of misplaced concreteness and turn it into something more than it is.

The chapter that follows the next one eventually considers another unifying schema, impishly referred to as Voegelin's ladder, which is based on a chart he once devised to help students with similar housekeeping chores. One of the strengths of this second alternative is the fact that it takes seriously the claims of spirituality, which has become a hot topic in leadership studies. En route to Voegelin's ladder, given its openness to such things as spirituality, we must consider the limits of reason. We have to hear the voices claiming that rationality and logic in leadership studies matter a great deal, but that they are nothing more than instruments, tools that are limited.

What remains then for us to do is place leadership within the flux of reality, re-connecting it finally to the broad sweep of human history as the comprehending context for all leadership. We should discover at the peak, as we emerge onto the rocks above the tree line, where the forest ends, that leadership actually plays a central role in the flow of history. It will be my contention that leadership is that which makes history human, a partnership with God, and therefore a profound opportunity to fulfill oneself.

These are grandiose words, appropriate to the high vistas perhaps, where the air is thin and the forest extends below us in every direction. We still have some hiking to do to reach that rarified atmosphere. Better if we resume now.

12

SYSTEMS, ALL THE WAY DOWN

Many of you know the story of the man who asked a little girl what holds up the earth. "A giant turtle," she answered. Puzzled, and a little amused, he asked her what holds up the giant turtle. "A bigger turtle," she answered politely. Hoping to make a point, the man pressed. "What holds that turtle up?" "An even bigger turtle!" When he tried asking one more time, she held up her hand and said, "Mister, it's turtles all the way down."

You would have a similar conversation with many who accept systems thinking. To them, everything is a system. Thus, everything is made up of systems. And everything is part of a comprehending system. "Mister, it's systems all the way down." Now that we have begun comparing leadership as a sociological form with other, more complex forms, such as elites and democracy, the question is bound to arise how these various forms are related. Are the rules that apply to simpler forms, such as leadership, applicable to the larger, more complex forms? Can we continue this process of synthesis indefinitely, to organizations, societies, and so forth? If we can successfully make the case for systems thinking, then we should be able to stop making these comparisons in this book and declare flatly that the same basic process applies, no matter what we are comparing. Each is a system comprised of systems and also part of a larger system.

This chapter considers briefly the extent to which systems thinking applies to leadership. In the first section, we meditate on systems thinking as a convenient method for making sense of the world. Those of you looking for a shortcut may proceed to the section that follows. In that section, we explore systems thinking, including a number of controversies yet to be resolved.

Primal images grounded in experience give birth to thought images and symbols we use to discuss them, as Voegelin taught us. Thought images bear a relation to each other by becoming a more complex image we can refer to as a schema, model, or mental map—an image depicting some theory or other about the way things work. Schemas pull together various thought images into some kind of unity or order.[1] Different schemas have their strengths and weaknesses. It was Alfred North Whitehead who admonished us to "seek simplicity, and then distrust it." Develop schemas, yes, but recognize their limitations. After all, no one schema represents reality completely. Other schemas have their advantages. Because the same object in reality can be schematized many ways, it helps periodically to contemplate new schemas, new complex thought images, for the purpose of disclosing aspects of reality that familiar schemas distort or neglect.

Systems thinking is one new possibility (Bass, 1990, p. 909).

In a section at the close of the chapter, intended partly as a contrast to systems thinking, we take a look at another way of bringing together all of the various lessons on leadership. Rather than subsume them all under systems thinking, we have found it useful in this book to arrange our thinking as symbol, concept, experience, and interpretation. By the close of this chapter, in other words, it will have become time for us to look back across the valley and get a composite image of where we have been. By doing so, we can find a place for systems thinking as a "conceptual scheme." In other words, rather than treat systems theory as the last word, we should integrate it into the larger project of leadership studies.

Just to make sure there is no mistake, we are examining systems theory as an example, one possibility among many, a schema that is potentially useful in its own right, standing in at this point of the argument for any one of a number of schemas attempting to do much the same thing. Time and time again in this book, we have reached such a fork in the trail, where we can with justification turn in different directions, and I have tried to draw your attention to the fact that we have choices, some better than others, but then, in order to continue our journey, we have made a choice and moved on. I am absolutely persuaded we could have chosen another path and still reached our goal. Nonetheless, there is a reason I have chosen this one, and not just because it is a placeholder for other possibilities.

A. MEDITATION ON METHOD:
THE CASE FOR SYSTEMS THINKING[2]

The first thing to do in this section is define a word. Aggregation is a process in the mind of gathering together into an increasing bundle. It does not matter what the mind is gathering—symbols, impressions, impulses.

Aggregation is the heart of induction. If the process never stops, aggregation eventually overwhelms the mind, like a bag that becomes too full, overburdening it with too many things, unless a way is found to organize the bundle conceptually. When it becomes overwhelmed, the mind struggles to economize and make sense of bundles by means of conceptualization, which is nothing more than a process of adopting schemas to reflect some kind of intelligible order in the bundle.[3]

As it turns out, the same bundle can be reflected in alternative schemas. Some of these schemas are better than others. For example, all other things being equal, the simpler schema is better. (This is a variation of Occam's Razor.) So also can it be said that the schema more accurately representing the bundle is better. Then again, different schemas might be better for different purposes.

It is also true that different bundles can be reflected by the same schema, such as the orbiting of electrons and planets, which crudely resemble each other, although in reality different bundles are usually reflected by different, alternative schemas. Nonetheless, all other things being equal, the schema that reflects a greater number of different bundles is better. The more things that conform to the same schema, the better the schema (Barzun, 1983, p. 127). That stands to reason.

The process does not end there. It simply moves to the next level of abstraction. Schemas themselves aggregate into bundles and threaten to overwhelm the mind at a higher level of conceptualization. There are bundles of bundles. Here we might speak of *magnitudes* of bundles. The problem, therefore, returns: this new bundle of bundles will overwhelm the mind unless a way is found to organize it into a comprehending schema (or *metaschema,* to coin a phrase). The proliferation of schemas requires its own schema. At this magnitude, the metaschema that fits a greater number of different magnitudes is better, all other things being equal (cf. Schütz, 1953/1962, p. 38).

Systems theory is a promising metaschema for just about any bundle at any magnitude of abstraction, and for that reason alone it deserves study—especially at a time in history when minds are so frequently at risk of being overwhelmed.

B. SYSTEMS THEORY[4]

Systems theory attempts to explain the behavior of all systems, including social systems of every magnitude. Social scientists in particular were involved in systems theory from the outset (Bausch, 2001, pp. 10–13). Vilfredo Pareto, for instance, coined the phrase "social system" for his writings on the economy, society, and politics (Parsons, 1977, p. 27). In the last two decades, several popular books on leadership refer to systems thinking (e.g., Wheatley, 1992; Senge, 1990).

A social system is a grouping of people who work together interdependently for a common purpose. Systems thinking considers the system as a whole, how its participants interact and fit together (Wheatley, 1992, pp. 139–155), so that leadership must be seen as a group activity or shared activity. It was thought at one time that systems seek equilibrium, and to qualify as systems they do *approach* it, but in social systems especially there is also a tendency away from equilibrium toward change and revitalization. A social system fluctuates or teeters between equilibrium and stability, on the one hand, and vitality, on the other. Indeed, one of the best analogies for a social system is the riverbed through which the changing waters flow (Capra, 1996, p. 171). The system channels change and over time is itself changed. In other terms, just as followers are the locus of individual change, systems are the locus of social change.

Participants in a system share a purpose and take action to achieve that purpose. In reality, the purpose might be impossible or vague, and it is likely to evolve. Participants might end up doing the wrong things or doing the right things in the wrong way. Systems test performance via feedback loops and make adjustments as needed. "Were people not following the plan?" "In light of experience, can we say there was something wrong with the plan?" As a result of this self-correcting process, leadership will occur at three places: operating the system, altering the system, and altering the *purpose* of the system. Leaders therefore serve three functions:

- helping to establish purpose (which is rare)
- helping to adopt and adapt methods to achieve that purpose
- taking action to see that other participants adopt these methods

In their consideration of the workings of the system, leaders should see the system as a whole largely because causation in systems is more subtle than meets the eye. Numerous factors contribute to outcomes, and there are likely to be time delays making it difficult to detect patterns of direct causation. In a manner of speaking, a system is the context for leadership, the pulsating and interlocking environment into which we are to synthesize the sociological form. Leadership is part of a larger network of interaction, that web we were talking about, which has its own statics and dynamics. Systems theory seeks to understand those statics and dynamics.

One of the motives for leaders to study systems theory is its diagnostic power when it explains why leadership on occasion goes awry. A leader who cannot think in terms of systems might intervene with the best of intentions and discover to her chagrin that one or more of the following happens:

- The leader intervenes at suboptimal points in the process.
- The leader treats a symptom rather than the disease.
- The leader fixes one problem only to make matters worse elsewhere.
- The leader overreacts and throws the rest of the system off balance.
- The leader accepts short-term gain that exacerbates long-term loss.
- The leader makes a seemingly rational decision that contributes to the problem, accelerating the trouble, like the depositors lining up for a run on the bank (Forrester, 1971/1973, pp. 80, 94f; Forrester, 1998, p. 5).

Ideally, the leader will see to it that discrete leadership moments serve the overall, long-term, system-wide purpose. That is to say, the system's purpose usually establishes the direction of leadership. But there is always that element of independence, detachment from the system, which characterizes leadership at its best, when it is purely leadership and not merely the execution of someone else's plan. Leadership contains an element of discretion. Otherwise, we are hard-pressed to call it leadership.

Systems themselves are classified in a variety of ways (e.g., open, closed, soft, autopoietic). A thorough understanding of systems theory would break these out and explain their relevance. As it happens, however, a thorough understanding of systems theory exceeds the scope of this chapter. Systems theory can be difficult to master and has generated a large and complicated set of terms and principles, including mathematical constructs, but these problems should not be ascribed to the theory itself, since the merit of a theory lies not so much in how easy it is to learn, but rather—once it is learned—how easy it makes our understanding of experience.

Systems theory has met with opposition. Jürgen Habermas famously quarreled with Niklas Luhmann about its rejection of the "transcendentally grounded world" we call reality (Habermas, 1985/1993, p. 370) and about its neglect of ethics (ibid., p. 376). It can seem to reject free will and creativity, and it can become too abstract to seem relevant to real-world problems.

Systems theory can also insinuate social engineering, as trained experts assume greater responsibility for leadership (Bausch, 2001, p. 124, quoting Habermas, 1974; Burnham, 1987, p. 295). Organizational complexity increasingly requires expertise, yet participants without that expertise are increasingly interested in being empowered to govern themselves (Bausch,

2001, pp. 104, citing Churchman, 1969, 314). That is a tension (competence versus participation) carried over from antiquity.

Compounding the tension, systems theorists presumed to unlock the laws of nature and thereby committed a sin against perspectivism. On one side, extreme advocates of systems thinking believe they have solved the mystery of the universe, while on the other side detractors consider systems to be elaborate images sufficiently abstract to mean very little in actual practice—abstract images that should never prevent ordinary people from enjoying a measure of autonomy. The truth probably lies somewhere in between.

C. FINDING A PLACE FOR SYSTEMS THEORY

Our ambition in these pages has been to develop and consider models or schemas of leadership that incorporate the widest number of studies and usages, embracing and ordering them all, if that is possible. In this regard we have concluded for the time being that there can be more than one of these—not because there is more than one reality, but because there is more than one way to conceptualize the one, paramount reality. Each schema has its strengths and weaknesses. Some are better than others. In addition, we have recognized that it might be possible to combine and integrate schemas into comprehending schemas we can refer to as metaschemas, which are schemas concerning schemas. Systems theory is one such metaschema.

Another metaschema (inspired by the work of Alfred Schütz and Edmund Husserl and implicit in much that has gone before in this book) describes four aspects of understanding (Schütz, 1962, p. 299). These aspects are not mutually exclusive. Each has its place. The merit of such a metaschema is to separate them conceptually and show their place. A person operates at all four aspects, although Schütz warned that in actual practice we tend to adopt one of these aspects as a fixed point of reference and distrust or take for granted the other three (ibid., pp. 299f). Frankly, that has to be done provisionally for the sake of making analytical progress, to avoid the confusion of trying to do too many things at once. Nonetheless, there is no reason to call one aspect "true" and the others "false." It is a matter of perspective (to employ, once again, a familiar word). What are these four aspects? Let me illustrate by using the word "apple."

Under the first aspect, the word "apple" is a specific set of letters in a particular sequence that can be defined, classified as a noun, translated into other languages, and otherwise used as a part of the English language. A person can look it up in a dictionary. "Apple" is a word, a symbol, a piece of language.

Under the second aspect, since the word is a symbol for other things, for objects in the real world that ordinary humans can experience (i.e., they can see it, pick it up, and taste it), we need to keep these two aspects distinct: the symbol (first aspect) and the concept to which it refers (second aspect). The concrete object to which it refers is a class of fruit, typified by a range of reddish color and a spherical shape, etc. "Apple" in this aspect means a concept, a mental unity, an assembly of experiences with a single name. That much is unremarkable. There is the word (first aspect) and the item in one's mind to which the word refers (second aspect).

Under the third aspect, we are not so much interested in the apple as a discrete object, a thing with certain typical properties. Rather, we are interested in the properties themselves, as they are experienced. It is not the apple; it is the sum of experiences with a concrete apple that would be of interest to us under this third aspect. In other words, there is a word (first aspect), an object to which the word refers (second aspect), and then there is the set of experiences that we use as the basis for concluding what an apple is (third aspect). That means we now have a symbol, a concept, and a set of experiences.

There is a fourth aspect, tying this together, as it were. It is the structure of inference one uses to move among experience, concept, and symbol, making sense of the other three aspects. Two persons in the same concrete situation might encounter the exact same apple, but one calls it too tart, while the other calls it too sweet. One might call it an apple, but the other (being French) might call it a pomme. One might prefer to eat it, but the other might regard it as an object in commerce or as a projectile. The fourth aspect explains the way a concrete person with a unique set of knowledge, memories, and interests puts it together in his or her mind. After all, one part of experience is the nature of the person having the experience.

The four aspects can be characterized quickly as the symbol, concept, experience, and interpretation. As we have already shown in this book, leadership falls within each of these. Perhaps it would be incumbent upon me now to run through the aspects as they pertain to leadership. This can be done profitably in two ways. The first way looks at the word "leadership" from the vantage point of an observer, a student of leadership, which means that we can understand leadership as a noun of some use in ordinary and scientific language (aspect 1), representing a type of interaction (aspect 2), based on certain experiences of interpersonal influence (aspect 3), which we interpret to be a meaningful construct for explaining social change (aspect 4). We have already been doing this throughout this book.

The second way looks at leadership as a participant might look at it, from all four aspects. This application of the metaschema will be a little different. (1) The leader is a symbol, a representative or representation of something else. (2) He or she symbolizes a vision (the goal, mission, objective, purpose), a conceptualization about the direction to be taken, which originates in conceptualizations of the way things are and the way things ought to be. (3) Leadership happens as a result of interaction, communication, the influence process that the leader and follower experience together. (4) Not everyone responds in the same way to the one we call the leader, of course, and that is partly because of the interpretation the follower makes with regard to the whole situation. Whereas I leap to serve the cause, you might dismiss the leader as a self-aggrandizing showman with a hidden agenda. Whereas I recognize the nature of the problem that the leader is trying to resolve and I agree that something has to be done, you might have more important things to do, according to a different set of priorities. You and I are likely to interpret the situation differently.

With this metaschema of four aspects in mind, we can place systems theory as a conceptual scheme in the second aspect, a mental product unifying disparate experiences into a discernible unit. That is its strength, certainly, inasmuch as it is broad and supple enough to include a wide variety of experiences, but it becomes a vicious abstraction if we were to hold that systems *are* reality, the very stuff we experience, which is simply untrue. No one experiences a system directly.

Controversies in leadership studies bubble up within this four-part metaschema. Controversies over systems theory are no exception. But the first obligation is to place the controversy within its proper aspect. That is one way to begin the process of resolving conflict. Is it a controversy of the first aspect, such as the controversies addressed by Joseph Rost, who catalogues and criticizes definitions of the word "leadership," going so far as to trace the origins of the word itself? Is it a controversy of the third aspect, such as the controversies addressed by Bruce Mazlish, who considers the imaginal origins of leadership? Is it a controversy of the fourth aspect, such as the controversies addressed by Wilfred Drath, who classifies three ways of interpreting events to mean leadership, even raising the awkward question whether the word really means anything at all? Controversies over systems theory, like I said, are controversies of the second aspect, about the most useful ways to conceptualize leadership. As such, it needs to be addressed in leadership studies, to be sure.

Systems thinking is a metaschema, but it is only part of the larger organizing schema attributable to Schütz. The next chapter offers yet another metaschema, and it might seem that the metaschemas are proliferating like summer flies, but that is inevitable at these levels of abstraction. It is helpful to appreciate the possible variety, while at the same time seeing how they integrate, since that is the long-term objective of leadership studies.

D. CHAPTER SUMMARY

From this vantage point, part way up the slope, we can gaze across the valley and in one glance see the contours of the valley. There was no way to see this from the depths of the valley. Up here, since the foliage is thinning, we can look down on the expanse where, in previous chapters, we had paid more attention to details. Here, we test the elasticity of our critical powers, moving with agility between points of view to complete our understanding of leadership.

The metaschema of Schütz orders not only the parts of this book, but also the entire range of leadership studies, and for that reason, it challenges students of leadership to complete their work by contemplating all four aspects, separately and together.

* Aspect one: leadership as *symbol*
* Aspect two: leadership as *concept*
* Aspect three: leadership as *experience*
* Aspect four: leadership as *interpretation*

The next chapter presents another model, which has the advantage of being broader, so to speak, than systems theory. It is also a metaschema, a way of structuring different approaches to the study of leadership, so that they can all coexist, with each in its rightful place. It has a long history, actually, with a record of intrasystematic consistency and considerable harmony with a wide range of experiences.

Its breadth reflects an inclusive image of what it means to be human. Humans are many things. They possess many faculties. They participate in the world on many levels. In order to develop a thorough understanding of leadership, therefore, we must examine our anthropological assumptions about the participants. Voegelin's ladder will help us do that.

13

VOEGELIN'S LADDER

The study of leadership frequently treats participants as rational maximizers, guided by logic as they make their choices in life. People are not so logical, of course, and one could argue that leadership especially consists of non-logical features, such as emotion and aspiration, as well as mystery, propaganda, and illusion. Of course, non-logical phenomena can be studied in a logical fashion, and to do that we have to use reason.[1]

It would be advisable, however, at some point during these studies, to recognize the limits of reason. This chapter begins to "frame" reason, so we get some idea of its limits. We can use reason to study non-logical things, yet there will always remain things that reason can never completely comprehend, partly due to the nature of reason and partly due to the nature of the reality we are trying to understand. A due respect for the limits of reason leads to caution and restraint. Not long ago, journalist Robert Kaplan concluded that "there is no greater attribute for a [leader] than humility built on an accurate assessment of his own limits" (2002, p. 153). Caution and restraint among scholars is a good thing. In the famous words of Ludwig Wittgenstein, from his *Tractatus Logico Philosophicus* (1922): "Whereof one cannot speak, thereof one must be silent."

Along these lines, this particular chapter builds a schematic structure with two dimensions: the horizontal and the vertical. First will be the horizontal dimension, pertaining to the limits of reason. The second dimension, which is vertical, presents a spectrum of ways to understand leadership, both its logical and its non-logical features. From there, we open out onto the increasingly popular topic of leadership and spirituality.

A. THE HORIZONTAL

A substantial number of studies come out of the Enlightenment tradition, in which reason serves as the supreme (if not the only valid) instrument for finding truth and choosing what to do. Meanwhile, the Enlightenment tradition has come under assault from two directions. We can locate these two directions horizontally: the first assault which I intend to present comes from the left, whereas the second assault comes from the right. These directions have not been assigned arbitrarily, as the first assault arises mostly on the political and cultural left of the spectrum and the second arises mostly on the right. It is by no means a strict *correlation*, yet the *connotation* of left and right helps to place the literature ideologically, so to speak. Nonetheless, despite the left/right imagery, we have to begin with the understanding that *both* assaults share in doubting the supremacy of reason. This they have in common.

1. Assault from the left. Reason itself is suspect. It is no longer enough to win an argument by appealing to reason. (Postmodernism gets involved in this assault.) The assault takes one of two paths: either (a) that reason serves as a legitimating cover for non-rational motives, i.e. that reason can be characterized as a superstructure (if you will) built up to gain or preserve power, or (b) that reason itself is fundamentally flawed and not to be trusted as an instrument for truth. This two-part assault concurs with the assault from the right as to the presence and permanence of non-reason, but it devotes more attention to the limits of reason than to the importance or value of non-reason, as we shall see. The two paths of the assault from the left work together, in parallel.

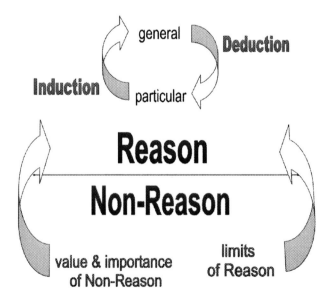

To trace the first path quickly, there is the accusation that reason, logic, science, and so forth, are more *rationale* than rational. Friedrich Engels, for example, pointed in this direction when he wrote about false consciousness, ideology, and societal superstructures. It is a version of cynicism, that people don't really mean what they say and that they justify themselves using argumentation. Reason is a smokescreen for something else. Find out about that something else and you get at what is really going on. Reason is little more than a façade, and the funny part supposedly is the extent to which most people do not even recognize their rationalizings. They do not penetrate their own façades.

Let us not overlook feminism's complaint that strict reason—logocentrism, to borrow a term—is the male's weapon to oppress the female and her leadership, which is based more on intuition and gestalt. One commentator went so far as to depict the emphasis in classrooms on reason—including facts, logic, and objectivity—as a "rape" of the feminine mind (Hoff Sommers, 1994, quoting Lerner, 198). Susan Mendus, writing for *The Oxford Companion to Philosophy*, had this to say:

> [S]ome feminists have questioned the appeal to rationality. . . . The claim that men and women are essentially rational beings is, it is argued, a gendered claim and one which reflects, not a universal truth, but only the preoccupations of Enlightenment philosophy (1995, pp. 270–272).

The same suspicion about the use of reason by those in power exists among other protected classes, such as minorities and the poor, as we had reason to mention earlier in this book.

There is the second path from the left, to the effect that reason is imperfect, not to be trusted, unable to support its claim to supremacy. Reason makes mistakes. It is limited. It often leads to catastrophic consequences. It seems to result in diametrically opposed conclusions. Today, one can doubt any proposition—any principle, finding, description, prescription, or definition—and some scholar will lend you credence. Richard Rorty said as much: "Since the time of Kant, it has become more and more apparent to non-philosophers that a really professional philosopher can supply a philosophical foundation for just about anything" (1982, p. 169).[2] In which case, reason becomes disqualified as a final arbiter. As Henri de Lubac once mentioned, "We are certainly cured of our infatuation for a world wholly explainable and indeterminately perfectible by pure reason" (1944, p. 86, citing Chardin).

From the left, then, we are urged to doubt the efficacy of reason, as well as the motives of those who employ reason.

2. Assault from the right. Reason is all well and good, but it cannot completely fathom reality. From the right, critics argue that certain aspects of life are impervious to its scrutiny. "The heart," wrote Pascal, "has its reasons that Reason does not know." Freud, for example, studied hidden irrational drives in the psyche. LeBon studied irrational drives in the mob. Edmund Burke referred to sentiment. Kierkegaard, to faith. Schopenhauer, to the will. Reason has its place, but it quickly finds itself subordinated or set aside in actual experience, and even though most people believe it is worthwhile to apply reason to non-reason for purposes of study, reason can never thoroughly grasp or contain it.[3]

Kenneth Boulding suggested a handy way of understanding this in three parts, something of a schema within a schema. There is what he calls an image we use to operate in the world. Part of it is conscious, the part we pay attention to, like the part of a building that shows up at night when illuminated by flashlight. Part of it is unconscious, the part we could pay attention to, if we choose to do so, like the parts of a building that are presently dark to us, but which we could see if only we move the flashlight. Boulding called this process of moving the flashlight "scanning." The third part of the image is subconscious, a part we cannot pay attention to, like the parts of a building behind the façade, where the flashlight cannot penetrate. All parts affect behavior (1956, p. 54). The trick is discerning what lies behind the façade.

Human beings have emotions, appetites, epiphanies, and tastes, and these can be overwhelming. We should respect them and not dismiss them as residual defects that triumphant Reason will eventually root out or repair. To a large extent, some of these non-rational aspects are the very things that give life savor, meaning, and purpose.

The assault from the right splits at this point, just as the assault from the left split. There is a difference, however. The assault from the left split into parallel paths, moving in the same direction. The two paths on the right move in diametrically opposed directions. One direction emphasizes the material or biological aspect of humanity, such as instinct. The other direction emphasizes the spiritual or transcendent aspect of humanity, such as aesthetics and revelation. Plato might have been the first to offer this image of a bipolar tension[4]—but in 1944 Henri de Lubac noticed the same tension between Nietzsche and Kierkegaard (part 1; chap. 2). He wrote at page 383, "How often the supraconsciousness is confused with the infraconsciousness!"[5] It is a fine and volatile distinction that serves as the basis for the vertical dimension of this schema. We turn to that now.

B. THE VERTICAL

> *"Man is a ladder placed on earth and the top*
> *of it touches heaven. And all his movements*
> *and doings and words leave traces in the*
> *upper world."*
>
> **— Martin Buber (quoted in Hitt, 1992, p. 3)**

Father de Lubac succinctly characterizes the vertical dimension. It originates in the assault from the right to the effect that non-reason matters a great deal in leadership and remains outside the sovereignty of reason.

In the previous section, we started to imagine two different paths for non-rational influences on leadership. One of them was higher (supraconsciousness), and one of them was lower (infraconsciousness). Given the renewed interest by leadership scholars in matters spiritual—and given the confusions that easily arise when trying to discuss them rationally—the following section begins to frame an answer to the question: "What does it mean to speak of higher things?" To get there, however, we would be advised to build the entire model first.

1. Below and above. It is possible to reason about non-rational things. Leadership is one example. Leadership involves non-rational things. Emotion, for example, tends to be thought of as non-rational. Kouzes and Posner insist that "[l]eadership is emotional. Period" (Shriberg et al., 1997, p. 189). Gardner made a similar remark, when he wrote that "in the tasks of leadership, the transactions between leaders and constituents go beyond the rational level to the nonrational and unconscious levels of human functioning" (1990, p. 14). The literature is full of claims to the effect that leadership involves non-rational things. Nonetheless, leadership can be studied in a systematic, scientific way. Perhaps the best place to begin is to note that these non-rational things tend to fall into one of two categories.

The one category or "path" would be things that we normally call material, biological, lower needs and drives, such as instincts, appetites, the will to power, and so forth. Writers who emphasize these non-rational things are trying to explain the foundations of leadership, such as why leaders feel compelled to lead to begin with and why followers respond. How far back into the material stuff will the explanation go? We might talk about impulses or urges. We might examine the psychological effects of a leader's height, health, resonant voice, posture, alpha animal traits signaling a primate coping-mechanism for the community, and so forth. The hypothesis is that humans tend to lead and follow in response to subrational forces, such as fear or fascination. Writers can go back from psychology to genetics, evolutionary biology, chemistry, and even, I suppose, electricity. This path looks at leadership as an outward phenomenon of a deep, organic process attributable ultimately to the impulses of vitality.

A distinct variation of this path we have already examined in some detail, and that is the power of myth. Writers such as Bruce Mazlish, James Hillman, and C. F. Alford have treated this variation with dexterity and depth. From within this variation come works on soul, which is something different from spirit. In simplistic terms, soul is down; spirit is up. This is important to remember, because soul and spirit are easily confused.

In other words, we can describe a vertical line, with paths going up and down in both directions. The first path, the one we have already started to describe (which Lubac labels "infraconsciousness") probes downward, toward the material foundations of human behavior. The second path goes in the opposite direction. With Lubac, we can call this path supracon-sciousness, and it includes things we normally understand as spiritual, aesthetic, moral, if not religious. It refers to a higher calling, a larger purpose, things such as destiny and vision, as though humans are beings with free will who aspire to something above or beyond themselves. Writers who emphasize these non-rational things are trying to explain the way that humans set goals and dream dreams. What are folks wanting to achieve? What do they hope to gain? Are we all part of something beyond our daily survival? Is there something more? This second path, traveling up our vertical line, looks at leadership as the means for fulfilling some cluster of aspirations.

The characterization of one path going down while the other path goes up connotes superiority, a hierarchy, as though going up were nobler, more elevated than the other way. Our language is full of similar metaphors equating "up" with "better." It is not necessary to accept that connotation. James Hillman has written extensively on behalf of going down—not toward the material specifically, such as chemistry, but toward myth and the soul (see, e.g., Hillman, 1975). Down is good, too. That is why it might seem more acceptable to speak of going *deeper*. That has a different connotation.

Changing the language we use does not change the value of the first, downward path, which is indisputable. Studies of leadership moving downward are perfectly legitimate. They form part of a complete treatment of the subject. We all have much to learn from the study of infraconsciousness. There is a non-rational foundation to our behavior. It is out of that foundation that humans emerge as they are. A thorough understanding of it can only help the cause. Just to highlight one example: Bernard Bass reports that several studies indicate leaders possess higher energy levels than non-leaders. Energy is an infraconscious factor that appears to be relevant to leadership (1990, pp. 89–90).[6]

It is the purpose of this section, however, to move in the other direction, upward, toward the spiritual—not to repudiate what lies below, but rather to seek to understand what seems to lie above. It too is comprised of the non-rational, and it too (in my opinion) can be studied rationally . . . up to a point. Chester Bowling, to cite one example, refers to a "nonrational epistemology" about leadership because the spirit lies in the "noncognitive realm" (2001, p. 370).

2. Voegelin's ladder. The image of a vertical line to order our thinking in this way received an explanation in a little-known essay by Eric Voegelin. In the *Southern Review* (1974), he published "Reason: The Classic Experience." It included an appendix, where he set out a table to show what he called "levels in the hierarchy of being" (CW 12, p. 290). It is reproduced with permission, as follows:

	PERSON	SOCIETY	HISTORY →
Divine Nous			
Psyche—Noetic			
Psyche—Passions			
Animal nature			
Vegetative nature			
Inorganic nature			
Apeiron—Depth			

In his words, then:

> The arrow pointing down indicates the order of formation from the top down. The arrow pointing up indicates the order of foundation from the bottom up. . . . The order of formation and foundation must not be inverted or otherwise distorted. . . . (CW 12, p. 290).

According to his principle of completeness, we must understand and appreciate each of the levels and not isolate any one of them. The ladder goes a long way toward illustrating what it would mean to have a comprehensive understanding of leadership: all of the cells on the ladder would be filled. Doing so would purportedly tie everything together.

Human beings operate at all levels simultaneously; these are simply different ways to approach the same reality. In other words, we are at one and the same moment physical objects operating according to physical laws—inorganic, vegetative, and animal—as well as psychological creatures with passions, beliefs, and imaginations. We fully occupy a reality between the two poles of transcendence and the apeiron. The temptation to pick one level and insist that it must be the *only* level he calls "hypostasis." It is a reductionist fallacy—unnecessary, for one thing, and unresponsive to the evidence (ibid., p. 290; Harvey, 2001, p. 378; Mazlish, 1990, p. 25).[7]

Not everyone agrees. There are writers who do choose one level, one way of understanding, and declare the rest to be illusory. Language of higher things rationalizes behavior, they might argue, cloaking it in legitimating words, almost to the point of deceit. They hold that claims of spirituality in leadership are little more than a pious fraud. Marxists take this position, for example.

For purposes of illustrating hypostasis, we might mention a few extreme instances. One hypostatic view holds that everything in the universe can be explained by mathematized physics. The rest is all fluff and hooey. Another view holds that everything can be explained by religious dogma. Yet another view seeks a single explanation in a psychology of myth. Barzun mentions an eighteenth-century book titled *Man as Machine*, followed in the next century by the declaration of man as an automaton. Since then, he writes, "man has been portrayed as a chemical, glandular, and electrical machine, [even] predestined and worked by the instrumentality of cells and genes" (2000, p. 367).

Voegelin's ladder makes room for many "viewpoints" so long as no one view presumes to exclude the rest. Leadership, as a phenomenon in reality, can be studied profitably at any one of the levels, from multiple perspectives, although the academic community is charged with integrating these findings periodically and keeping them in good order. This it has not done adequately, which is why all of the interest lately in spirituality has forced the issue.

3. Leadership < > Spirituality. At the pinnacle of Voegelin's ladder we would find that level where we can start to make sense of spirituality, even though there it implicates or refers to something even higher, beyond which we cannot go, transcending humanity. The highest level represents the point where humanity intersects with the divine. For that reason, it will have to remain incomplete, tinged with mystery, allusive. Such is the nature of spiritual things.

Despite its inscrutability, we have to take it seriously and do our best to understand it, for several reasons.

(a) There has been a revival of interest among academics in management, organizational behavior, and leadership studies, so we have take some account of their work.

(b) Academics have become increasingly interested largely because spirituality has been invoked by participants as meaningful, if not determinative, for their experiences of leadership (Harvey, 2001; Mitroff & Denton, 1999).

(c) Leaders and scholars alike have examined the possibility that spirituality has instrumental value (Mitroff & Denton, 1999, p. 86). Corinne McLaughlin assembled multiple findings, concluding that "[s]pirituality could be the ultimate competitive advantage" (2002, citing Mitroff).

(d) It is not just a competitive advantage. Spirituality pertains to morality and ethics (Marsden, 1997, p. 85; see generally MacIntyre, 1981/1984). Debates and investigations into the origins and validity of moral claims frequently refer to spirituality.

(e) At the very least, claims of spirituality deserve as much respect as other diverse claims in a pluralistic society (Marsden, p. 86). It will not do to bar them at the gate.

4. What people are saying. Spirituality is hard to define.[8] Different traditions will offer versions. Frequently, people who claim to experience it simply refuse to give more than a vague description, saying that such things are ineffable. Specifically with regard to leadership, however, a number of writers have made the attempt, directly or indirectly.

Once again, therefore, we might justifiably imitate Aristotle, who in similar situations would look around to find what people are already saying about the topic. For the sake of brevity, I restrict myself here to a few writers. Their remarks do not actually *prove* the importance of this nonrational, supraconscious realm, but they do illustrate a widespread belief in its importance among people who have spent considerable time reflecting on leadership. Many authors refer to the leader's "higher" purpose. The leader is not to be merely utilitarian, using or deploying followers in order to achieve results. Rather, a leader answers to a higher calling, grounded in something sublime, transcendent, or holy, and it is that fealty, that dedication which positions her to lead others. What exactly are they saying?

Christians certainly urge the connection of leadership with spirituality. John Maxwell has made a career in the Christian publishing industry by beginning with scriptural precepts and drawing conclusions about what leadership is (or ought to be). Much of this literature is unapologetically anti-intellectual, grounded in fundamentalist dogma—which does not mean that it is necessarily wrong or useless. Among intellectuals from within the Christian tradition, Irving Babbitt and Richard Weaver made similar claims some time ago about the connection between spirituality and leadership, and their voices have been too long neglected in leadership studies.[9] In fairness, of course, Christianity is not the sole basis for connecting spirituality and leadership.

Not all of the persons writing about spirituality have an explicitly religious perspective. Some are simply groping for words that intend much the same thing as spirituality. Their work is secular. Stephen Covey, who happens to be a Christian, refers to one of the roles of a leader as one who has "a compelling vision and mission. Pathfinding deals with the larger sense of the future. It gets the culture imbued and excited about a tremendous, transcendent purpose" (Shriberg et al., 1997, p. 180). Kouzes and Posner use comparable language. Among their "ten most important lessons" is the following:

> [L]eaders must envision an uplifting and ennobling future. . . . We expect leaders to take us to places we have never been before—to have clearly in mind an attractive destination that will make the journey worthwhile. (ibid., p. 186)

They conclude by urging leaders "to seize the opportunities for greatness" (ibid., p. 189). James MacGregor Burns describes transforming leadership as raising leader and follower "to higher levels of motivation and morality [because followers] can be lifted into their better selves" (ibid., p. 213, quoting Burns, 1978). Peter Vaill "equates *visionary leadership* with a spiritual process through which people seek ways to bring out the best in themselves and, consequently, the best in others" (ibid., p. 35; emphasis supplied).

Charles Handy insists that "life is about more than surviving—there could be something glorious about it, it could contribute to a better world. That leaves one with a personal challenge, to do something glorious with one's life. It is also, I believe, a challenge for every organization and every business" (1998, p. 118). In addition to these voices are the books reviewed recently in *The Leadership Quarterly* (2001). Let us take a closer look at what all of these writers are claiming.

5. Leadership *implies* spirituality. Leadership, like spirituality, is a relationship grounded in a purpose, and that purpose reflects the aspirational character of its participants. Participants experience and respond to the

tension of existence. Leadership originates in a desire to change the present, to improve something about one's existence and bring it into alignment with an ideal, no matter how slight. Leadership embodies those aspirations, representing a level of faith we have as humans that together we can participate in approximating those ideals. Aspiration justifies leadership.

Humans obviously aspire. They envision a future that is different, better somehow, from the one they presently occupy. They believe things can get better. And rather than sit around hoping for that to happen on its own accord, like manna from heaven, humans tend to get up and do something about it. They participate in trying to improve the world. This drive to realize better days takes shape, moving from need to idea to purpose, and then humans get down to work. To the extent they work together toward some common purpose, issues of leadership become comprehensible. The very existence of common or collective purpose makes leadership possible.

This purpose belongs to the spiritual realm, no matter how mundane. It might not rise to the level of praising God or winning salvation for the soul, but it belongs to the spiritual realm. Within that spiritual realm of dreams, desires, designs, and decisions, we may try to make a profit, assault an enemy ridge, or pass legislation. It could be any one of a number of objectives. With this in mind, one long-term project for every pragmatist leader, it seems to me, would be sorting through these various aspirations, reconciling most, and prioritizing them into some kind of coherence. That coherence ultimately fits into the coordinates of two classic questions of self-awareness: (a) who am I? and (b) why am I here? All purposeful action presumes to answer those two questions of identity and vocation. Consequently, so too would leadership presume to answer those questions, for both the leader and the followers.[10]

Max Scheler, writing extensively on spirit, regards it completely as "guidance and direction" (1928/1961, 62, 68). Spirit sublimates drives or instinct by detaching a person momentarily from the immediate press of events (dictated by the infraconsciousness and its encounters with the world) to contemplate another way, another possible condition, which it then pursues by channeling energy. Spirit inspires leaders to realize a vision and permits them to inspire followers to do the same. In this way, leaders experience spirit within themselves and evoke spirit in others.

Suppose that a leader articulates a vision about the kind of shipping department she expects to be supervising at a manufacturing facility. That is her purpose. She is painting a verbal picture of the future she wants to bring about, and she is trying to get her subordinates in the shipping department to share that vision, to buy in to it, so that together they may work to make it a reality. That is the typical kind of aspiration in leadership studies—worldly, narrow, common. No one disputes that some leaders articulate more elevated visions, such as world peace and eternal bliss, so the point I am trying to make is that they are the same thing in essence. The supervisor has taken a piece of the whole vision for a better world (presumably where everyone profits and workers go home proud of their labors, while customers experience delight) and has applied that to a specific set of circumstances, for a specific set of people, and for a specific task. Her vision is part of a larger vision.

The literature on leadership and spirituality appears to be asking leaders and the scholarly community to take seriously the spiritual dimension of even the most mundane projects, to contemplate the way in which a leader's immediate vision fits a larger vision. "Are you just cutting stone or are you building a cathedral?"

That is what I understand the literature to intend.

C. A PRESCRIPTION

Voegelin's ladder depicts a hierarchy in which higher levels form the lower ones. Lower levels constrain what the higher levels can do. And as the levels get higher on the chart, levels that are relatively lower actually resist formation and (in a manner of speaking) push back. Animal appetites frequently crowd aside rational thought, as Maslow rightly understood; rational thought has been clever in stigmatizing spirituality as delusion or superstition. Part of what this book intends is the restoration of hierarchy, as a matter of prescription, reestablishing the rank order, so that first and foremost a leader is attuned to her purpose, subordinating her powers to that purpose, with each descending level forming the levels that fall below it. To do that, she must be aware of the constraints placed upon her ambitions by these lower levels. Aspiration that is oblivious to real-world constraints is un-realistic, overweening (we might say), at risk of becoming utopian, oppressive, even stupid.

Nonetheless, it is true that people in their personal lives usually fail to hold this hierarchy together in good order, knowingly or not, which is one reason they respond to leaders who do. Voegelin's ladder is almost a template for patterns of domination, as persons operating from a higher level are more likely to lead—but I would not push the analogy that far. It does tend to reinforce the claim that people are likely to follow leaders with integrity, where integrity means the integration of the entire person, up and down the ladder.

There is something to be said for the ancient distinction that one either conforms to the order of being or rebels against it (Niemeyer, 1995, p. 47, citing Camus, 1956). To the extent leadership expresses human freedom, as we shall aver in the last chapter, it might resemble rebellion, since conformity to some abstract "order of being" appears to renounce freedom and subjugates the individual to something external to or independent of human life. Freedom can mean Promethean revolt.[11] That turns out not to be the case, since at each progressively higher level, a person enjoys greater freedom, not less, so that a person who throws his lot in with animal appetite is actually less free than one who throws his lot in with rationality, and so forth up and down the ladder. This would be so even though he might experience his choices as supremely responsive to impulse and call it freedom. Nearly every ancient philosophical and religious tradition saw through this self-deception.

It might be helpful to approach things from another perspective. All of the literature espousing spiritual leadership originates with an accusation, whether implicit or explicit, that not every person in a leadership position now is sufficiently spiritual. There would be no call for making a prescription if everything were just fine. Spiritual leadership stands in contrast to something else. By uncovering what constitutes that "something else" we go a long way toward understanding what is intended by spirituality.

What, then, is the literature on spiritual leadership trying to combat? Three types of leader come to mind. First would be the obtuse leader, oblivious to issues of spirituality, a person who never looks up from the sidewalk. The goal here is to get the obtuse leader to look up and look around with a loftier vision. He or she is a leader with a low ambition or a poor imagination, sometimes petty, of the sort that thrives in bureaucracy. Second would be the demonic leader, subservient to dark and mysterious forces hostile to humanity and to God. The goal here is to equip good leaders for the spiritual warfare they believe is going on around them, to cloak them in the armor of foreknowledge. Studies of tyrants and cult leaders fit here. The third type of leader that the literature intends to set up in contrast to spiritual leaders would be the spiritually diseased leader, one who by all accounts means well and thinks that he or she is attuned to the spirit, when that turns out to be untrue, or insufficiently true. This third type responds to the promptings of the spirit in a mistaken, fitful, or distorted way. They aren't getting it quite right, and their disease jeopardizes the very things they claim to be trying to achieve.

Our little typology deserves closer scrutiny. It is not my purpose to proclaim it as authoritative. It does, I think, suggest one of the directions the conversation ought to be taking, toward a morphology of the leader who all of these writers think needs their advice. Whether a leader is dull, malign, or sick—and what can be done about it—would seem to be relevant to the prescriptions they hope to make.

As we have had reason to notice over and over on our walk through these woods, leadership implicates deep philosophical questions—questions of logic, epistemology, ethics, and the like—and the next chapter returns to this one question in particular, about the relationship of freedom and order. Before making this final turn, however, we should probably summarize what we have just been doing.

D. CHAPTER SUMMARY

We are human beings trying to understand human behavior. At some point in our ruminations, we are obliged to make plain our anthropological framework. *What does it mean to be human?* Our answer to this question will pertain to our conceptualization of ourselves as observers, as well as our conceptualization of the participants in leadership.

Scholars are inclined to value rationality, and they should. Scholars themselves tend to be very smart, and as scholars they tend to be rewarded for their intelligence, so they come to rely heavily on their intellectual powers. Rationality lies at the heart of their work. I think it is important to make controversies surrounding the limits of reason explicit.

Another reason to make these controversies explicit is the assumption behind many investigations: that participants in leadership are themselves rational. This is an assumption—a useful assumption, in many instances—but an assumption, nonetheless, that we would do well on occasion to doubt, in deference to the empirical evidence that leadership is just as much non-rational, if not more so.

These controversies gave us an excuse to make plain our anthropological framework, namely Voegelin's ladder, which presents a broad and variegated image of humanity. This framework not only assists in our studies of leadership, as, for example, in classifying previous research; it also suggests a way of structuring our prescriptions for leadership.

Promptings of the spirit form aspirations, which take shape in the mind of a leader as purpose that will depend on reason to design and then execute a plan in light of existing constraints. Spirituality informs ethics, which in turn relies on our intellectual powers to prepare a response to the demands of a paramount reality. To the extent we are going to teach others how to lead, therefore, we should in my opinion ground their ambition in their life's vocation and equip them intellectually to integrate their whole life and their circumstances as a precondition for their attempts to lead, attempts which in truth are little more than messing in the lives of other human beings who have their own callings and dreams.

14

LEADERSHIP IN THE FLUX

These past few chapters exist solely to illustrate that after one has separated out some topic or subject matter to analyze and study, there remains the synthesizing task of reconnecting it with its context, like placing the zebra conceptually back into its habitat. Leadership is no exception, which is why we have found it necessary to fit leadership into several larger contexts, such as the organization or society, among the many webs of influence. The largest contexts would be human history and the human condition, as grand themes which sound pretentious. It certainly requires more than a single chapter in one man's book to do them justice, so we have to content ourselves mostly with intimations and platitudes. Nonetheless, something should be said at this level of abstraction in order to complete the hike, reaching the summit and standing there to gaze as Olympians on the expanse of forest where we ordinarily live and move and have our being.

Before making the final ascent, let us build some momentum by recalling how we got here.

Leadership can be studied as a sociological form. Like all forms, it comes into existence out of the flux of life in order to serve some purpose or constellation of purposes of the participants. If existing sociological forms had been sufficient, it would have been unnecessary to create this one—the participants would not have gone in search of anything new—so the creation of leadership is itself an example of life transcending its forms.[1] Yet leadership is itself a form. James remarked, "Leaders give the form" (1880, p. 446). It is just that they also break the preexisting form. That is what they are doing, at one and the same time: transcending one form and giving birth to a new form.

In the course of time, life will set in motion forces to transcend this form. In the meantime, leadership tends to persist and withstand the strains brought on by the forces of life. Leadership frequently persists by means of solidifying into something intended to last, such as a pact, organization, or, on a larger scale, social stratification into elites. There is at any given moment a tension between pressures to change and pressures to persist. As pressure to burst this sociological form increases, three things can happen. The form can collapse under the onslaught, so that new forms replace it, like an overrun village; the form can ossify and become irrelevant, like the Maginot Line in an age of blitzkrieg; or the form can adapt to change, so that it prevails by making concessions to the demands of life.

- Slavery would be one example of an overrun form, persisting in only a few remote cultures.
- Racial kinship is becoming increasingly irrelevant in the pluralistic West.
- Apprenticeship appears to be a form that has adapted since the Middle Ages, from its feudal character to one that fits within the structure of contemporary labor unions.

The third alternative reconciles the persistence of forms with the flux of life and proves to be the most enduring. This is so for the *Denkbild*, if you recall, in that it must approach a perfection of form while at the same time reflecting the primal images from which it emerges. Since primal images change, the *Denkbild* has to be adaptable; that is, it has to be able to incorporate change as part and parcel of its nature. Otherwise, a better alternative will present itself. This means that the best *Denkbild* will be so structured as to *anticipate* the need to adapt. That two-fold measure of intrasystematic consistency (perfection of the form) and correspondence (adaptation to the flux of life) determines its usefulness or "cash value" as a form. (Any resemblance at this point to pragmatism is fully intended.)

This third alternative of a form adaptable to circumstances can be illustrated by reference to a classic element in elite theory that we noted in an earlier chapter. We might look at it again.

An Italian with one of the all-time great names, Vilfredo Pareto, made a number of contributions to sociology. One of his most enduring contributions was an explanation of the so-called circulation of elites (1901/1991). According to his observations and studies, every society is governed by an elite, a ruling class (a fact which numerous other theorists had already noticed). What interested Pareto was the *permeability* of the elites, the dynamics by which one elite accommodates or replaces another (ibid., p. 36).

Many of those who govern really cannot sustain themselves in power. They lack the requisite virtues. Quite a number do not even *want* to persist. By the same token, many who are not governing presently feel that they should be and so in many ways strive to prove themselves worthy. For the well-being of the community, the social structure should adapt to the upward pressure of the ambitious newcomers. In some cases, the prevailing elite refuses to yield and resists being displaced, which is good in a way: it demonstrates their commitment and stirs them to action. However, an impermeable elite totally incapable of squashing or diverting opposition will eventually topple, probably with great violence, as in the French Revolution, when the worthier leaders of the masses felt they had no choice but to wrest control. In some cases, of course, an elite refuses to assert itself and squanders its position by capitulation. Their presence in history is harder to detect, since their time in power was so brief and undistinguished. One thinks of the first government formed after the Russian Revolution. Pareto respected an elite that found a way to preserve itself by means of raising up to its level the worthiest members of the lower classes while at the same time finding a way to marginalize or demote the least worthy members of their own class.[2] Such an elite exemplifies what I have been talking about: a form that persists by adapting to change.

Near the beginning of this book, we contrasted the theory underlying leadership studies with a theory holding that in actuality leaders do *not* really make a difference, as Tolstoy believed. Leadership studies stands directly opposed to determinism, in whatever version that takes. The argument was put succinctly in an out-of-way place. In 1985, the historian Arthur Schlesinger, Jr., wrote a short introductory essay on leadership for a children's biography of Margaret Thatcher. He explained that by their lives, by their example, leaders demonstrate to the rest of us that we are indeed free. We are not helpless victims of biology or economics. A leader's greatest value (he argued) lies in urging us to exercise our freedom and take actions we otherwise would not have taken, to prove to ourselves that we have choices, and (perhaps most liberating) to encourage us to change the context of our lives. Oddly enough, it was a philosopher widely characterized as a determinist who said much the same thing. As Karl Marx famously put it in 1845: "philosophers have only *interpreted* the world in various ways; the point is, to *change* it" (*Theses on Feuerbach*, XI).

Leaders demonstrate that within the flux of life, we too live, and we can enter that flux to alter its course.

William James, so frequently cited in these pages, took an intermediate position in his great 1880 article on patterns of historical causation. He stood between determinists and those who held to the so-called Great Man

Theory. He said much the same thing as Schlesinger, that societal change results from the "acts or the example of individuals" (p. 446). In so doing, he opposed simple determinism and certainly fatalism: individuals can and do make a difference. However, the person we hope to characterize as a leader does not inspire ordinary folks to exercise *their* freedom and express *their* genius so much as he gives form to the flow of events and interjects new ideas or new methods that the rest of us resist or adopt or integrate gradually. In other words, leaders do not necessarily make leaders out of the rest of us. They lead. Whether we ever realize our own genius (or feel adequately the afflatus of existential freedom or whatever it is that Schlesinger regards as the primary outcome) is, to James, coincidental. And on this point, I concur with James, even though it takes nothing away from the central message that leadership exhibits and exemplifies freedom.

Think of it this way. Leadership is an event in history, a shift or surge in the flow of history that helps to give history a discernible shape. At one time, history itself was thought to be the record of leaders, a chronicle of the impact of explorers and kings, but then historians began to study statistical correlations, impersonal forces, trends, to such an extreme that leaders became little more than colorful flotsam—good copy and "merely" symbolic of reality. Today, leadership studies recognizes the causal significance of individuals to the course of history. Leadership studies exists explicitly to increase or improve the role of leaders. Leadership studies prepares students to assume responsibility for the trajectory from the present to the future—in other words, to make history.

That is why, early in this book, we emphasized the importance of studying the past: to learn from the past, certainly; to understand the present; and ultimately to shape the future. Understanding where you *were*, where you are now, and how you got here prepares you to go somewhere else. Leadership can be understood as a mechanism by which trajectories change, no matter how slightly, in the histories of people together. Leadership is part of what makes the flux of human existence into something we can think of as history.[3]

Leadership is an interpretation of the causal importance of individual human lives.

An attentive reader might object that all of this talk about free will and the impact of leaders contradicts the various assertions in this book about the course of history, as though history's patterns prove that we are *not* free. The argument might go something like this. If we live according to patterns, then we are not free. If, for example, the flux of life—that disembodied force we seem to have personified—runs along in some kind of dialectical order, from A to B to C, then how can it be meaningful to say that the future could be otherwise? Once we find a pattern, either it can come to an end, in which case it no longer holds and its usefulness to us tomorrow is zero, or it *cannot* come to an end, in which case leadership would be futile, like kicking against the goad. So which is it, you might wonder, freedom or order? Leadership or determinism?

A thorough response to this objection would have to include the following elements.

(a) First, it is a false dilemma. Freedom is meaningless without the doing. Freedom proves itself in action. Freely chosen behavior is in effect an ordering force. That action becomes part of the raw stuff from which we derive any sense of history.

(b) Just because the patterns in history might have predicted that you would choose to do X, in no way does this show that your choice of X was determined. You freely chose what someone else could predict. The social sciences do this all the time. When prices go down, people tend to buy more of a product, all other things being equal. When the price goes up, they buy less. That pattern of economics in no way forces me to make my purchases. I could do otherwise. I just do not tend to. Even so, at the moment of purchase, I am a free agent, doing what I like in the circumstances.

(c) The historical pattern we have been considering in these pages is a pattern incorporating the possibility of change. It does not hold that human interaction conforms to a rigid set of laws forever and ever, amen. Instead, it shows the tendency of humans to try new things, make adaptations, and otherwise experiment through life. These patterns of history are patterns of change, specifically describing the human capacity to transcend the past and present. It is a pattern of freedom.

(d) Most patterns in history depict broad tendencies. They trace the path of whole societies and cultures. Within those societies and cultures, one will find numerous counter-examples and acts of resistance. Reactionaries fight rearguard actions, while radicals make their bootless plea. By analogy, when a sports reporter describes the ebb and flow of a football contest, there might have been a story line to the game, but there were always two teams playing against each other, struggling until the final gun. Before the teams took the field, the outcome was in doubt. The game still had to be played. They played in freedom. So, even as the pattern emerges, it allows for plenty of innovation and choice. Leadership expresses human freedom. It is part of the process by which free people find their way in the world.

(e) The next response to the false dilemma of freedom vs. order might seem strange at first. Those who despise philosophy are likely to snort and roll their eyes at what I am about to say, but it really does need to be said. With this painfully abstract assertion we reach with labored breath the peak of the mountain, the absolute summit, at high altitude. I take this assertion largely from an observation by Heidegger about the philosophy of Aristotle (1995, §14), and it goes something like this. Purpose should be contrasted with boundlessness. A previous chapter explained that for Aristotle, experienced *need* yields an *idea* that crystallizes into a *purpose*. Once purpose becomes action, it expresses freedom fully, because that means I am doing what I choose. That is the epitome of freedom, is it not? Freedom entails boundedness, a being bound to purpose. "How can free choice," you might ask, "mean that one is in any sense bounded?" Until a person decides, he has many potential courses of action, but the very word "decide" means "to kill alternatives"—the openness of the moment closes around a single course of action. Out of formlessness, aimlessness, a purpose takes discernible shape and enters the world, giving definition to one's life, even if only for the moment. The irony is that freedom expresses itself in boundedness, and that boundedness closes off alternatives and binds. Nobody gets anywhere, nobody achieves anything, nobody advances until operating from out of a condition of freedom by means of some form of action. We are free, yet we are fated to launch ourselves out of freedom toward something we purpose, so that self-constraint, self-discipline exemplify freedom best. It is a paradox.

Binding oneself to another person, whether to the leader or to a follower, for the sake of some purpose—chosen freely, we presume—introduces a degree of constraint right there, constraint by that other person, by her desires and limitations. Simply by entering into the relationship with someone else, you become bounded by her (Simmel, 1908/1950, p. 188). This is why leadership solely for the sake of *using* other people is more constrictive than leadership for the sake of *serving* other people would be. Using a stepladder makes one beholden to the ladder, while at the same time it makes possible what otherwise would have been impossible. A person is both liberated and constrained by the instrument one chooses.

There is a profound difference between engaging with another person *despite* constraints and engaging with another person *because of* those constraints. If I want to form a new political party, I must account for the foibles, passions, and canniness of my fellow citizens. The party takes shape despite the people I have to work with, who forget to call back on the telephone, secretly plot to betray the new party, or fear the ramifications of joining. Leadership despite constraints is far less liberating than leadership entered into in order to remove or ameliorate constraints.

In either case, leadership has to do with changing the world and fulfilling individual purposes.

By saying this, we arrive at a critical moment. Leadership studies could breed arrogance as graduates set out to change the world and fit it to their wishes. They learn techniques for getting their way and imposing their will on the world and the people around them. There is, in my opinion, a great audacity to leadership. People are rightly ambivalent about their leaders and leadership in general (Simmel, 1908/1950, p. 193). It is presumptuous to want to lead others. But that audacity expresses only half of the message. The other half tempers leadership, and we have seen it in a number of different disguises throughout this book.

We considered in this book the extent to which morality serves as a constraint on leadership. We took a giant step back to contemplate the vast, intricate webs of influence within which any leadership takes place. Nobody absolutely determines anything. There is always some countervailing pressure, some intractable sector of the public, some higher authority. Leadership is an overcoming of resistance, a struggle to bring into being, a vocation to suffer. Even in the methods proposed by this book, we spoke up in favor of humility, openness, and fallibilism. And there is something to be said for teaching leadership as an inoculation *against* tyrannical leadership: the more that followers understand leadership, the greater their resistance to its abuses—or, the greater their chances of making conscious what had often been happening to them unconsciously. Besides, more leaders, widely distributed throughout a community, soften the harsh and wild tendencies of any one person arrogant enough to presume (Coser, 1971, p. 186). In other words, leadership studies can be characterized not as feeding audacity but keeping it in check.

Leadership could foster arrogance. It certainly has in the past. There is something to be said for confidence, if not boldness, as an expression of freedom, inasmuch as we are free beings with considerable latitude to live our lives. There is also something to be said, however, for wisdom about its enjoyment.

That is why, in the chapter on spirituality, we began to take a hard look at the purposes of leadership. What does it ultimately serve? For leadership always serves something, some beneficiary or ideal, whether it is the leader's own vanity, the follower's security, an organization's perpetuation, or some other objective above and beyond the relationship itself. Leadership is, in the words of James MacGregor Burns, basically about "achieving purpose" (1978, p. 18). That purpose, or *telos*, also serves as a constraint on the audacity of leadership—even on the worst kind of selfish tyranny, because that means there is something the leader is supposed to achieve, something that defines him and gives his leadership one shape and not another.

We all serve gods, of a sort. Leadership is one way that we do this.

Even at the moment of purest liberation, when we break out of the past and break out of tradition or taboos, we show ourselves beholden and in thrall. In this sense, leadership exemplifies the human condition and warrants study as one of the more vivid and problematic forms of that condition, capable of serving the highest that is in us while at the same time holding us back, whether in brutality or the quietude of alienation. We find ourselves within an inescapable tension. It is a deep forest.

Kenneth Thompson suggests that we should study leadership only if we think rigorously about three issues, because if we fail to do so, our efforts will have been wasted. First, there is ambivalence about leaders and leadership itself, rooted in our ambivalence about the use of power. (We were just talking about that.) Second, there is widespread uncertainty about the nature of leadership itself, especially given its inherently tensional character. Third, there is only a dim perception what the future requires of its leaders, because it seems necessary to draw from the "wisdom of the past," as he puts it, while also opening up to innovation, novelty, the likes of which we cannot now predict (1984, pp. 131–133).

This book represents my best effort at a contribution to these rigors, especially to the second issue, the prevailing uncertainty about the nature of leadership itself. I have decided that the ambivalence, uncertainty, and "dim perception of the future" that Thompson worries about are inherent, part of the constitution of our study, never to be resolved—at least not without distorting reality. That is my tentative position.

As I said, the forest is deep.

In conclusion, I want to thank you for letting me be your guide on this tour. It is my wish that you come to *inhabit* this forest and find it home.

NOTES

PREFACE

1. Voegelin, CW 11, p. 137 ("An analysis should start from the meaning of words accepted at the time by the general public").

2. Bernard Bass (1990) makes a suggestion that is similar. "The search for the one and only proper and true definition of leadership seems to be fruitless, since the appropriate choice of definition should depend on the methodological and substantive aspects of leadership in which one is interested" (p. 18). He concurs that we probably need to delimit the object of our studies as we set out on our journey, but that there may not be one such thing as leadership. For him, the word, standing alone, is arguably too big. Thus, leadership studies would consist of multiple sub-definitions.

CHAPTER 1

1. Bergson explains "analysis ad infinitum" in *The creative mind,* chap. 6 (reprinted in Barrett & Aiken, 1962, pp. 303–331).

2. Similar boundary crossings will be required, in two respects. First, as stated earlier, programs in leadership education in contemporary colleges and universities exist within different schools and departments, such as education, business, political science, military science (and ROTC), and even technology. Leadership studies has no common academic home. This fact alone prevents cooperation. Second, leaders exist in different realms of life. There are business leaders, military leaders, political leaders, etc., and each realm has its distinctive qualities or attributes that make comparisons from realm to realm awkward. Lessons from one realm do not always translate to another. For these reasons, true interdisciplinarity is difficult, because it requires boundary crossings without ignoring the boundaries. Don Levine wrote that any "healing response needs to be one that connects different parts of the community while fully respecting what

appear to be irreducible differences" (1995, p. 297; see pp. 290–294). This book accepts that challenge.

3. The word "science" will be used here in the narrower sense popularized by Samuel Coleridge (Fontrodona, 2002, pp. 129f) and characterized by what has come to be known as the scientific method. To clarify, this entire book is a work of science in the broader, Aristotelian sense.

4. Some writers on leadership are starting to deride science and the scientific approach generally. Katherine Tyler Scott, publishing a paper she presented in 2000, asserts that the latest paradigm in leadership "is the seeming antithesis of the Scientific paradigm" (pp. 45–54, quoting at p. 45).

5. William James issued an apt warning, however, against letting the science distort our understanding of reality. Yes, of course, science detects trends, patterns, order in nature, but it also runs the risk of replacing genuine observation with laws and concepts, as though these were the reality. He argues, for instance, against the "misuse of concepts . . . using them not merely to assign properties to things, but to deny the very properties with which the things sensibly present themselves" (1909/1996, pp. 218f). He added, "It is but the old story, of a useful practice first becoming a method, then a habit, and finally a tyranny that defeats the end it was used for" (ibid., p. 219). "The essence of life [after all] is its continuously changing character; but our concepts are all discontinuous and fixed" (ibid., p. 253). For a more complete discussion, see the following chapter.

6. The best compendium of the scientific study of leadership is *Bass & Stogdill's handbook of leadership* (3rd edition) (1990). On a regular basis, scholarly journals such as the *Leadership Quarterly* and the *Administrative Science Quarterly* extend this work.

7. Two of the most respected advocates of this "hermeneutic" view are Hans-Georg Gadamer and Jacques Derrida (Skinner, 1985, chaps. 2 & 3).

8. One journal presently dedicated to this approach is *Philosophy of Management.*

The point about logic and theorizing goes to Eric Voegelin's observation that there are two arguments over theory, as we shall discuss in a later chapter: i.e., the intrasystematic consistency of the theory and its correspondence to lived human experience. History and science emphasize the correspondence of theory to experience, in the hope of verifying what we can know; this third umbrella on logic and theorizing emphasizes intrasystematic consistency, the validity of that which we tend to think and believe. The fourth part on the imagination we will have to examine in some detail, and it can be said to lie back of the other three.

9. Karl Marx, for one, resisted the possibility. "Philosophy must seriously protest when it is confused with imagination." The book at my disposal where this quotation appears (Mazlish, 1984a) eventually comes to the conclusion that this is precisely what Marx did: he confused philosophy with imagination.

10. Toward the end of his enormous handbook, Bernard Bass emphasizes "that no one approach is fully adequate, by itself, to understand the leadership process. . . . [W]e require the use of multiple methods" (1990, p. 897). For this reason, James MacGregor Burns refers to leadership as a master discipline subsuming other disciplines. He says, "You can't do leadership, you can't study leadership, unless you think politically, philosophically, and psychologically. Leadership borrows extensively from the other fields, but it also contributes a lot to these other fields" (2003, p. 5).

CHAPTER 2

1. Bernard Bass made a similar assertion, writing "that the possibilities are far from exhausted. Leadership presents a lively, challenging field for research and innovative applications" (1990, p. 913).

2. For a reader on pragmatism, see Menand (1997). In it, Menand identified a number of recent works about pragmatism by such luminaries as Hilary Putnam, Richard Bernstein, and Richard Posner.

3. A recent article in the *Leadership Quarterly* titled "The Leadership of Pragmatism" by M. Mumford and J. v. Doorn does nothing of the kind and bears no relationship to pragmatism (2001). Two books that do apply pragmatism to management generally are Nahser, 1997, and Fontrodona, 2002. In addition, there is a useful article by S. Rosenthal and R. Buchholz titled "Leadership: Toward new philosophical foundations" in the *Business and Professional Ethics Journal* (1996). The authors conclude that "the framework of American pragmatism [is] well suited to provide the powerful new philosophical position which [James MacGregor] Burns sees as necessary for developing what he calls a 'school of leadership'" (ibid., p. 38).

4. The word "concept" is being chosen here in preference to similar words, such as "idea" or, as we shall examine later, the German *Denkbild*. (See Barzun, 1983, p. 57.)

5. Small wonder that in 1993 Joseph Rost found literally hundreds of definitions for the term "leadership" dating back centuries.

6. Peirce wrote about a pursuit of "the truth we do not yet know" (Nahser, 1997, p. 60). For that pursuit, we must remain open, curious, and humble. The signs and symbols presented to us require interpretation, so we should

remember "there might be some *other* meaning the sign could have" (Nahser, 1997, p. 67; emphasis supplied).

7. Whitehead was to give this tendency a different name, a name that has become more famous: the Fallacy of Misplaced Concreteness.

8. Later, we shall have reason to refer to this as the patent world. Incidentally, James found even more vivid language to describe this pluralistic universe when he wrote: "It is a turbid, muddled, gothic sort of affair without a sweeping outline and with little pictorial nobility" (quoted in Menand, 1997, p. 389). Freud had reason once to call it "primeval pulp" (Mazlish, 1990, p. 49).

9. Simmel observes that one response to the experience of fragmentation is mysticism, a faith in a unity that cannot be experienced in any other way, a fusion on a spiritual level, "for there is no other way of channeling the unbearable multiplicity and unfamiliarity of all things into one, except through our soul" (1904/1997, p. 36). In this, Simmel resembles the ancient Greek philosopher Heraclitus.

10. Please note: *participants* in leadership engage in interpretation, which is one reason for *students* of leadership to understand the process of interpretation, but it is also true that students of leadership engage in interpretation themselves, so interpretation takes place at two levels. Leadership studies can be thought of as a process of interpreting interpretations. The formal study of these processes goes by the name of hermeneutics, as we mentioned earlier.

11. For a comparable remark, see Hilary Putnam, in Menand, 1997, p. 361.

12. Using lightning and thunder to illustrate antecedents and consequences is misleading, however, since we know that in human affairs X might cause Y today and Z tomorrow. So far as we can tell, the patterns of causation between people are not so fixed. Followers might have responded to one leadership tactic with enthusiasm at first. Later, the enthusiasm wanes. A leader can go to the well once too often. This is part of the reason patterns in leadership are so hard to pick up and why they turn out to be unreliable in actual practice.

13. Richard Bernstein denies that pragmatism is a method. His explanation appears in Menand, 1997, p. 383. We will proceed as though it were a method.

14. Menand, 1997, p. xxiv ("Peirce regarded truth as a matter of community consensus"). Bernstein agrees with Peirce when he identifies as one of pragmatism's five substantive themes "the need to nurture a critical community of inquirers" (quoted in Menand, 1997, p. 387).

15. By the same token, pragmatism encourages action as the bottom line and not endless navel-gazing, for "its admonition to act on beliefs with-

out waiting for philosophical confirmation of their validity . . . is the essence of pragmatism" (Menand, 1997, p. xix). Elsewhere, Menand informs us that all pragmatists believe "in the virtue of experimentation" (ibid., p. xxxix).

CHAPTER 3

1. In echoes of Ecclesiastes, Montaigne once complained, "There is more ado to interpret interpretations than to interpret things; and more books upon books than upon any other subject; we do nothing but comment upon one another. Every place swarms with commentaries" (quoted in Ormiston & Schrift, 1990, p. 1).

2. The astute reader might notice in the following pages a version of phenomenology (or, more precisely, phenomenological philosophy), which is a tradition in twentieth-century philosophy, although this chapter is by no means a definitive example. That was never the intention. By inserting such a big word as "phenomenology" into this book, I am really only pointing toward it, inasmuch as phenomenology means too much or too many different things to expect more than will have been suggested in these pages. That notwithstanding, phenomenology has been identified by Bernard Bass as one of the "most prominent" new methods for studying leadership (1990, p. 892).

3. That theory does not have to be explicit in order to be operational (Bass, 1990, pp. 375–379).

4. Jongbloed and Frost offer a near facsimile to leadership when they speculate that leaders accomplish very little in the world: all they do is influence how others perceive what does happen. In other words, leaders interpret events and enable others to interpret events, without producing substantive outcomes. They alter perceptions to change the meaning of things, which to Jongbloed and Frost is no small feat, but in their opinion leaders rarely if ever get anything done (1985, p. 100).

5. The words "symbol" and "sign" are closely related. In this work, we shall hope to avoid misunderstanding by trying not to use the word "sign." (See Peirce, 1997, p. 170.)

6. As a technical matter, Bergson insists there are at least two ways to experience the world that are most definitely not "concurring and mutually determining," namely intuition and analysis, since "from intuition one can pass on to analysis, but not from analysis to intuition" (Barrett & Aiken, 1962, p. 317).

7. In its way, this book echoes Don Levine, who concludes his masterwork on sociological theory by calling for a dialogical approach (1995, chap. 16).

8. This problem with ordinary usage we will have to take more seriously later, under the rubric of perspectivism.

9. Voegelin held that what scientists and theoreticians do is different *in kind* from what people do in ordinary usage. We are to have a different purpose and different standards (1952, p. 53). We are not simply improving on their work. Even then, he insisted that we work from the same class of experiences and take seriously the language people use about those experiences (ibid., p. 64).

10. Habermas had this to say: "Ordinary languages are incomplete and provide no guarantee for the absence of ambiguity" (quoted in Ormiston & Schrift, 1990, p. 219). Communication is consequently ruptured, broken, yet somehow we seem to muddle through. How is that? We have to interpret ordinary language, to bridge over those ruptures by means of something referred to as understanding. Understanding makes consensus possible—though obviously we do not always succeed. The remedy to ambiguous language and misunderstanding was thought to be a more precise language, such as mathematics and its cousin symbolic logic, but that will never suffice. We also have to rely on powers of interpretation.

The imagery of the bridge allows us to make one further observation. In order for pedestrians to cross over a bridge, they don't need to understand why it stays up. Most people simply want bridges to stay up, although the engineers had better know. In a corny sense, leadership studies is the engineering of bridges. Leadership studies would be equivalent, in this sense, to engineering studies, as a specialized activity for ordinary use.

11. Elsewhere, Ortega went much further. In *Meditations on Quixote*, he wrote about "the barbarous, brutal, mute, meaningless reality of things. It is sad that it should reveal itself to us thus, but what can we do about it! It is real, it is there: it is terribly self-sufficient. Its force and its single meaning are rooted in its sheer presence. Culture is memories and promises, an irreversible past, a dreamed future. But reality is a simple and frightening 'being there.' It is a presence, a deposit, an inertia. It is materiality" (1914/1961, p. 145).

12. Part of Voegelin's concern in writing about second realities was his opposition to something known as scientism, which he regarded as a distortion of the scientific spirit.

CHAPTER 4

1. Straddling the categories is a book titled *The Leadership Secrets of Santa Claus*, published in 2003 by WALK the TALK Company.

2. We might name this mischievously Newton's First Law of Leadership: every person in a state of uniform leadership tends to remain in that state of leadership unless an external force is applied.

3. And it is a troubling possibility that coercion falls within this type, since the leader might establish domination on superior strength and powers of intimidation. Historically, people fear defying divine authority. Nobody wants to cross God's anointed, though obviously it happens. Coercion can fascinate as well as terrify.

4. The author appreciates the critical help of David Frantz and J. Mark Thomas on this section.

5. Interestingly, Simmel explained at one point that the intellect carries forward the past in its memory as two things: "objectification in concepts and pictures" (1971, p. 360). "Concepts and pictures" are much the same thing as thought images and primal images.

6. Cassirer used different words to make a similar and stronger assertion about what he calls the localist theory of cases: "[T]he whole development of language as of thought in general must proceed from the intuitive, from the 'concrete and vital' to the conceptual" (1921/1953, p. 208).

7. For a concise explanation of external realism, which this kind of argument presupposes, see Searle, 1998, chap. 1.

8. Chauncey Wright, one of the precursors of pragmatism, mentioned these arguments in 1877 (White, 1972, p. 123, citing *Philosophical Discussions; cf.* Barzun, 1983, p. 76). Simmel explained the significance of these two arguments in his essay "The Conflict in Modern Culture" (1918/1971, p. 387). Life comes into the world as forms and then struggles to transcend its forms. Forms persist according to their degree of perfection. Life persists according to its irresistible flux. *Denkbilder* succeed to the extent that they approach perfection as part of a formal structure of thought, as part of a coherent theory, but they also have to remain true to the hard, cold, shifting facts of reality. An imperfect form does not deserve to persist, and an irrelevant form has no purpose. To difficulties of "contradiction" and "discrepancy of fact," William James added a third: unsatisfied desire, which Voegelin does not mention here (White, 1972, p. 206).

9. What Voegelin is describing in this quotation is precisely the basis for the rest of this book, because existing symbolizations about leadership clash and have become wildly confused, forcing everyone back to the primal images we have about leadership, and to do that rigorously in a time of transition we sacrifice some of the intrasystematic consistency that has built up over time in leadership studies.

10. A more thorough application of Voegelin's entire work exceeds the scope of this book. Nonetheless, it might help to keep in mind that the imagination operates *between* the reality we experience as impressions and the symbols that we employ, like a porous membrane between two substances

(OH-5, pp. 37–38)—and when a symbol such as leadership becomes problematic, we are advised to return to the primal images. If we do not, we might forget ourselves and start to believe that our symbols *are* reality: this error leads directly, in his opinion, to deformations and spiritual disease. Again, this is Whitehead's fallacy of misplaced concreteness.

11. Elsewhere, Voegelin wrote: "Differentiation of a segment does not abolish the truth of reality experienced compactly; there is no simple succession in which historically later truth makes an earlier one obsolete" (CW 28, pp. 180f).

12. Voegelin described the same process as it pertains to differentiation. Just as exemplary individuals emerge to alter our image of what it means to be human, so also exemplary individuals notice or detect differentiations. He wrote:

> These advances in differentiation do not occur in the sense that suddenly, through a kind of biological mutation all over the world, all men pass on from a more compact to a more differentiated insight into their order. Rather, these insights occur in determinate men, who, again, are in determinate societies, and very often they do not immediately penetrate beyond the bounds of the given society. Very often they are ineffective even within the bounds of this society, for the one who is immediately understanding is always only one individual human being, and whether he is a prophet or a philosopher makes no difference." (CW 31, pp. 205ff)

13. I begin this book with the simplest dyad of one leader and one follower. At this stage of the argument, some experts protest that, empirically, leadership emerges out of *groups* or that leadership is a response to *group* dynamics (e.g., Hughes et al., 1996, p. 6, citing Roach & Behling, 1984). They might object to my reliance on dyads as misleading, since we usually think of leaders as leaders of *groups,* empowered and hedged in by *groups.* For them, the fundamental unit of study is the *group* and not the one-on-one relationship. But the phenomenon can be studied at different magnitudes, all the way from simple dyads to vast international conflict (Karmel, 1977, p. 477). I simply prefer to begin at this magnitude, for reasons other scholars can recite (e.g., Northouse, 1997, p. 110; Alford, 1994). Put simply, the follower's situation—including the involvement of a group—certainly affects leadership and might even constitute the set of forces giving rise to leadership in the first place. This does not mean that the study of leadership must begin with a study of groups. In fact, I find beginning from groups less analytically useful (contra Northouse, 1997; Born, 1996, pp. 65f). We began our ascent at the valley floor at the simplest level. Group dynamics add a layer of complexity that leadership studies would eventually have to incorporate.

On this controversy, Rost stakes out his peculiar position by insisting that leadership can exist at any magnitude *but* the dyad. For him, as we have just seen, leadership becomes possible only among three or more persons (1993, pp. 55, 105, 110).

14. *Leadership without easy answers* (1994) by Ronald Heifetz demonstrates this kind of work.

15. Drath has reported he was unfamiliar with Voegelin's work at the time (personal communication).

CHAPTER 5

1. Painful to consider, therefore, is the observation by Peirce "that to be deep one must be dull" (1997, p. 110).

CHAPTER 6

1. Wren and Swatez provide a useful schema along these lines in Wren, 1995, chap. 36.

2. Racial profiling became a controversy for law enforcement on just these grounds. If the practice had no utility whatsoever, it would have fallen into disuse on its own.

3. The Czech intellectual Jan Patočka made a similar observation in his lectures on European philosophy. He credited the ancient Greek Democritus with making an important first step in this direction. Reality presents itself partially, in a "misshapen, distorted way. . . . [E]verything [he said] has to be apparent, [i.e.] separated from reality. . . . For this reason the philosopher tries to somehow remedy this misshapenness and this distortion" (2002, p. 76).

4. A similar approach appeared in Bolman and Deal (reprinted in Wren, 1995, chap. 50).

5. For a brief explanation of the work bond as the simplest, most basic relationship in organizations, see Hummel, 1994, pp. 125–128.

6. It is possible that the motivations that led to the formation of leadership could have led to the formation of a love affair, for example, or a rivalry. This is why it becomes difficult to distinguish forms that seem so similar. Part of leadership studies would be the process of differentiating leadership from education, seduction, marketing, conquest, and so on. And in doing so, we must remind ourselves to distinguish the forms themselves and not confuse them with the contents that led to their formation.

7. Similar problems arise when analysis stands accused of fragmenting and (in the words of Barzun) "distorting" reality (2000, p. 214). Analysis breaks apart

conceptually what couldn't exist apart in fact. Writers on leadership have been right to express their reservations (e.g., Wheatley, 1992). Analysis is a distortion, however, only to the extent one neglects the companion obligation of synthesis or pretends away the compact experience being analyzed, as though it never happened as such, for that would be reductionism. In both abstraction and analysis, we possess tools of great power, so long as we appreciate their limitations and don't become like the man with a hammer for whom everything is a nail. Today, there is a tendency to resist tools or instruments because in one way or another they have been abused in the past or relied on to the exclusion of all others. An IQ test is one mistrusted tool. Corporal punishment would be another. Out of a healthy fear of abuse, some people go to the extreme and call for its abolition, when a more balanced approach might be best.

CHAPTER 7

1. In 1984, Chemers referred specifically to Hollander (1970) and Graen et al. (1975; 1977) on issues of leader/follower exchanges (Wren, 1995, pp. 92ff)—not to mention Burns (1978) and what he labeled transactional leadership. For a simplified overview of Simmel's principles of social exchange, see Turner et al., 1998, pp. 224f.

Please note that participants are not necessarily conscious of what they are doing exactly or why. They operate according to infraconscious and supraconscious drives or motives, emotions and appetites, as well as conscious designs as rational maximizers. There is no reason to assume full consciousness or rationality.

2. For purposes of clarification, convergence alone does not create leadership. It is probably more often the case that these two conditions converge and nothing at all happens. They are necessary, but not sufficient, conditions.

3. On this point, passivity should not be used interchangeably with apathy, as we shall see.

4. Haugaard (1997) has questioned ascribing leadership to some "hidden force which lies behind reality." He wrote that Marx and Nietzsche do much the same thing, as though human behavior were simply the fulfillment of a prescribed plan or direction, the evidence of something else we cannot perceive directly. He thinks that this approach "implies a derogation of the autonomy of the individual, and the possibility of historical contingency" (p. 3).

When Heidegger delves into Aristotle's understanding of a thing's potential or capacity to take some particular action, he insists, "The potential is . . . what is not yet present. A capability can be called present . . . only if it is engaged in its enactment. Only the builder who is building has capability" (Heidegger, 1981/1995, p. 146). Until that time, what can we say with any certainty? What evidence do we have? Power reveals itself in force.

This does not preclude us from talking intelligibly about potential or capability, inasmuch as we have to start discerning as a matter of science what potentialities must be present in order for an event to take place. A fire needs oxygen. We want to be able to say this with confidence, so we can start making predictions that without X there can be no Y. Haugaard is simply trying to prevent us from treating these "potentialities to follow" as uniform.

He is also hoping to remind us that a potentiality can be offset by the presence of another condition, such that X will contribute to Y *unless* there is a Z. To borrow an example, a pauper might be induced to prostitute herself. (How many wealthy women do?) A pauper might be so induced *unless*, for example, she possesses certain countervailing values that make such a lifestyle repugnant to her. Haugaard would object if we were to opine as social scientists simply that poor women are potential prostitutes, although in a sense they are. I would have discovered the planet Neptune if I had lived at the time it was first discovered and if I were trained in astronomical observation and if I had sufficient equipment and if I were truly interested, etc. I had the potential, you see, if only. . . .

5. Any resemblance to the experience of doubt articulated by Peirce previously is intentional.

6. Oakeshott tends to be claimed by the political right. Interestingly, Gemmill and Oakley on the political left agree with the diagnosis that followers project their anxieties onto the leader, which enables them to regress into a "psychic prison" (1992, p. 114). Problems in life are then blamed on defective or nonexistent leadership (p. 118), while followers get "to return to the symbiotic environment of the womb" (p. 126). Gemmill and Oakley extend the critique, however, to accuse leadership studies of "offering ideological support for the existing social order" (p. 115). The existing social order Gemmill and Oakley refer to elsewhere as "the pathological status quo" (p. 124). By studying and teaching leadership, we encourage this process and legitimate these psychic prisons. For this, we deserve to be called the "leadership mafia" (p. 119).

7. It can be said with some asperity there are two kinds of leaders: those who believe the world should be different and those who believe their place in the world should be different.

8. An important qualification: There is one ordinary use of the term "leadership" we will be tempted to reject, since we are not required to validate every first-degree construct. When people follow someone who is oblivious to them, such as a role model who is unaware that anyone is paying attention to what he or she is doing, we frequently want to say that the role

model is "leading" followers. We might want to call it inadvertent or unintentional leadership. Technically, this is not leadership at all. It is something else. There is no question that it happens, of course, as followers emulate, mimic, fall in line behind, and otherwise respond to the example being set, but there is no mutual orientation between them, so there is no relationship, and there is no direction being set by a leader as a result of the role model's intentions. You cannot say whether the follower is doing what the role model wants done. The role model *influences* others, but we are inclined to conclude that he or she is not *leading* them. Even if we were to yield as a matter of definition, we would still want to reject it for purposes of leadership education, since this is not what interests us in the field of leadership studies. A leader can lead by example, which French and Raven refer to as Referent Power, but in those cases the leader *would* be oriented to the follower and intend that the follower follow the example being set. All that being said, there is reason to include these experiences in our studies, at the margins, as will become evident in a subsequent chapter when we broach the subject of phantom leadership, i.e., leadership in which the follower imagines there to be a leader when in fact there is none. For the time being, there is no reason to see it as any kind of refutation of my argument that such things do happen.

9. See Solomon, in Ciulla, 1998, p. 93.

This would seem to be the place to consider a certain combination of elements that we shall try to keep apart. It is not at all uncommon for the follower to blend or interweave her image of the leader (on the one hand) with the vision that leader inspires (on the other). They often go together. The follower associates the leader with the task.

To be sure, most leadership events are relatively simple and uncomplicated in this regard: a person makes a specific request and the other person responds. It would be easy to differentiate the "image" from the "vision." On some occasions, the image seems contrary or alien to the vision, and many consultants advise would-be leaders to avoid such dissonance. Even so, image and vision do often combine in the minds of the followers. John Kennedy is often associated with the race to land on the moon, Henry Ford with the assembly line, Winston Churchill with Britain's dogged resistance to the Nazis, and so forth. Finally, as we have already mentioned, sometimes *the image is the extent of the vision,* which constitutes a recipe for style without substance, celebrity without basis, or as the Texan says, "The fellow is all hat and no cattle." The image of the leader is the vision.

Nonetheless, the sociological form requires that the leader bear some idea of the direction the follower should take.

CHAPTER 8

1. The concept of "power over" has been extensively treated in Wartenberg (1990).

2. This tendency is behind the counter-tactic of leaders who adopt open door policies and manage by walking around, to close distances and demystify the leader's space.

3. For Simmel, writing just after the turn of the century, "All social forms are defined to some extent in terms of the dimension of interpersonal distance" (Levine, 1971, p. xxxv; see, e.g., Simmel, 1971, chap. 10). Bernard Bass dug up this apt quotation from the *Odyssey:* "The leader, mingling with the vulgar host,/ is in the common mass of matter lost" (1990, p. 3, citing book 3, line 297).

4. Mazlish spoke to this dimension ten years later in his study of the revolutionary ascetic, where he observes that a certain type of leader tends to lead the movement without intimacy and in fact is likelier to succeed *without* it— an observation made in another context by F. G. Bailey, who distinguishes the mass followers (at a distance) from the daily staff (intimate) (1988, p. 6).

5. See, e.g., Simmel, 1971, p. 343; Bass, 1990, pp. 694–703, 899. This dimension becomes relevant in Pareto's famous hypothesis about the circulation of elites, about which more later.

6. Regarding societal culture, see Bass, 1990, chap. 34; regarding organizational culture, see Bass, 1990, pp. 586–594.

7. For a thorough treatment of different academic approaches to understanding power, see the 1986 book titled, suitably enough, *Power,* edited by Steven Lukes. See also Hillman, 1995.

8. Heidegger, 1995, p. 60; see Aron, 1986.

9. One of the best places to begin would be the compilation by Joanne Ciulla titled *Ethics: The Heart of Leadership* (1998).

10. The terms "moral" and "ethical" are not technically identical in meaning, but they both reflect an interest in the Good, which is our starting point.

11. Taking this one step further, Machiavelli will be cited for the proposition that the ends justify the means, which largely nullifies the use of morality as a standard at all. If anything, for Machiavelli the leader must occasionally be immoral.

12. Kirkpatrick and Locke (among others) completely overlook this distinction (1995, pp. 138f.).

CHAPTER 9

1. If the two sentiments that go with the two trends make us all sound like brats, well, I am not sure MacIntyre would reject the implication.

2. Voegelin is by no means the only theorist to take the following approach. One could also cite Jan Patočka, for example, and Isaiah Berlin.

CHAPTER 10

1. See Harter, 2003.

2. Max Weber gives the typical example of hierarchy in the bureaucratic structure (1922/1958, chap. 8; see Simmel, 1908/1950, part 3).

3. Heidegger's exposition of this issue is especially revealing (1981/1995).

4. Different writers use different terms, such as circle, class, and status group (Mills, 1956, pp. 365f, n. 4).

5. Different writers use different terms for these strata, such as the patricians and plebeians, or the bourgeoisie and the proletariat, and these terms are not always interchangeable with the terms "elite" and "masses."

6. Michels once went further, however, to conclude as a matter of sociological law that "men, in every enterprise requiring collective action, must submit their particular movements to the rule of the single will of a leader" (Michels, 1927/1949, p. 151; see Machiavelli, *Discourses* I:9). If anything, he notes, democracy lends itself to the consolidation of power, not so much in a class or cabal, but rather in a single person, il Duce or der Führer.

CHAPTER 12

1. These schemas can be thought of as configurations (Marías, 1961, p. 178, n. 14).

2. I appreciate the critical help of Mark Dean on this section.

3. Peirce referred to these schemas or conceptualizations as hypotheses, if you recall.

4. The article on which this section is based was co-authored by Nathan Harter and Associate Professor Julie Phillips of Purdue University, whose partnership and kind permission are hereby gratefully acknowledged. For a more complete statement, see our entry on systems theory in *The Encyclopedia of Leadership* (2004).

CHAPTER 13

1. For a useful treatment of the many meanings of the word "reason," see Levine, 1985, especially chaps. 7, 9, and the appendix.

2. James held much the same viewpoint (see Barzun, 1983, p. 131.).

3. This is why, for instance, Peirce insisted that we also require instinct and sentiment (Fontrodona, 2002, p. 93).

4. E.g., Voegelin OH-3; p. 231; see generally Voegelin, CW 12, chap. 10.

5. See also Hughes, 1958, p. 16 ("Man as an actor in society . . . was seldom decisively influenced by logical considerations: supra- or infra-rational values of one sort or another usually guided his conduct").

6. No one can ignore the material factors of leadership. In reference to Napoleon III, Bass has quoted Emile Zola: "A grain of sand in a man's flesh and empires totter and fall" (1990, p. 155). Bass then considered the effects of ill-health on leaders at the onset of World War I, plus specific crises in the American presidency attributable to physiological conditions. Later, he foresaw the importance to leadership studies of breakthrough findings in genetics (1990, p. 911).

7. Ortega once wrote the following: "The sole false perspective is that which claims to be the only one there is" (1923/1961, p. 92).

8. For a brief digression on the meaning of the word "spirit" and its European cognates, see Barzun, 2000, pp. 220–224.

9. I have been anticipated by George Panichas, whose article comparing the two first appeared in *Modern age* in the summer of 1996 (Panichas, chap. 5).

10. It would be logical to credit the leader with having the greater influence on determining both identity and vocation for both parties. In a sense, the leader helps the follower to answer who *he* is and what *he* is meant to be doing.

11. This is the central defect in Marxism, as well as in other ideological disasters.

CHAPTER 14

1. Mazlish, 1990, p. 255 ("Almost always, leadership will be defined in opposition to that of prior leadership").

2. Ortega delivered a fascinating account of just such an elite in an essay titled "Concord and Liberty" (1940/1946). The economist Ludwig von Mises illustrated how free market capitalism achieves a remarkable fluidity of talent (1944/1983, p. 15). See also Simmel, 1908/1950, pp. 279f.

3. Karl Jaspers identified this as one of three characteristics of the leap that humanity made into history itself (1949/1953, p. 46). It can even be said that history and humanity emerged together, with "a continual thrusting forward on the part of *single individuals*. They call the rest to follow them" (ibid., p. 47).

REFERENCES

Alford, C.F. (1994). *Group psychology and political theory*. New Haven: Yale University Press.

Aristotle. (1952). *The works of Aristotle* (vol. 1). Chicago: Encyclopedia Britannica. Reprinted for *Great books of the Western world* from W.D. Ross (Ed.). *The works of Aristotle*, by arrangement with Oxford University Press.

Aron, R. (1986). "Macht, power, puissance." In S. Lukes (Ed.). *Power* (chap. 13) (W.D. Halls, Trans.). Oxford: Basil Blackwell. (Original work published 1964.)

Babbitt, I. (1979). *Democracy and leadership*. Indianapolis: Liberty Fund. (Original work published 1924.)

Bailey, F.G. (1988). *Humbuggery and manipulation*. Ithaca: Cornell University Press.

Bardwick, J. "Peacetime management and wartime leadership." In F. Hesselbein, M. Goldsmith, & R. Blanchard (Eds.). (1996). *The leader of the future* (pp. 131–139). San Francisco: JosseyBass.

Barker, R. (2001). "The nature of leadership." *Human Relations* 54:4:469–494.

Baron, R., & J. Greenberg. (1986). *Behavior in organizations* (3rd ed.). Boston: Allyn and Bacon.

Barrett, W., & H. Aiken (Eds.). (1962). *Philosophy in the twentieth century* (vol. 3). New York: Random House.

Barzun, J. (2000). *From dawn to decadence*. New York: Harper Collins.

Barzun, J. (1983). *A stroll with William James*. Chicago: University of Chicago Press.

Bass, B. (1990). *Bass & Stogdill's handbook of leadership* (3rd ed.). New York: Free Press.

Bausch, K. (2001). *The emerging consensus in social systems theory*. New York: Kluwer Academic/Plenum.

Bellamy, R. (1987). *Modern Italian social theory*. Stanford: Stanford University Press.

Bennis, W., & B. Nanus. (1985). *Leaders*. New York: Harper & Row.

Bentley, E. (1957). *A century of hero-worship* (2nd ed.). Boston: Beacon Press. (Original work published 1944.)

Berger, P., & T. Luckmann. (1966). *The social construction of reality*. New York: Doubleday.

Bergstrom, A. (2003, Winter). "An interview with Dr. Bernard Bass." *Leadership Review*. Retrieved on 1-22-03 from http://www.leadershipreview.org/2003winter/article3_winter_2003.asp.

Berlin, I. "The purpose of philosophy." In H. Hardy (Ed.) (2000). *The power of ideas*. Princeton: Princeton University Press. (Original work published 1962.)

Bernstein, R. (1992, Winter). "The resurgence of pragmatism." *Social Research* 59:4:813–840.

Blake, R., & J. Mouton. (1964). *The managerial grid.* Houston: Gulf Publishing.

Block, P. (1993). *Stewardship.* San Francisco: Berrett-Koehler.

Bobbio, N. (1995). *Ideological profiles of twentieth century Italy* (L. Cochrane, Trans.). Princeton: Princeton University Press. (Original work published 1969.)

Bobbio, N. (1996). *Left and right* (A. Cameron, Trans.). Chicago: University of Chicago Press. (Original work published 1994.)

Born, D. "Leadership studies." In P. Temes (Ed.). (1996) *Teaching leadership* (pp. 45–72). New York: Peter Lang.

Boulding, K. (1956). *The image.* Ann Arbor: University of Michigan Press.

Bowling, C. (2001). [Review of the book *The spirit of leadership*]. *The Leadership Quarterly* 12:369–371.

Buber, M. (1952). *Eclipse of God.* Evanston, IL: Harper Torchbooks.

Burnham, J. (1987). *The Machiavellians.* Washington, D.C.: Gateway Editions. (Original work published 1943.)

Burns, J.M. (2003, Fall). "We're operating on a frontier." *Compass: A Journal of Leadership* 1:1:5–8.

Burns, J.M. (1978). *Leadership.* New York: Harper Torchbooks.

Calder, B. (1977) "An attribution theory of leadership." In B. Staw & G. Salancik (Eds.). *New directions in organizational behavior* (pp. 179–204). Chicago: St. Clair Press.

Campbell, J. "The cutting edge of leadership." In J. Hunt & L. Larson (Eds.). (1977) *Leadership: The cutting edge* (pp. 221–235). Carbondale, IL: Southern Illinois University Press.

Capra, F. (1996). *The web of life.* New York: Anchor.

Carnall, C. (1990). *Managing change in organizations* (pp. 98–101). New York: Prentice-Hall.

Carroll, L. (1862–1863/1991). *Through the looking glass.* Project Gutenberg and Duncan Research Shareware Release 1.5 of *Through the Looking-Glass.* http://www.cs.indiana.edu/metastuff/looking/lookingdir.html [accessed 5 January 2002].

Cassirer, E. (1953). *The philosophy of symbolic forms* (vol. 1) (R. Manheim, Trans.). New Haven: Yale University Press. (Original work published 1921.)

Cassirer, E. (1945). *Rousseau, Kant, Goethe* (J. Gutmann, P.O. Kristeller, & J.H. Randall, Jr., Trans.). Princeton: Princeton University Press.

Chemers, M. "Contemporary leadership theory." In J.T. Wren (Ed.). (1995) *The leader's companion* (pp. 83–99). New York: Free Press. (Original work published 1984.)

Ciulla, J. (2003, November 6–8). "Mapping leadership studies." International Leadership Association Annual Conference, Guadalajara, Mexico.

Ciulla, J. (Ed.) (1998). *Ethics.* Westport, CT: Quorum Books.

Clemens, J., & D. Mayer. (1999). *The classic touch.* Chicago: Contemporary Books.

Conger, J., & R. Kanungo. (1988). "The empowerment process: Integrating theory and practice." *Academy of Management Review* 13:3:471–482.

Conrad, J. (1910). *Heart of darkness & The secret sharer.* New York: Harper & Brothers.

Copleston, F. (1966). *A history of philosophy* (vol. 8, part 2). Garden City: Image Books.

Coser, L. (1971). *Masters of sociological thought*. Chicago: Harcourt Brace Jovanovich.

Coser, L. (1956). *The functions of social conflict*. New York: Free Press.

Dahl, R. (1986). "Power as the control of behavior." In S. Lukes (Ed.). *Power* (chap. 3). Oxford: Basil Blackwell. (Original work published 1968.)

Davis, S. (1996). *Leadership in conflict*. New York: St. Martin's Press.

de Grazia, S. (1989). *Machiavelli in hell*. Princeton: Princeton University Press.

deMott, B. (1993, December). "Choice academic pork: Inside the leadership-studies racket." *Harper's* 61–77.

de Sanctis, F. (1960). "Long live Italian unity." In D. Jensen (Ed.). *Machiavelli: Cynic, patriot, or political scientist?* (pp. 22–26). [Problems in European Civilization] Boston: D.C. Heath & Co. (Original work published 1956.)

Dobson, A. (1989). *An introduction to the politics and philosophy of José Ortega y Gasset*. New York: Cambridge University Press.

Drath, W. (2001). *The deep blue sea*. San Francisco: Jossey-Bass.

Ealy, S. (2002). "Compactness, poetic ambiguity, and the equivalences of experience." American Political Science Association Annual Meeting, Boston.

Eco, U. (1989). *Foucault's pendulum* (W. Weaver, Trans.). San Diego: Harcourt Brace Jovanovich.

Eco, U. "Towards a semiological guerrilla warfare." (1983). In *Travels in hyperreality* (pp. 135–144) (W. Weaver, Trans.). New York: Harcourt Brace Jovanovich. (Original work published 1967.)

Eliade, M. (1991). *Images and symbols* (P. Mairet, Trans.). Princeton: Princeton University Press. (Original work published 1952.)

Fontrodona, J. (2002). *Pragmatism and management inquiry*. Westport, CT: Quorum Books.

Forrester, J. (1998 December 15). Designing the future. Retrieved 1-16-03 from http://sysdyn.mit.edu/sdep/papers/Designjf.pdf.

Forrester, J. (1971, 1973). *World dynamics* (2nd ed.). Cambridge: Wright-Allen Press.

Foucault, M. "Truth and power." In P. Rabinow (Ed.). (1984) *The Foucault reader* (pp. 51–75). New York: Pantheon. (Original work published 1977.)

Franklin, J. (1996, December). "My lifelong apprenticeship." *Reader's Digest* 149:896:49–53.

French, J.R.P., & B. Raven. (1959). "The bases of social power." In D. Cartwright (Ed.). *Studies in social power* (pp. 150–167). Ann Arbor: Institute for Social Research, University of Michigan.

Freud, S. (1959). *Group psychology and the analysis of the ego* (J. Strachey, Trans.). New York: W.W. Norton & Co. (Original work published 1921.)

Friedrich, C., & C. Blitzer. (1957). *The age of power*. [The development of Western civilization (E. Fox, Series Ed.)]. Ithaca: Cornell University Press.

Frisby, D. (1992). *Simmel and Since*. New York: Routledge.

Gardner, J. (1990). *On leadership*. New York: Free Press.

Gemmill, G., & J. Oakley. (1992). "Leadership: An alienating social myth?" *Human Relations* 45:2:113–129.

Ginsberg, M. "The sociology of Pareto." In J. Meisel (Ed.). (1965). *Makers of modern social science: Pareto & Mosca* (pp. 89–107). Englewood Cliffs: Prentice Hall. (Original work published 1936.)

Gladwell, M. (2000). *The tipping point.* New York: Little, Brown & Company.

Gramsci, A. (1957, 1992). *The modern prince and other writings* (L. Marks, Trans.). New York: International Publishers.

Greenberg, J. (1996). *The quest for justice on the job.* Thousand Oaks: Sage.

Grob, L. "Leadership: The Socratic model." In B. Kellerman (Ed.). (1984). *Leadership: Multidisciplinary perspectives* (pp. 263–280). Englewood Cliffs: Prentice-Hall.

Habermas, J. (1993). *The philosophical discourse of modernity* (F. Lawrence, Trans.). Cambridge: MIT Press. (Original work published 1985.)

Habermas, J. (1991). "Georg Simmel on philosophy and culture" (M. Deflem, Trans.). *Critical Inquiry* 22:3:403–414. Adapted for www.sla.purdue.edu/people/soc/Mdeflem/zsimhab.html [Accessed 12-18-2000].

Handy, C. (1998). *The hungry spirit.* New York: Broadway Books.

Handy, C. (1994). *The age of paradox.* Boston: Harvard Business School Press.

Harter, N. "Elite theory." In J.M. Burns, G.R. Goethals, & G.J. Sorenson (Eds.). (2004). *Encyclopedia of leadership.* Sage Reference.

Harter, N. (2003, Summer). "Between great men and leadership: William James on the importance of individuals." *Journal of Leadership Education* 2:1.

Harter, N. (2003). "Multiple leaders among volunteers." *Journal of Management Systems* 15:1:51–58.

Harter, N. (2001). "Luxury, waste, excess, and squander." *Reason in Practice: The Journal of Philosophy of Management* 1:2:75–81.

Harter, N. (1998). "Defining leadership." American Political Science Association Annual Meeting, Boston.

Harter, N. (1992, October/November). "Thinking about diamonds and organizational vision." *The Journal for Quality and Participation* 15:14–16.

Harter, N., & J. Phillips. "Systems theory." In J.M. Burns, G. Goethals, G. Sorenson (Eds.). (2004). *The Encyclopedia of leadership.* Sage Reference.

Harter, N., & D. Evanecky. (2002, Summer). "Fairness in leader-member exchange theory: Do we all belong on the inside?" *Leadership Review.* http://www.leadershipreview.org/.

Harvey, J. (2001). "Reflections on books by authors who apparently are terrified about really exploring spirituality and leadership." *The Leadership Quarterly* 12:377–378.

Haugaard, M. (1997). *The constitution of power.* New York: Manchester University Press.

Hayek, F.A. (1955). *The counter-revolution of science.* New York: Free Press.

Heidegger, M. (1995). *Aristotle's metaphysics Θ 1–3* (W. Brogan & P. Warneck, Trans.). Bloomington: Indiana University Press. (Original work published 1981.)

Heidegger, M. (1977). *The question concerning technology and other essays.* St. Louis: Harper & Row. (Original work published 1954.)

Heifetz, R. (1994). *Leadership without easy answers.* Cambridge: Belknap Press.

Heilbrunn, J. "Can leadership be studied?" In P. Temes (Ed.). (1996). *Teaching leadership* (pp. 1–11). New York: Peter Lang. (Original work published in 1994.)

Heinemann, F.H. (1979). *Existentialism and the modern predicament*. Greenwood Publishing Group.

Hersey, P., & K. Blanchard. "Situational leadership." In J.T. Wren (Ed.). (1995). *The leader's companion* (pp. 207–211). New York: Free Press.

Hillman J. (1995). *Kinds of power*. New York: Currency Doubleday.

Hillman, J. (1975). *Re-visioning psychology*. New York: HarperCollins.

Hitt, W. (Ed.). (1992). *Thoughts on leadership*. Columbus, OH: Battelle Press.

Hoff Sommers, C. (1994). *Who stole feminism?* New York: Touchstone Book.

Hollander, E.P. "Leadership and power." In G. Lidzey & E. Aronson (Eds.). (1985). *The handbook of social psychology* (3rd ed.). New York: Random House.

Hughes, H. S. (1958). *Consciousness and society*. New York: Vintage Books.

Hughes, R., R. Ginnett, & G. Curphy. (1996). *Leadership* (2nd ed.). Chicago: Irwin.

Hummel, R. (1994). *The bureaucratic experience* (4th ed.). New York: St. Martin's Press.

Hummel, R. (1993). "A call for a philosophy of administration." *Administrative theory and praxis*. 15:1:52–54.

Jaki, S. (1990). *The only chaos and other essays*. Lenham, MD: University Press of America.

James, W. (1996). *A pluralistic universe*. Lincoln: University of Nebraska Press. (Original work published 1909.)

James, W. (1995). *Selected writings* (G.H. Baird, Ed.). London: Everyman Library.

James, W. (1970). *The meaning of truth*. Ann Arbor: University of Michigan Press.

James, W. (1950). *The principles of psychology* (vol. 1). New York: Dover. (Original work published 1890.)

James, W. (1907). *Pragmatism*. New York: Longmans, Green, and Co.

James, W. (1880, October). "Great men, great thoughts, and the environment." *Atlantic Monthly* 46:276:441–459.

Jaspers, K. (1953). *The origin and goal of history* (M. Bullock, Trans.). New Haven: Yale University Press. (Original work published 1949.)

Jennings, E. (1960). *An anatomy of leadership*. New York: Harper & Brothers.

Johnson, P. "Antipodes: Plato, Nietzsche, and the moral dimension of leadership." In P. Temes (Ed.). (1996). *Teaching leadership* (pp. 13–44). New York: Peter Lang.

Jongbloed, L., & P. Frost. (1985). "Pfeffer's model of management." *Journal of Management* 11:3:97–110.

Kaplan, R. (2002). *Warrior politics*. New York: Vintage Books.

Keegan, J. (1987). *The mask of command*. New York: Penguin.

Keulman, K. (1990). *The balance of consciousness*. University Park: University of Pennsylvania Press.

Kirkpatrick, S., & E. Locke. "Leadership: Do traits matter?" In J.T. Wren (Ed.). (1995). *The leader's companion* (pp. 133–143). New York: Free Press. (Original work published 1991)

Kotter, J. (1988). *The leadership factor*. New York: Free Press.

Kouzes, J., & B. Posner. (1987). *The leadership challenge*. San Francisco: Jossey-Bass.

Kuhn, T. (1970). *The structure of scientific revolutions* (2nd ed.). Chicago: University of Chicago Press.

Lerner, R., A. Nagai, & S. Rothman. (1996). *American elites*. New Haven: Yale University Press.

Levine, D. (1995). *The sociological tradition*. Chicago: University of Chicago Press.

Levine, D. (1985). *The flight from ambiguity*. Chicago: University of Chicago Press.

Levine, D. "Introduction." In G. Simmel. (1971). *On individuality and social forms*. Chicago: University of Chicago Press.

Lipman-Blumen, J. "Why do we tolerate bad leaders?" In G. Spreitzer & T. Cummings (Eds.). (2001). *The future of leadership* (chap. 11). San Francisco: Jossey-Bass.

Lubac, H. de (1949). *The drama of atheist humanism* (E. Riley & A.E. Nash, Trans.) (part 1). San Francisco: Ignatius Press. (Original work published 1944.)

Lukes, S. (Ed.). *Power*. Oxford: Basil Blackwell.

Lyotard, J. "The postmodern condition." In K. Baynes, J. Bohman, & T. McCarthy (Eds.). (1996). *After philosophy* (chap. 2). Cambridge, MA: MIT Press. (Original work published 1984)

Machiavelli, N. (1950*). The discourses on the first ten books of Titus Livius* (C. Detmold, Trans.). New York: Modern Library. (Original work published 1531.)

Machiavelli, N. (1991). *The prince* (R. Price, Trans.). New York: Cambridge University Press. (Original work published 1532.)

MacIntyre, A. (1981, 1984). *After virtue* (2nd ed.). Notre Dame, IN: University of Notre Dame Press.

Malcolm X. (1965). *Autobiography*. New York: Ballantine Books.

Mangan, K. (2002, May 31). "Leading the way in leadership." *The Chronicle of Higher Education*.

Manz, C., & H. Sims, Jr. (1989). *Super-leadership*. New York: Berkley Books.

Marcuse, H. (1992). *One-dimensional man*. Boston: Beacon Press.

Marías, J. "Notes." In Ortega y Gasset, J. (1961). *Meditations on Quixote* (pp. 166–192) (E. Rugg & D. Marín, Trans.). Urbana: University of Illinois Press. (Original work published 1957.)

Marsden, G. (1997). *The outrageous idea of Christian scholarship*. New York: Oxford University Press.

Marx, K. (1967). *Writings of the young Marx on philosophy and society* (L. Easton & K. Guddat, Trans.). Garden City: Anchor.

Marx, K., & F. Engels. (1947). *The German ideology* (parts 1 & 3)(R. Pascal, Ed.). New York: International Publishers. (Original work published 1932.)

Mazlish, B. (1990). *The leader, the led, and the psyche*. Hanover: Wesleyan University Press.

Mazlish, B. (1984a). *The meaning of Karl Marx*. New York: Oxford University Press.

Mazlish, B. (1984b). "History, psychology, and leadership." In B. Kellerman (Ed.). *Leadership: Multidisciplinary perspectives* (pp. 1–21). Englewood Cliffs: Prentice Hall.

Mazlish, B. (1981, Spring). "Leader & led, individual & group." *The Psychohistory Review* 9:214–237.

Mazlish, B. (1976). *The revolutionary ascetic*. New York: McGraw-Hill.

McClain, B. (n.d.). Advice for those who want to read Eric Voegelin. http://www .salamander.com/~wmcclain/ev-advice.html [accessed 7-29-00].

McGill, M., & J. Slocum, Jr. (1997). "A little leadership, please." *Organizational Dynamics 26*.

McLaughlin, C. (2002). Spirituality in business. *The Center for Visionary Leadership*. Retrieved 1-17-03 from http://www.visionarylead.org/spirituality_in_business.htm.

Meindl, J., S. Ehrlich, & J. Dukerich. (1985). "The romance of leadership." *Administrative Science Quarterly* 30:78–102.

Menand, L. (2001). *The metaphysical club*. New York: Farrar, Straus & Giroux.

Menand, L. (Ed.) (1997). *Pragmatism*. New York: Vintage Books.

Mendus, S. "Feminism." In T. Honderich. (1995). *The Oxford companion to philosophy* (pp. 270–272). New York: Oxford University Press.

Michels, R. (1949). *First lectures in political sociology* (A. de Grazia, Trans.). Minneapolis: University of Minnesota Press. (Original work published 1927.)

Michels, R. (1949). *Political parties* (E. Paul & C. Paul, Trans.). Glencoe, IL: Free Press. (Original work published 1915.)

Mill, J.S. (1988). *The logic of the moral sciences*. LaSalle, IL: Open Court. (Original publication dated 1872.)

Mills, C.W. (1956). *The power elite*. New York: Oxford University Press.

Mitroff, I., & E. Denton. (1999, Summer). "A study of spirituality in the workplace." *Sloan Management Review*, 40:4:83–92.

Morgan, G. (1986). *Images of organization*. Newbury Park: Sage.

Moulakis, A. (2000). "Voegelin and Strauss on Machiavelli." Discussion paper prepared for The Voegelin Society panel, American Political Science Association, Washington, D.C.

Nahser, F.B. (1997). *Learning to read the signs*. Boston: Butterworth-Heinemann.

Newstrom, J., & K. Davis. (1993). *Organizational behavior: Human behavior at work* (9th ed.). St. Louis: McGraw-Hill.

Niemeyer, G. "Enlightenment to ideology: The apotheosis of the human mind." In W. Rusher (Ed.). (1995). *The ambiguous legacy of the Enlightenment* (chap. 3). Lanham: University Press of America.

Northouse, P. (1997). *Leadership: Theory and practice*. Thousand Oaks: Sage.

Nye, R. (1977). *The anti-democratic sources of elite theory: Pareto, Mosca, Michels*. Beverly Hills: Sage.

Oakeshott, M. "The masses in representative democracy." (1991). In *Rationalism in politics and other essays* (new & expanded ed.) (pp. 363–383). Indianapolis: LibertyPress. (Original work published 1961.)

Olson, R. (1962). *An introduction to existentialism*. New York: Dover.

Ormiston, G., & A. Schrift (Eds.). (1990). *The hermeneutic tradition*. Albany: State University of New York Press.

Ortega y Gasset, J. (1985). *Meditations on hunting* (H. Wescott, Trans.). New York: Charles Scribner's Sons. (Original work published 1943.)

Ortega y Gasset, J. (1984). *Historical reason* (P. Silver, Trans.). New York: W.W. Norton.

Ortega y Gasset, J. (1961a). *The modern theme* (J. Cleugh, Trans.). New York: Harper Torchbooks. (Original work published 1923.)

Ortega y Gasset, J. (1961b). *Meditations on Quixote* (E. Rugg & D. Marín, Trans.). Urbana: University of Illinois Press. (Original work published 1914.)

Ortega y Gasset, J. (1957). *Man and people* (W. Trask, Trans.). New York: W.W. Norton.

Ortega y Gasset, J. (1946). *Concord and liberty* (H. Weyl, Trans.). New York: W.W. Norton. (Original work published 1940.)

Ortega y Gasset, J. (1944). *Mission of the university* (H.L. Nostrand, Trans.). New York: W.W. Norton. (Original work published 1930.)

Panichas, G. "Irving Babbitt and Richard Weaver." (1999). In *The critical legacy of Irving Babbitt* (chap. 5). Wilmington, DE: ISI Books. (Original work published 1996.)

Panichas, G. (1996, Fall). "Reflections on leadership." *Modern Age* 38:307–311.

Pareto, V. (1991). *The rise and fall of elites* (H. Zetterberg, Trans.). New Brunswick: Transaction. (Original work published 1901.)

Parsons, T. (1977). *Social systems and the evolution of action theory*. New York: Free Press.

Patočka, J. (2002). *Plato & Europe* (P. Lom, Trans.). Stanford, CA: Stanford University Press.

Peirce, C.S. (1997). *Pragmatism as a principle and method of right thinking* (D. Turrisi, Ed.). Albany: State University of New York Press.

Peirce, C.S. (1955). *Philosophical writings of Peirce* (J. Buchler, Ed.). New York: Dover. (Original collection published 1940.)

Pfeffer, J. (1977). "The ambiguity of leadership." *Academy of Management Review* 2:104–112.

Popper, K. (1965). *Conjectures and refutations*. New York: Harper Torchbooks.

Pruyne, E. (2002). *Conversations on leadership*. Cambridge: John F. Kennedy School of Government.

Rapoport, A. (1974). *Conflict in man-made environment*. New York: Penguin.

Robbins, S. (2003). *Organizational behavior* (10th ed.). Upper Saddle River, NJ: Prentice Hall.

Rorty, R. "Pragmatism and philosophy." In E. Baynes, J. Bohman, & T. McCarthy. (1987). *After philosophy* (pp. 26–66). Cambridge: MIT Press. (Original work published 1982.)

Rorty, R. (1982). *Consequences of pragmatism*. Minneapolis: University of Minnesota Press. (Original works published 1972–1980.)

Rosenthal, S., & R. Buchholz. (1996). "Leadership: Toward new philosophical foundations." *Business and Professional Ethics Journal* 14:3:25–41.

Rost, J. (1993). *Leadership for the twenty-first century*. Westport, CT: Praeger.

Scheler, M. (1961). *Man's place in nature* (H. Meyerhoff, Trans.). New York: Noonday Press. (Original work published 1928.)

Schlesinger, A., Jr. "On leadership." In Garfinkel, B. (1985). *Margaret Thatcher* (pp. 7–11). New York: Chelsea House.

Schütz, A. (1962). *Collected papers* (vol. 1)(M. Natanson, Ed.). The Hague: Martinus Nijhoff. (Original works published 1940–1955.)

Searle, J. (1998). *Mind, language and society*. New York: Basic Books.

Sells, B. (Ed.). (2000). *Working with images*. Woodstock, CT: Spring.

Senge, P. (1990). *The fifth discipline*. New York: Doubleday-Currency.

Shelley, P.B. (1966). *The selected poetry and prose of Shelley* (H. Bloom, Ed.). New York: Signet Classic.

Shriberg, A., C. Lloyd, D. Shriberg, & M.L. Williamson. (1997). *Practicing leadership*. New York: John Wiley & Sons.

Simmel, G. "Religion and the contradictions of life." (1997). In *Essays on religion* (chap. 5) (H.J. Helle & L. Nieder, Eds. & Trans.). New Haven: Yale University Press. (Original work published 1904.)

Simmel, G. (1971). *On individuality and social forms* (D. Levine, Ed.). Chicago: University of Chicago Press.

Simmel, G. (1955). *Conflict and the web of group-affiliations.* New York: Free Press. (Original works published 1923 & 1922.)

Simmel, G. (1950). *The sociology of Georg Simmel* (K. Wolff, Trans.). Glencoe, IL: Free Press. (Original work published 1908.)

Skinner, Q. "Introduction." In Skinner, Q. (Ed.). (1985). *The return of grand theory in the human sciences* (pp. 1–20). New York: Cambridge University Press.

Steyrer, J. (1998, Winter). "Charisma and the archetypes of leadership." *Organization Studies.* http://www.findarticles.com/cf_0/m4339/5_19/65379679/p1/article .jhtml?term=Steyrer [date accessed: 8-8-01].

Stogdill, R.M. "Personal factors associated with leadership." In Wren, J.T. (Ed.). (1995). *The leader's companion* (pp. 127–132). New York: Free Press. (Original work published 1948.)

Strauss, L. "Niccoló Machiavelli." In L. Strauss & J. Cropsey (Eds.). (1987). *History of political philosophy* (3rd ed.) (pp. 296–317). Chicago: University of Chicago Press.

Thompson, K. "The dilemmas & antinomies of leadership." In R.S. Khare & D. Little (Eds.). (1984). *Leadership: Interdisciplinary reflections* (pp. 9–20, 131–133). Lanham, MD: University Press of America.

Tolson, J. (1995, Winter). "At issue: The trouble with elites." *Wilson Quarterly* 19:1:6–8.

Turner, J., L. Beeghly, & C. Powers. (1998). *The emergence of sociological theory* (4th ed.). Cincinnati: Wadsworth Publishing.

Vail, P.B. (1989). *Managing as a performing art.* San Francisco: Jossey-Bass.

Voegelin, E. (2000). *Collected works* (vol. 11, chaps. 9, 14) (E. Sandoz, Ed.). Columbia: University of Missouri Press. (Original works published 1962 & 1980.) (Cited as CW 11.)

Voegelin, E. (1999). *Collected works* (vol. 31) (D. Clemens & B. Purcell, Eds. & Trans.). Columbia: University of Missouri Press. (Cited as CW 31.)

Voegelin, E. (1998a). *Collected works* (vol. 2) (R. Hein, Trans.; K. Vondung, Ed.). Baton Rouge: Louisiana State University Press. (Original work published 1933.) (Cited as CW 2.)

Voegelin, E. (1998b). *Collected works* (vol. 3) (R. Hein, Trans.; K. Vondung, Ed.). Baton Rouge: Louisiana State University Press. (Original work published 1933.) (Cited as CW 3.)

Voegelin, E. (1998c). *Collected works* (vol. 24) (B. Cooper, Ed.). Columbia: University of Missouri Press. (Cited as CW 24.)

Voegelin, E. (1990a). *Collected works* (vol. 12, chaps. 5, 8, 10). Baton Rouge: Louisiana State University Press. (Original works published 1970, 1971, & 1974.) (Cited as CW 12.)

Voegelin, E. (1990b). *Collected works* (vol. 28, chaps. 2, 5) (T. Hollweck & P. Caringella, Eds.). Baton Rouge: Louisiana State University Press. (Cited as CW 28.)

Voegelin, E. (1987). *Order and history* (vol. 5). Baton Rouge: Louisiana State University Press. (Cited as OH-5.)

Voegelin, E. (1978). *Anamnesis* (G. Niemeyer, Trans.). Columbia: University of Missouri Press. (Original work published 1966.)

Voegelin, E. (1956). *Order and history* (vol. 1). Baton Rouge: Louisiana State University Press. (Cited as OH-1.)

Voegelin, E. (1952). *The new science of politics*. Chicago: University of Chicago Press.

Vondung, K. "Introduction." In Voegelin, E. (1998). *Collected works* (vol. 3, pp. xi–xvii). Baton Rouge: Louisiana State University Press. (Cited as V-3.)

Vondung, K. "Introduction." In Voegelin, E. (1998). *Collected works* (vol. 2, pp. ix–xx). Baton Rouge: Louisiana State University Press. (Cited as V-2.)

von Mises, L. (1983). *Bureaucracy*. Grove City, PA: Libertarian Press. (Original work published 1944.)

Wartenberg, T. (1990). *The forms of power*. Philadelphia: Temple University Press.

Weaver, R. (1948). *Ideas have consequences*. Chicago: University of Chicago Press.

Webb, E. (1981). *Eric Voegelin*. Seattle: University of Washington Press.

Weber, M. (1990). *Basic concepts in sociology* (H.P. Secher, Trans.). New York: Citadel Press. (Original work published 1913.)

Weber, M. (1958). *From Max Weber* (H.H. Gerth & C.W. Mills, Trans.). New York: Oxford University Press. (Original work published 1922.)

Wheatley, M. (1992). *Leadership and the new science*. San Francisco: Berrett-Koehler.

Wheatley, M., & M. Kellner-Rogers. (1996). *A simpler way*. San Francisco: Berrett-Koehler.

White, M. (1972). *Science and sentiment in America: Philosophical thought from Jonathan Edwards to John Dewey*. New York: Oxford University Press.

Whitehead, A.N. (1933). *Adventures of ideas*. New York: Mentor Books.

Whitehead, A.N. (1955). *Symbolism*. New York: Capricorn Books. (Original work published 1927.)

Wills, G. (1994). *Certain trumpets*. New York: Simon & Schuster.

Wren, J.T. (Ed.). (1995). *The leader's companion*. New York: Free Press.

The author also wishes to note his general reliance on *The Oxford companion to philosophy,* edited by Ted Honderich. (1995). New York: Oxford University Press.

Index

Abduction, and leadership studies, 11
Abstract ideas, study of, 3
Aggregation, 156–157
Alienation, 125
Analysis and reality, vi
Argument, three reasons to study,
    67–68
Aristotle, 141
    and ignorance, iv
    and morality, 115
Aspirations
    drive to attain, 174–175
    real world constraints and, 176
Attribution, leadership element, viii

Barzun, Jacques, 77
Behavior, non-rational foundations
    for, 170
Belief, pragmatist definition, 28
Bernstein, Richard, 78–79
Berry, Patricia, 46, 47
Betti, Emilio, 70
bin Laden, Osama, 114, 115
Boulding, Kenneth, 46–47, 167–168
Bowling, Chester, 170
Burns, James MacGregor, 109–110, 174

Cassirer, Ernst, 39–40
Change, leadership element in, viii
Charismatic domination, 50
Coercion and leadership, 109
Collectivism, lowest-common-
    denominator (LCD), 120–121
Constructs
    arriving at, vi–vii
    first-degree, 39, 42
    second-degree, 39, 42
Contingency approach, 80–81
Coser, Lewis, 83–84

Creative powers, preserving one's own,
    124

Darwinism, social, 122
Deduction and Leadership Studies, 9–11
Deformative reification, 131
de Lubac, Father, 168, 170
Democracy and elites, 148–150
Denkbilder, 180
DePree, Max, 110
Destruction, politics of personal, 133
Differentiation
    described, 54–59
    and leadership, 59–60
    of leadership studies, 2
Direction, leadership element, viii
Disciplines, new, 1
Drath, Wilfred, 46, 162

Elites
    circulation of, 180–181
    democracy and, 148–150
    and engagement in leadership, 147
    joining, 146
    and leaders, 147–148
    non-political, 148
    societies and, 145–146
    and spirituality, 172–173
    and webs of influence, 138
Elite theory, 145–150
Emotivism
    defined, 120
    and trends in the popular mind,
        120–121
Engels, Friedrich, 166
Enlightenment tradition, assaults on, 168

Facts and reality, 31
Feminism and strict reason, 166–167

213